Piman Shamanism and Staying Sickness

Dúajida ceremony painting by Louis Valdez

Piman Shamanism and Staying Sickness (Ká:cim Múmkidag)

Donald M. Bahr,
anthropologist

Juan Gregorio,
shaman

David I. Lopez,
interpreter

Albert Alvarez,
editor

The University of Arizona Press
Tucson, Arizona

About the Authors . . .

DONALD M. BAHR, who conceived this presentation, spent twenty-four months during the 1960s in the Papago village of Santa Rosa, Arizona. Bahr received his B.A. and Ph.D. degrees in anthropology from Harvard University, and in 1967 became Assistant Professor of Anthropology at Arizona State University. His published writings focus on Piman myth and ritual oratory as well as on the Piman theory of sickness.

JUAN GREGORIO was the shaman personally interviewed by Don Bahr and whose theory of sickness comprises this corpus of texts. One of the first men from his Papago village to be educated in Anglo-American schools, he was an interpreter for Catholic priests and for many years a farm laborer, meanwhile planting his own crops at Santa Rosa and becoming a shaman and ritual curer for sicknesses concerned with war. Gregorio was keenly interested in the work leading to publication of this study, but died in 1971 before typesetting was completed — with the book in press.

DAVID I. LOPEZ, interpreter of Gregorio's discourse, as a child often stayed with his Papago shaman grandfather in Santa Rosa. He attended school through the tenth grade. Lopez has worked as a farm laborer and, at home, as cowboy, farmer, and custodian at the Santa Rosa school.

ALBERT ALVAREZ, editor of Gregorio's texts in this book, also is the grandson of a Papago shaman. He was the first student in a linguistic training program for American Indians at the Massachusetts Institute of Technology. Prior to that, he attended school on the Papago reservation, dividing his boyhood between his grandparents' home and the farm labor camps of southern Arizona where his parents worked. From MIT Alvarez returned to the reservation at Sells, Arizona, to work as a linguist and day laborer. His writings on the sound system of Papago and Papago puns have been published in linguistic journals.

THE UNIVERSITY OF ARIZONA PRESS

Frontispiece: In the *dúajida* the shaman sings, holding a rattle in one hand and a feather in the other. The tab hanging from the shaman's pocket is from his packet of tobacco for rolling cigarettes. The coffee can is used both as an ashtray and to receive strengths sucked from the patient. *Courtesy of Papago Tribe and U.S. Public Health Service. Photo by Helga Teiwes-French.*

I. S. B. N.-0-8165-0303-6
L. C. No. 72-92103

José Lewis Brennan, Pioneer Ethnographer

José Lewis, known to some non-Indians as José Lewis Brennan, was the Papago Indian who traveled with W. J. McGee of the Bureau of American Ethnology as interpreter on an 1894 field expedition from the San Xavier (Papago) Indian Reservation in southern Arizona to Seri Indian country in Sonora, México. Doubtless as a result of his acquaintance with ethnologist McGee, José Lewis wrote in Papago and in English translation a series of observations concerning Papago culture. These were done in 1897 for the Smithsonian Institution and include materials on sickness, the berdache, "backward" people ("contraries"), warfare, salt-gathering expeditions, political organization, folktales, and language.

José Lewis, who was born in the Papago village of Vainam Kug ("Iron Stands"), again served as interpreter in 1901-02, this time for Frank Russell among the Pima of the Gila River Indian Reservation. The orthography used by Lewis in his holograph manuscripts is virtually identical to that used for the Piman texts in Russell's volume on Pima Indians. It appears that it was Lewis rather than Russell who actually collected and transcribed the one hundred pages of published Piman materials in Russell's book. Indeed, José Lewis was a pioneer in ethnographic and linguistic studies of his own people. He died among the Gila River Pima and was buried in Blackwater on that reservation. Photographs of handwritten pages from his original notebooks, on deposit at the Smithsonian Institution, are reproduced in this book.

Contents

TABLES

ILLUSTRATIONS

Foreword

Well-being, long life, and happiness are among man's universal desires. All human societies have devised means to attempt to fulfill these desires, just as every culture has members whose special task it is to cope with threats to their attainment.

Surprising as it may seem, little is known in a comparative way of the variety of beliefs concerning good health characteristic of different cultures. In this cultural sense as well as individually, we all have our bodies of theory of afflictions – but for the most part our philosophies of sickness are implicit and unconscious. We can state in an objective way the kinds of things we regard as afflictions; we can discuss their symptoms; and, if we are medical doctors, we profess to know something about their diagnoses and cures. There are, however, culturally based and culturally biased assumptions underlying our theories of disease – including that of the scientific dogma of western medicine – and they are these assumptions which are so poorly understood. Thanks to a large body of ethnographic data, we have long been able to compare the *forms* of sickness, diagnosis, and cure among different cultures. But we have stood incapable of comparing their *meanings*. The philosophical underpinnings of thought, whether thought concerning sicknesses or anything else, have always been harder to discern than the tangible or readily perceived aspects of objects or of actions.

The present study, one which has been developed through the collaboration of a Papago Indian shaman, a Papago Indian translator, a Papago Indian linguist, and a non-Indian explicator, provides us with an introduction to the study of the Piman theory of sickness. It also provides us with a modest step toward a comparative study of theories of sickness.

With the help of his Papago colleagues, ethnologist Donald Bahr has been able to apply a system of logic peculiar to his own culture to reveal the system apparently inherent in the Piman theory of disease. In general, there seem to be two kinds of afflictions: those which Pimans classify as "sicknesses" and those which they do not. Of the "sicknesses," there are those that "stay" – which are peculiar to Piman Indians and are not shared by other human beings – and there are those that "wander" – contagious afflictions which fail to respect race, culture, age, or sex.

Although this study is concerned primarily with "staying sickness," the concept can be explained only by contrasting it with other Piman forms of affliction. Staying sicknesses, in addition to being restricted to Piman Indians, are not contagious even from Piman to Piman. They are caused by the "ways" and "strengths" of "dangerous objects." Such sicknesses, which are the primary concern of Piman shamans, can affect only human beings and not other kinds of animals. More significantly, they involve a sense of transgression against the dignity or propriety with which dangerous objects were endowed at the time of creation. It is thus that sickness and morality became intertwined.

The principal role of the Piman shaman is as diagnostician rather than as curer. A patient's body is the stratified repository for a lifetime's acquisitions of sickness-causing "strengths." It is the job of the shaman to divine which of these strengths are causing the sickness. Once divined, the curers – who may be any Pimans – can take over. How and why all this comes about are explained in detail in Bahr's analysis which is divided into three parts: staying sickness, diagnosis, and cure. Earlier discussions of Piman sicknesses have been preoccupied with the ethnographic facts, with the things people do and use to acquire good health. Such preoccupation has permitted sketching in the shadows of Piman beliefs about sicknesses; the present study attacks their substance.

Today when Piman (and other American Indian) theories of sickness are being forced to compete with often-conflicting western theories, we hear a great deal of patronizing talk about the psychotherapeutic value of treatment by medicine men. We are even told that western doctors sometime condescend to allow medicine men to treat Indian patients in hospitals. Beneath this liberality, however, there remains the cock-sure belief that scientific medicine, the kind involving x-ray pictures or data which can be stuffed into computers, is the far superior approach.

Anyone who reads this multi-authored book will gain new respect for the Piman practices. There is nothing simple or uncomplicated in the Piman approach to sickness. The Piman theory of human afflictions, here laid bare for the first time, is as sophisticated as any in the world. "The purpose of the [shaman's] diagnosis," states Bahr, "is to make people aware of the sickness they have." What could a Jung or a Freud add to this?

It should be remembered, moreover, that the study which follows is only a beginning. It is the attempt to understand and to make explicit what one Piman shaman, in this case a Papago Indian, means by the choice of the words he uses in answering questions about sickness. There are probably more than a hundred additional Piman shamans (Bahr's estimate is one hundred and fifty), no two of whom would be expected to give precisely the same answers to the same questions. The curers, in contradistinction to the shamans, have not been interviewed at all. Neither have the patients. And nowhere has there been an effort to detect and to explain the origins and natures of the "ways" of the more than forty "dangerous objects" whose strengths are capable of imparting staying sickness. Finally, the Piman theory of afflictions is but one aspect of what the people themselves refer to as *'ó'odham hímdag*, the "Piman way." The four authors have forced the door slightly ajar, enabling us to glimpse ahead and to wonder in excitement and anticipation at what the "way" shall be.

The method of analysis presented here is at once simple and complex. Bahr, the anthropologist, Alvarez, the linguist, and Lopez, the translator, let Juan Gregorio, the shaman, do the talking. They then dissect his speech and come to grips with the meanings of his words in English. It is finally left to Bahr to do the intellectualizing, to superimpose his own theoretical ideas on what Gregorio is presumed to have meant by what he said. Although the approach is by no means a new one, so far as I know this is its most rigorous application to the study of a subject as intricate and complicated as a theory of afflictions. To make clear how the analysis is done it has been essential to publish the texts in both Piman and English. The result is a model for future efforts of its kind. We might even hope, indeed, that the method will soon be applied to a similar study of the western theory of afflictions. Western medicine and its practitioners have long been in need of such an analysis. All of us should profit by an awareness of the sicknesses we might have.

This book discloses a nonwestern theory of disease which is as subtle and as sophisticated as any other such theory. It affords an introduction to this subject as well as an introduction to the world view of a whole people. It presents a method of analysis which if applied elsewhere will make it possible to compare theories of afflictions and even systems of philosophy in modes in which we previously have not been able to compare them. From such comparisons there should arise a greater understanding of man and of the human condition.

Many years ago George Herzog collected a Piman text which contained the prophecy "that other people [who may be understood to be Anglo-Americans] will do the thing which the Pimans must not do, namely, to kill the earth." Perhaps if nonnative Americans will begin to listen, and intensively so, as we have failed to do for more than four hundred and fifty years, the prophecy will be denied. This book teaches us one method of paying heed.

BERNARD L. FONTANA
Ethnologist, Arizona State Museum,
University of Arizona

GUIDE TO THE PIMAN TEXTS

Sounds of Piman

The sound system of Gregorio's dialect of the Piman language is fully and technically discussed by Alvarez (1969). This analysis shows a system of twenty-nine different sounds: fifteen consonants, ten vowels, and four additional sounds which are neither consonants nor vowels. The sounds are listed below together with their nearest English equivalents. These English equivalents are only approximate guides to pronunciation.

Consonants

p as in *p*in
b as in *b*in
t as in *t*in, but with tip of tongue between the teeth
d as in *d*in, but with tip of tongue between the teeth
ḍ as in po*d*, with tip of tongue well behind the teeth
c as in *ch*urch
j as in *j*ump
k as in pi*ck*
g as in pi*g*
m as in *m*outh
n as in *n*ose
ñ as in Spanish ca*ñ*on, English ca*ny*on
s as in *s*ip
ṣ as in *sh*ip
l as in cu*rl*

Vowels

i: as in P*e*te
e: as in t*oo*l, but with the lips spread instead of rounded
u: as in t*oo*l
a: as in p*o*d
o: as in b*oa*t

The short vowels *i, e, u, a,* and *o* are the same, only shorter in duration

Neither Consonants nor Vowels

w as in *w*agon
y as in *y*ellow
' as in oh-oh (glottal pause)
h as in *h*eart

This system for writing Piman is very similar to the system employed by Dean and Lucille Saxton in their *Papago & Pima to English Dictionary* (1969). The only differences are the following: Where Alvarez writes *ḍ, c, ṣ, ñ, i:, e:, u:, a:,* and *o:*, Saxton writes *D, ch, sh, h, ih, eh, uh, ah,* and *oh,* respectively.

Translations

Gregorio's spoken texts have the initial appearance of poetry because we have rendered them into lines. In general, each line is the beginning of a sentence or the beginning of a clause within a complex sentence. We have used periods sparingly and have left a double space between a line ending with a period and the next line. Thus, the texts appear as long sentences, almost of paragraph length, composed by many lines connected by "and," "but," "if," "which," "because," and "well and."

Frequently rather than use a period we have joined sentences with a comma. We decided in favor of a comma when we thought the following line of text added to or modified the previous line. Thus we reserved periods for the termination of what we considered complete chains of thought. We also used commas within lines – again arbitrarily – to designate phrases. In this instance it was a choice between a comma or no punctuation; we used commas when we thought they would help the reader relate the line of Piman to the line of literal translation.

We have also divided some texts into multi-sentence topical units; these are marked by capital letters. The question which elicited a text is indicated by the letter *Q*. Further divisions in the text are marked by the letters *A*, *B*, *C*, etc., which indicate shifts from one topic to another.

Each line of Piman is given a literal and a free translation. The literal translation consists of word for word equivalents. The English equivalents follow the Piman word order.

The literal translations leave much to be desired. This enterprise was dependent upon the extent to which Piman wordings and word order can be matched with English, that is, the degree to which Piman sentences can be word for word "turned into English." Not every element of written Piman that looks like a word, because it stands alone in the transcript, can be given a single English equivalent. In some situations we supply no equivalent, and in others we supply an English phrase; depending upon the context, we may give one equivalent at one time and another at other times. Still, we think the literal translations are useful as they allow the reader to follow the pace and emphasis of Gregorio's speech and indicate the degree of content we extracted from Gregorio's words.

One abbreviation is used in the literal translations. This is "ss" which stands for sentence straightener, a term employed by Alvarez with reference to a Piman subordinator, *m*, which is used to form complex sentences. The subordinator appears in constructions which translate into English as "if . . . ," "which. . . ," "who . . . ," and "that. . . ."

The free translations match English with Piman in terms of lines rather than words. Thus, they read more smoothly than the literal translations. A further function of the free translations is to provide background information on subjects Gregorio alludes to without specifically naming. In this sense the free translations explicitly communicate more information than either the literal translations or the Piman originals. This additional information is presented in brackets.

The bracketed information is important in view of Gregorio's tendency to be sparing in his use of nouns, preferring at times to omit them completely from a line of text or to use pronouns – "that-one," "something," or "whatever" – in place of the thing to which he is referring. Thus the bracketed information is necessary and, additionally, it indicates our comprehension of his words. The identifications were first made by Lopez and Bahr and later verified by Alvarez.

We used single quotation marks to indicate terms whose meanings are uncertain. One may refer to this use of single quotation marks as the "so-called" convention. Whenever the reader finds a term in single quotation marks he may apply this convention by reading "so-called" into the sentence prior to the quoted item. Certain English terms, for example, 'evil spirits', were put into single quotation marks when we wished to refer vaguely to the concept of evil spirits. The reader should recognize that we are naming a concept, or several concepts whose application to the problem at hand remains unclear or suspect; these quoted terms are insecure in Piman doctrine as we know it and they are without known equivalents in Piman.

Our corpus of texts was gathered in twenty-four taped sessions with Gregorio. It consists of about three hundred texts, not all of which are cited in this study. In addition to a chronological numbering system for texts printed in this book, text 1 through 53, texts are parenthetically cited – for example (tape 16.5) – according to the session in which they were collected, 1. through 24., and the place of the text within those spoken during a given session, .1 through .20, for example. Thus, a text parenthetically identified as (tape 16.5) was the fifth text spoken during the sixteenth session.

List of Texts

PART I

TOWARD A PIMAN THEORY OF SICKNESS

And you will not be the ones to kill the staying earth,
I will leave it to them,
and they will do it.
And these will kill the staying earth,
and even if you don't know anything,
and you will just be feeling fine,
and you will see it
when it happens.

"Elder-Brother Shaman's Prophecy,"
a text collected by George Herzog from the
Gila River Pimas in the 1920s

1. Intent of the Study and Contributions of Coauthors

For a year and a half Donald Bahr questioned a Papago shaman concerning the sicknesses of his people. The materials analyzed in this study are the transcribed texts of his answers obtained between February 1967 and October 1968. Bahr had known the shaman – Mr. Juan Gregorio of Santa Rosa, Arizona – for seven years. Mr. Gregorio died on 5 October 1971. The shaman gave his full support to this project and consented to be listed as a coauthor although it should be understood that the preparation of this book was not his idea.

The book grew out of Bahr's interest in the nature of Piman theorizing on sickness. It was known at the outset that shamans play a crucial dual role: guardian of Piman health and preserver of Piman consciousness of their humanity as Indians. It was not known whether this role is explicitly recognized by shamans and, if so, whether it is the object of reflection and discussion. Bahr wanted to study the intellectual content of a shamanic theory of sickness and, moreover, he hoped that this study would be supportive of the shamans' role.

It was anticipated that a book would be needed to cover the topic properly and that the materials required for such a book should be gathered in the Piman language. The decision to limit the study to the theories of a single man was made, first, in order to transfer *to a shaman* as many as possible of the functions normally associated with authorship. These include the selection of an expository style, the duty to make interpretations and explanations, and the right to judge which things are important and which are not. Bahr felt that in many anthropological studies the role of the native informant is confined to stating facts while the functions subsumed under authorship devolve on the anthropologist. This state of affairs he wished to reverse. In his situation the reversal required considerable involvement on the part of the anthropologist for no Piman seemed willing to undertake the project of his own accord.

The second factor instrumental in the decision to limit the project to a single shaman concerns linguistics. Piman shamans do their theorizing orally in Piman. The anthropologist interested in writing a book on Piman theory must meet them on their terms. At the beginning of the study Bahr's knowledge of Piman was severely limited. Thus, in order to comprehend a shamanic theory on sickness it was necessary to learn the language. This put a special and contradictory burden on the shaman: On the one hand, he was urged to speak on his own level as if addressing an audience of Pimans and, on the other hand, it was frequently necessary to ask him to repeat himself and to explain the meanings of words. Bahr felt that only one shaman should be asked to work under these conditions.

Gregorio became the shaman because Bahr knew him better than any other. He consented to give tape-recorded lectures in Piman on any question asked, provided the question was asked in Piman. The answers would stay within the bounds of what Gregorio considered legitimate public knowledge.

As will be seen from the texts included in this book, Gregorio spoke at length in an intellectually disciplined manner in response to short, open-ended questions. This was precisely what was required, particularly in the early phases of the project when the questions were relatively blind. In beginning sessions Bahr commonly sat through the lectures holding a microphone with only a vague grasp of the meaning of Gregorio's words. As the project advanced the questions became longer, better focused, and explicitly keyed to statements made in earlier sessions. In this manner Gregorio was shown that his lectures had been understood and Bahr was assured of his comprehension.

The work of the other authors, Lopez and Alvarez, was linguistic. Mr. David Lopez of Santa Rosa, Arizona, assisted in the translation of Gregorio's texts throughout the period they were gathered. Lopez did not attend the sessions with Gregorio or suggest questions. His task was to examine the tape recordings with Bahr, concentrating, first, on what Gregorio literally had said and second, on how the literal content of his answers could be understood with regard to allusions, alternate expressions of meaning, and internal organization. Lopez did not pass judgment on the validity or completeness of Gregorio's answers.

In short, Lopez guided Bahr through the content and style of Gregorio's speech. Lopez' bilingual fluency was crucial to the project in that from the beginning Bahr was able to make the maximum use of Gregorio's ability to speak at length on theoretical topics. It is doubtful that Gregorio would have been as informative had he been forced to speak English. Although as a young man his competence in English probably matched that of Lopez, a young man, it seems the major development of his thinking on sickness occured while, as an aging man, he refrained from speaking English. In his later years Gregorio spent many hours each week talking with his patients in Piman about sickness. He preferred not to speak English, hence his English speech was pained compared to his fluency in Piman.

Mr. Albert Alvarez, a trained linguist from Sells, Arizona, completes the roster of coauthors. After Lopez and Bahr translated the texts of the present corpus and the latter's analysis of them had been completed and submitted as a doctoral thesis, Alvarez began his task of correcting the transcriptions and revising the translations. The translations are intended to match Piman words or phrases with English counterparts.

Alvarez edited the texts with the idea that they might be used for classes in the Piman language. Thus, the orthography used is that which he has developed for use by Pimans (Alvarez 1969; Alvarez and Hale 1970).

2. Shaman's Role, Traditionally and in This Study

Let us first consider two background questions on Piman theorizing: Who is authorized to speak about theories of sickness? To whom are these statements made? Although there exists common knowledge about sickness, it seems that Pimans rarely reflect upon the substance of this knowledge. It appears as if the ordinary person knows only platitudes or simple maxims about sickness, while the right to "get to the bottom" of these matters is limited to shamans. If he knows more than platitudes or thinks about sickness in depth, the ordinary Piman seems unwilling to declare these things for to do so is to imply that he is a shaman. Before settling on this project, Bahr had found that most Pimans deferred answering his questions about sickness with such remarks as, "I don't know about that because I am not a medicine man." We interpreted these statements to mean: "I have no right to represent the truth as Pimans know it about sickness. If you want to ask about such things you should speak with a shaman."

With whom do the shamans normally speak about sickness? They do not ordinarily discuss theory with their fellow shamans, nor does there appear to be an apprenticeship system wherein new shamans are given instruction by older ones. The main occasions for listening to a shaman's interpretations occur when, as a patient, one asks about how an affliction fits into the general pattern of Piman sickness.

We conclude that shamans are the sole authorized theorizers on Piman sickness. They aim their theorizing at patients rather than at students or at other shamans. The principal product of their theorizing, then, is that body of common knowledge which is accepted by the public, but which the public feels incompetent to expand upon or to evaluate critically. It is only when a person receives the call to be a shaman that he begins to speak with authority on the thoughts that underlie the common knowledge.

As a nonpatient Bahr was making an unusual request and as a nonshaman he was beginning an odd piece of work. Although he could have sought permission to sit in the background of Gregorio's sessions with patients he decided against this procedure, anticipating that the verbal exchange between shaman and patient would reach a level Bahr would find excessively particularistic and allusive.

He needed schooling in the usages and rationales basic to Gregorio's explanations. This was accomplished in private sessions. We assume that this kind of discussion differed from Gregorio's normal sessions with patients. Thus, although one may reasonably posit that he enacted a customary role in conveying doctrine to his own people, it is doubtful whether the lectures he delivered to us were drawn intact from his stock of "natural" statements. We may equally propose that these texts mark the beginning of a new shamanic endeavor especially designed to build a general theory.

A Piman theoretical discourse on sickness exists, for not only can we speak in Piman about Piman concepts, but we have identified terms in common usage as probable candidates for theoretical systematization. It will be seen, however, that many of the analyses of Piman theoretical terms were imposed by Bahr and were not established by the shaman. This raises the speculation of whether a basic incompatibility exists between Bahr's intellectual orientation and those of the Piman shamanic tradition; for example, whether the former's penchant for systematization, "logical" progression of ideas, and generalization is incompatible with the latter's penchant for ambiguity, modesty, unconsciousness, or whatever other qualities may appear essential to the Piman shaman's manner of intellectualization. Such speculation will not be laid to rest by this book. On the contrary, it will probably be awakened, particularly in the minds of Piman readers.

In an attempt to specify the sense in which the book is the anthropologist's and not the shaman's, we will retrace the stages of our relationship. Its overall development was for Bahr a period of acquiring and digesting texts which culminated in writing a book on them; for Gregorio it was uniformly a matter of responding to our questions. Like an oracle, the shaman never spoke unless presented with a question. He gave no overt guidance at all. This was a hinderance because Bahr would have appreciated advice at the outset – and admonitions as to the limitations of what one could learn merely by asking a shaman questions. On the other hand, the fact that Gregorio would entertain any question enabled Bahr to set his own pace and to approach the shaman in the manner of an ignorant and curious, but spiritually detached, inquirer.

While we lacked overt guidance from Gregorio – and can only speculate as to the covert guidance he gave by entering into some subjects and withholding others – we had a source of orientation which was unknown to him, namely the general anthropological literature on shamanism and sickness and the specific studies on Piman culture. We conceived of this literature as a product which Gregorio and we should attempt to match or build toward.

We accomplished this objective in an indirect fashion. Instead of beginning with a direct question about an important idea such as "What are the causal agents of sickness? ," we aimed to acquire a corpus of texts in which the desired technical concepts gradually would become clear. Furthermore, direct English question on the "causal agency of sickness" was nonpermissible because we did not want to force Gregorio to answer a question in reference to a specialized term. Even if this term did have an exact counterpart in his thinking, he might not have been aware of it because he would be unfamiliar with the English. For the same reason – only more so, because our Piman was more limited than his English – we did not search initially for a way to say "causal agency of sickness" in Piman.

We began by asking simpler and more commonplace questions, for example, "What sickens babies? " Gradually the desired technical terms accumulated as we mastered expressions of common knowledge on sickness and asked additional questions about that knowledge.

As previously stated we tried to elicit theoretical statements from Gregorio. On some topics his theorizing is explicit and, in our opinion, brilliant. Certain of his ideas align him with Western European scholars whose works we have read. Specifically, we have found him to be "Freudian" and "Durkheimian" – at least in the sense that we think he would have found the doctrinal principles of these thinkers congenial.

Our own contributions to the technical vocabulary and thus to theorizing were confined largely to those topics where Gregorio's statements seemed to lack an idea which Bahr, as a vicarious participant in Piman theory-building, considered significant. To our regret, these contributions tended to place us in the position of a "Frazerian"; that is, they were required when it was a problem of the magical, the ineffable, or the inscrutable. Among these topics are spirits, the shaman's charisma, and visions.

It remains for further study to discover whether these topics are in fact unelaborated in the minds or in the public utterances of Piman shamans and whether they comprise the soft underbelly of Piman thinking on sickness. Based upon our research we must conclude that Gregorio had little to say about magical processes – so little, in fact, that we never learned how to say "magic" in Piman. Nor did we learn how to say "spirit," although our own interpretation shows a crucial, logical place for spiritual objects during diagnosis and cure. We have, then, two English terms for the technical vocabulary which were not given by Gregorio.

To conclude, we suspect that the readers of this book will find that Gregorio's richest areas of theorizing have been on topics which Anglo-Americans will regard as valid, that is, compatible with Anglo-American views on sickness. He is vague on those subjects which Anglo-Americans tend to distrust, and it is precisely here that Bahr has intervened to represent a plausible systematization on behalf of Piman theory. Thus, of the four coauthors, Bahr can be held primarily responsible for such criticisms which seem the most likely to arise concerning fallacy or superficiality in our presentation.

3. Piman Culture and History From Gregorio's Vantage Point

From our perspective the largest extension of Piman culture in effect surpasses the boundary of Gregorio's known world. The widest possible usage of the term "Piman culture" would include Piman-speaking Indians in a long, narrow area stretching from southern Arizona through the neighboring states of Sonora and Sinaloa, Mexico. Thus defined, the following groups, from north to south, constitute Piman culture: the Gila River Pimas, the Papagos, the Lower Pimas, the Tepehuan, and Tepecano. Of these, only the first three were known to Gregorio, a Papago. The Tepehuan and Tepecano are thus unclassified according to his distinction between the Pimans and other peoples.

As a Papago, Gregorio's egocentric method of differentiating among the Piman Indians makes the finest distinctions among the Papagos who live close to him. He normally spoke of people who live nearby simply by identifying them with their home villages. He spoke of spatially more distant Pimans in terms of larger territorial groupings consisting of several villages. The latter groupings correspond at least in part with dialects of the Piman language and presumably also with historically distinct aggregates of people. Into this latter grouping fall the Gila River Pimas and the Lower Pimas, as well as speakers of several dialects of Papago. The former grouping – spatially close Pimans – is named by village and consists of all villages of speakers of his own dialect, as well as some nearby villages whose people speak dialects of Papago different from Gregorio's.

This distinction between classifying other groups according to villages versus classifying them according to dialects corresponds to a distinction between the circle of nearby, familiar, and frequently interacting people and that of relative strangers. Most of Gregorio's patients belonged to the former category. Furthermore, when he spoke about differences in the practices and beliefs relating to sickness, he generally did so in terms of his own circle versus the speakers of other dialects.

At the next remove in Gregorio's scale of familiarity we have what approximates a racial distinction between Pimans and other Indian tribes, Mexicans, blacks, whites, and others. For our purposes the most important attribute of non-Pimans is that, in Gregorio's opinion, the main category of Piman sickness does not apply to them; Pimans and only Pimans are afflicted by sicknesses of this special group which constitute the main subject matter of our study. These sicknesses are referred to as *ká:cim múmkidag*, or "staying sickness."

The Piman distinction just outlined between the circle of familiar people and relative strangers allows us to envision a plurality of Piman histories, so that each dialect group can be discussed as a separate manifestation of Piman culture. From Gregorio's vantage point these groups have had separate histories from the beginning of time. He knew little about the histories of the non-Piman tribes, the Spaniards, the Mexicans, or the Anglo-Americans. Based upon present evidence it appears that by far the greatest elaboration of mythical or historical epics occurs in reference to the differentiation among dialect groups, rather than between Pimans and non-Pimans.

Finally, turning to the recent acculturation of Pimans within Gregorio's familiar circle, we note that Spaniards and Mexicans remained outside the territory occupied by his people. Gregorio's ancestors made pilgrimages to Spanish missions and left their homes to work in Mexico, but unlike most other Piman groups Gregorio's people apparently have always experienced the Hispanos as agents of civilization whose settlements were outside the Piman homeland.

Between the beginning of Anglo-American contact, around 1850, and the setting aside of the Papago Reservation, in 1916, mines and ranches were established in the territory of his people. In themselves these temporary settlements had little impact on his people's sense of autonomy within their own portion of the world. U.S. government Indian programs, and the commerce and labor market of the Anglo-Americans who settled in Arizona, however, led his people to substitute Anglo-American goods for much of their own and to accept Anglo-American education, charity, and other concepts. These events took place during Gregorio's lifetime, about seventy-five years. As he put it, "I never dreamed as a boy that I would now be talking with you in my house with an electric light on." We feel it is especially important that his theory of sickness remains intact and functional supporting his sense of the autonomy of Piman society in the face of the changes of the last fifty years.

PART II

THE NATURE OF *KÁ:CIM* SICKNESS

What is the meaning of ká:cim múmkidag*?*
Look, something is called like that
of the diversity of our sicknesses,
and it never wanders,
and it is just right here,
whenever it is close to the people.
Look, I will explain something clearly,
which is that the ocean lies over there,
well, look, as for that something is quite apparent,
that it is there, and there it stays,
and it never wanders.
It just stays there through the years
for as long as it lies, that one.

Juan Gregorio, text 48

1. Classification of Afflictions

The *ká:cim múmkidag*, or staying sicknesses, form a select group among the various human afflictions recognized by Piman theory. They are the "Indian sicknesses" that afflict only Pimans, are diagnosed only by Piman shamans, and are cured by native ritual curers.

In Gregorio's classification there are only two categories of real "sicknesses" (*múmkidag*) and there is a multitude of other "afflictions" (*pi 'áp'edag*) which are not sicknesses in the strictest sense. The two proper categories of sickness are the *ká:cim* or "staying" and the *'óimmeḍdam* or "wandering" sicknesses. Among the multitude of nonsicknesses are such afflictions as venomous bites, indigestion, sorcery, and broken bones.

The sections of part II explore aspects of this Piman classification. By comparing the *ká:cim* sicknesses with the "wandering" ones and with various kinds of nonsicknesses, we will expose the basic qualities of the *ká:cim* which are at the heart of Piman doctrine.

When we say that Gregorio's classification excludes many afflictions from the ranks of proper sicknesses, our criterion is a linguistic one stemming from his use of the Piman words *múmkidag,* "sickness," and *múmkicud*, "to cause it to sicken." Gregorio was quite reluctant to use these words in speaking about what we term "nonsicknesses," while he used them freely and constantly in speaking about the "staying" and "wandering" sicknesses.

Discussion of the system of classification will commence in section 2 with the distinction between staying and wandering sicknesses. This will yield a general description of the causes of *ká:cim* sickness. Later sections will explore aspects of this basic scheme by comparing staying sickness with the following nonsicknesses: forebodings, sorcery, venomous bites, "dirty stuff," infant deformities, and childhood retardations.

The causal agents of *ká:cim* sickness are the "ways" and "strengths" of "dangerous objects." The following examples are typical of Gregorio's speech on the matter:

Húawĭ géwkdag 'o múmkicud g hémajkam.
Deer strength sickens people.

Bán géwkdag 'o múmkicud g hémajkam.
Coyote strength sickens people.

Bá'ag hímdag 'o múmkicud g hémajkam.
Eagle way sickens people.

It can be seen that a kind of "way" or "strength" is said to be the thing that "sickens people."

For the wandering sicknesses a different pattern of speech is evident. Instead of a "way" or a "strength," the actual name of a sickness is said to be the causal agent, for example:

Cúcul híwdag 'o múmkicud g hémajkam.
Chicken pox sickens people.

On examination this pattern, which echoes Anglo-American usage,* yields a "germ theory" approach to causal agency.

Pimans view germs as microscopic particles which wander through the world, enter humans, and manifest themselves as symptoms. It will be shown in section 2 that the basic *ká:cim* scheme relating "dangerous object," "way," and "strength" does not hold for the germ-caused sicknesses.

Each variety of *ká:cim* sickness is named for the kind of "dangerous object" whose "way" and "strength" causes it. A total of approximately forty kinds of dangerous objects, each with its *ká:cim* sickness, has been reported by Gregorio and other sources (Brennan, 1897; Russell, 1908; Underhill, 1946). [See table 2 for a list.]

Ká:cim sicknesses become known to Pimans through the diagnoses of shamans. The shaman traces the patient's symptoms, which frequently are ambiguous, to the "strength" and "way" of a kind of "dangerous object." This process depends on each shaman's knowledge of the varieties of *ká:cim* sickness.[1] The historical record summarized in table 2 gives an overall impression of unity among Piman shamans: the areas of agreement among the sources are more impressive than the differences.

We recapituate these remarks on classification with two concrete examples. First, when Bahr asked about the "kinds of things that sicken the head," Gregorio responded, "Many things sicken the head." He used the important word *múmkicud* just as Bahr had in his question. The shaman then listed a series of causal agents – eagle way, hawk way and jimsonweed way – and discussed the *ká:cim* sickness associated with each.

Second, at a later point in the same session Bahr posed the question, "What things sicken the intestines? ", again using *múmkicud.* Gregorio responded that these afflictions are "a different kind of thing." The intestines, we learned, are not afflicted by any of the known varieties of *ká:cim* sickness. Gregorio explained the conditions under which a purely

* For example: "He was struck down by cancer," "Chicken pox is going around," and "He caught cold."

physiological condition, constipation, occurs: If people eat an excess of cow fat and later expose themselves to the cold, the fat hardens in the intestines causing constipation.* Throughout this discussion he avoided using the words *múmkidag* and *múmkicud*, using instead more vague words – such as "damage" – or more specific words – such as "to get hard." Gregorio was saying that constipation is not a "sickness" in his opinion, since it is neither caused by a "way" or "strength" nor by germs; it is one of the multitude of nonsickness afflictions.

Thus we see how only afflictions of a select group are considered to be *ká:cim* sicknesses. The causal agencies attributed to *ká:cim* sicknesses, "way" and "strength," differ from the causal agents attributed to most of the other human afflictions. In a word they are magical – unconstrained by time and space. When Gregorio talks about the cause of the other afflictions the materialistic reader will find himself on common ground: wandering sicknesses are caused by germs; "dirty stuff" (a nonsickness in Gregorio's view) is a dietary disorder; and even sorcery, which is mysterious in some respects, can at least be traced to the material actions of a human enemy.

In contrast the causal chain leading to a *ká:cim* sickness involves two mysterious entities, "way" and "strength." When the patient misbehaves toward a dangerous object, he is said to have trespassed on the "way" of that class of objects – but mystery surrounds the process by which a "way" discovers that a violation has taken place. Because of this violation the "strength" of that class of dangerous objects will create symptoms in the patient's body – but the actual means of the "strength's" entry are mysterious. The actions which cause *ká:cim* sicknesses generally occur long before the patient becomes sick, so long before that the patient has forgotten what he did and, therefore, he requires the services of a shaman to diagnose the sickness.

As we pursue the special properties of "strength" and "way" as causal agents we will discover the distinctive moral aspect of the *ká:cim* sicknesses. In trespassing against a dagerous object's "way," the patient is said to have committed an impropriety against rules which were set down for Pimans at the time of creation. The *ká:cim* sicknesses were intended specifically for Pimans as a race of chosen people. This becomes an issue in the distinction between *ká:cim* and *'óimmeḍdam* (wandering) sicknesses. The "ways" of the former are justified by the "commandments of propriety" issued by "whatever made us and turned us loose on the surface of the earth" – a god named "Elder-brother Shaman." The commandments govern various important roles – parent, hunter, cowboy – as they relate to dangerous objects –

* The indigenous forms of fat, from deer meat and cactus seeds, do not have this disadvantage.

animals, spirits, and the rest of the forty-odd kinds of things. In contrast the germs of of *'óimmeḍdam* sicknesses are said to spread freely by contagion without regard to the social role or moral state of the victim.

People contract *ká:cim* sicknesses because they have behaved improperly toward a dangerous object which was endowed with dignity at the time of creation. In comparing these sicknesses, which are curable, with another kind of affliction, the incurable deformities of babies, we will see how the former stem from infringements against the rights of inhuman species. *Ká:cim* sicknesses are cured by rituals which appeal to the dignity of the offended object as a species legitimately different from people. Deformities differ in that they arise from making fun of freaks, that is, creatures whose legitimate status as a member of a species is denied by the fact of their abnormality. Pimans consider deformities incurable because the offended creature does not have the dignity granted a member of a species and this dignity is indispensable to curing.

TABLE 1

PIMAN CLASSIFICATION OF AFFLICTIONS
(*pi áp'edag*)

We emphasize that the classification is based on the theories of a single shaman and is not sacrosanct. Other Pimans may think differently about the classification's two basic claims: that there are only two categories of sickness and that these categories are named *ká:cim* and *'óimmeḍdam.*

SICKNESS (*múmkidag*)	NOT SICKNESS*
Staying Sickness (*ká:cim múmkidag*)	Forebodings
– Caused by dangerous objects which have ways and strengths	Sorcery
	Venomous bites
– Caused by parts of dangerous objects, the whole forms of which have ways and strengths	Dirty stuff
	Infant deformities
	Childhood retardations
Wandering Sickness (*'óimmeḍdam múmkidag*)	Constipation
– Caused by various noxious substances such as germs, heat, or pus	

* This is not an exhaustive list of afflictions which are not considered sicknesses.

2. Causal Agencies

In the following assessment of Gregorio's use of the word *múmkicud*, "to cause it to sicken," it will be evident that he uses this verb primarily in reference to *ká:cim* sicknesses. The sole other well-attested pattern of usage is with reference to the contrasting category of *'óimmeḍdam* (wandering) sicknesses. Two benefits will derive from this inquiry into the usage of *múmkicud:* first, we will present all of the reported varieties of *ká:cim* sickness; second, we will study the scheme of causal agency which is common to all *ká:cim* sicknesses and which contrasts these with wandering sicknesses. The second task will receive the greater share of our attention, for, in discharging it we will introduce concepts which will figure prominently throughout the study: dangerous object, strength, way, commandment, and propriety.

In our interpretation the grammatical subject of a sentence with *múmkicud* stands for the causal agent of a sickness. These subjects may be divided into three groups.

1. Dangerous objects, *s-ta-'é:bidam há'icu*, for example, coyote, *bán*. These objects have a kind of strength (e.g., coyote strength, *bán géwkdag*) or a kind of way (e.g., coyote way, *bán hímdag*). Dangerous objects appear in the names of *ká:cim* sicknesses (e.g., coyote sickness, *bán múmkidag*).
2. Parts of dangerous objects. These possible subjects of *múmkicud* are said to be "parts of" or "inherent properties of," *cú'idag*, the above group of dangerous objects. The following examples illustrate this usage.
    a. *Ñú:wǐ 'á'an 'o ha-múmkicud, c wuḍ abṣ 'o ñú:wǐ cú'idag.*
    Buzzard feather sickens them, and it is a property of the buzzard.
    b. *Céwagǐ 'o ha-múmkicud, c wuḍ abṣ 'o wí:gita cú'idag.*
    Cloud sickens them, and it is a part of [the ritual called] *wí:gita.*

    These subjects of *múmkicud* differ from the first group because although they may be the causes of sicknesses – by our definition any subject of *múmkicud* is a cause of sickness – they do not have a way or strength of their own and neither do they have a sickness named after them. Roughly speaking they are the particular tangible things which cause trouble: feathers, food, footprints, nests, gopher holes, and ritual effigies. They are singled out for avoidance or care according to the commandments of the way of each kind of dangerous object.

3. Wandering sicknesses, *'óimmeḍdam múmkidag*, for example, flu, *s-tóñjig*, literally, "hotness" or "fever." These possible subjects of *múmkicud* differ from the others owing to the nature of the strength associated with them, because Gregorio does not use the word "way," *hímdag*, in reference to them, and because of the manner in which they are named.

Subjects of *múmkicud:* dangerous objects

Table 2 represents all the subjects of *múmkicud* mentioned by Gregorio, plus Russell's findings from the Gila River Pimans (1908) and Underhill's findings from the several Piman dialects spoken on the Papago reservation (1946). The forty-eight items of the list are ordered according to citation by these sources.

We doubt that the list is exhaustive of any native's knowledge; for example, Gregorio's contributions to the list probably do not exhaust his knowledge of the things that sicken people.* The list is intended both to locate the published examples of things that cause sickness within a larger context of possible subjects of *múmkicud* and also to indicate the most frequently mentioned causes of sickness among the Pimans.

In addition to being scored according to their sources, the items are either marked with one, two, or three stars. The items marked by one star belong to the first group of possible subjects of *múmkicud*, dangerous objects; those with two stars belong to the second, parts of dangerous objects; those with three stars belong to the third group, wandering sicknesses.

Dangerous objects

The subjects of *múmkicud* marked by a single star include the things most commonly identified by students of Pimans as the causes of sickness. Each item is equated with its own kind of sickness, the complete description of which would include: (1) the things people do to the object such that they contract the sickness; (2) the symptoms of the sickness; and (3) the ritual cure, *wúsota* or *wúsosig*, of the sickness. (See the Appendix [p. 284] for a tabulation covering the texts reported by Gregorio, Russell, and Underhill on each sickness with regard to these three points.)

* We never presented Gergorio with a question which required him to tell "everything."

Furthermore, it is with respect to this group of the possible subjects of *múmkicud* – dangerous objects – that the shaman makes his diagnosis. For example, at the end of a diagnostic session the shaman may say: "Coyote, ocean, and gila monster are doing it to you; these are making you sick, and you will have to get cured for each."

This first group of causal agents differs from the second group – parts of dangerous objects – in that each of the former has its own strength, way, and status as a recognized "whole" kind of sickness. Each bona fide *ká:cim* sickness must have way and strength.

The word we translate as "way" is *hímdag*. Lopez offers the following English equivalents for the term: "characteristic ways of acting," "the way it goes," "the things it does," "religion [of people]."

When the way of a dangerous object is spoken of as a causal agent of sickness, way refers to the collective rights of the dangerous object. These rights refer to things which the kind of dangerous object does – his or its actions – or is – his or its physical parts – or has – an animal's house. If people infringe upon these things they become sickened. Thus an individual deer is dangerous because he is an instance of the species whose way is understood to interact with human conduct according to definite rules.

Géwkdag, strength, when cited as a causal agency denotes the substantial or quasi-substantial thing which enters the patient's body and creates the symptoms of a sickness. People suffer because the strengths of dangerous objects enter their bodies and, only then, can the shamans or ritual curers exorcise the strengths to cure the sickness. The following examples of Gregorio's usage of *géwkdag* and *hímdag* will illustrate their integral relationship to dangerous objects.

1. *Pégi, k hab 'á'aga maṣ wuḍ húawĭ géwkdag, húawĭ múmkidag, c pi o ha-'áp'et, hégai.*

   Well, and it is called deer strength, deer sickness, and it damages them [the people] (text 12).

   In this case *pi 'áp'et*, "to damage," is used in place of *múmkicud*, "to sicken." Had Gregorio not doubly named the causal agent by pausing after "deer strength" to add "deer sickness," we presume he would have selected *múmkicud* to be the verb of the sentence, as in ". . . *húawĭ géwkdag, c o múmkicud, hégai*."

2. . . . *mo wuḍ cú:wĭ hímdag, géwkdag, k c hab júñcug.*

   . . . It is jackrabbit way, strength, and it makes it [the patient or the patient's body part] do it [become afflicted] (tape 1.14).

   Again the agent responsible for the sickness is doubly named way and strength. *Júñcug* is here used in place of *múmkicud*. We believe that *múmkicud* could be substituted for *júñcug* in this

TABLE 2

CAUSAL AGENTS

	Gregorio	Russell	Underhill
Butterfly*	X	X	X
Buzzard*	X	X	X
Coyote*	X	X	X
Deer*	X	X	X
Devil*	X	X	X
Eagle*	X	X	X
Enemy*	X	X	X
Gila monster*	X	X	X
Gopher*	X	X	X
Horned toad*	X	X	X
Owl*	X	X	X
Quail*	X	X	X
Rabbit*	X	X	X
Rattlesnake*	X	X	X
Turtle*	X	X	X
*Wí:gita**	X	X	X
Wind*	X	X	X
Badger*	X	X	
Bear*	X	X	
Dog*	X	X	
Hawk*	X	X	
*Húidam**	X	X	
Lightning*	X	X	
Lizard: *cúsukal**	X	X	
Mouse*	X	X	
Cow*	X		X
Housefly*	X		X
Jimsonweed*	X		X
Lizard: *jénaṣat**	X		X

	Gregorio	Russell	Underhill
Ocean*	X		X
Whore*	X		X
*Pihuri**		X	X
Roadrunner*		X	X
Bee*	X		
Cat*	X		
Cloud**	X		
Híhiwdag, sores [chicken pox, small pox] ***	X		
Híwkalig, roughness [measles] ***	X		
Hé:ñ ṣómaigig, coughing snotness [whooping cough] ***	X		
Paint**	X		
Saint*	X		
S-hé:pĭ, cold***	X		
Ṣómaigig, snotness [the common cold] *	X		
S-tóñjig, hotness, fever [flu] ***	X		
Caterpillar*		X	
Ground squirrel of the mesas*		X	
Sun**		X	
Frog*			X

clause in answer to the question, "What does the strength do? " The answer would be "it sickens," *múmkicud 'o.*

3. *Cem hékid 'o s-kó:simcud, heg 'ámjeḍ hégai cúkud hímdag, géwkdag.*

   It [causal agent] always makes him [the patient] want to sleep, from that one owl way, strength (tape 3.9).

   S-kó:simcud, "to make it want to sleep," is here used instead of *múmkicud* to name a particular kind of sickness. In this example, we believe Gregorio chose the former because it is a more informative verb.

Expressions of causal agency

We have just seen examples of sentences with

SUBJECT	PREDICATE
deer strength deer sickness	damages them
jackrabbit way [jackrabbit] strength	causes it to do it
owl way [owl] strength	causes it to want to sleep

One of the above examples is more specific than "sicken": to make sleepy; and the others are more vague: to damage. It seems that a wide range of predicates can be understood as varieties of sickening, simply because the agent of sickening is the strength or way of a dangerous kind of object. The same predicates – none of which is *múmkicud* – could occur in sentences which have nothing to do with sicknesses; there are many other forms of damage and other reasons why people become sleepy. We conclude that subjects compounded with way or strength permit the inference that sickening is being discussed, even when the verb *múmkicud* is not spoken because, generally, "to sicken" is the effect strengths and ways have on Pimans.

Even when strength and way are absent from the subjects of sentences with *múmkicud* we should understand that they are implicit. Furthermore, the subjects of sentences with *múmkicud* generally refer to classes of dangerous objects – for example, coyote as a dangerous kind of thing – or, implicitly, to the way or strength which is generic to such a class of things.

Sentences with "coyote" in the subject and "sicken" in the predicate do not refer to acts of sickening caused by individual coyotes. We have never heard a Piman speak of acts of sickening in the latter sense, that is, to identify a particular coyote and to specify the moment in which the animal caused sickness. We maintain that this manner of speaking about coyotes as causal agents is incompatible with the doctrines on *ká:cim* sicknesses. Text 1 exemplifies Gregorio's thoughts concerning causal agents.

TEXT 1 (Tape 1.9)

A

Héu'u,	b 'o má:s	hía	'í:da,	'ab ha-amjeḍ	hégam
Yes,	appears	on the one hand	this-one,	about them	those-ones

'á'al	hémajkam
babies	persons

Yes, it is like that about babies

mo há'icu	'am hab si má:s
ss something	there really appears

that something [dangerous] is very important then

mat o 'al cémajk.
ss will be small.

when it [baby] is small.

Ha'icu	'o hab wuḍ gógs	c hég múmkicud	g 'áli.
Something	is dog	and that-one sickens	the baby.

The thing is [the] dog and that [class of thing] sickens the [class] baby.

Há'icu	hab wuḍ 'ép nánhagio,
Something	is also mice,

Something else is [the class] mice,

c hég	'ép múmkicud	g 'áli,
and that-one	also sickens	the baby,

and that also sickens the [class] baby,

kó'owĭ	'o 'ep múmkicud	g 'áli,
rattlesnake	also sickens	the baby,

[the kind of thing that is a] rattlesnake also sickens the [class] baby,

cú:wĭ 'ep múmkicud,
rabbit also sickens it,
rabbit also sickens it,

hóhokimal 'ep múmkicud hégai.
butterflies also sicken that-one
butterflies also sicken that one.

Ñé:, há'ap 'o a'i si táṣo 'am hab má:s, 'í:da.
Look, that-way only clearly there appears, this-one.
Look, that's about all that seems clear about it [inventory of things that sicken babies].

B

C 'im hab ṣa'i dá:m, g ṣa'i gé'e hémajkam
And there on top, the slightly big person
And further on there is the adult

mo 'am há'icu hab hí cú'ig
ss something on the other hand is
in which case there is something else [dangerous]

mo hég 'áb hab 'ép si má:s . . .
ss that-one against also really appears . . .
which has to do with that [the adult] . . .

mañ hé'ekia há'icu 'am hab 'i káij
ss I several something there spoke
several of which I have mentioned

. . .mo hé'ekia há'icu ha-múmkicud,
. . .ss several something sickens them,
. . .which are the several [kinds of] things that sicken them [adults],

ká:w, cíaḍag, húawĭ, ge ṣú:dagĭ, bá'ag, wíṣag.
badger, gila monster, deer, ocean, eagle, hawk.
badger, gila monster, deer, ocean, eagle, hawk.

Há'icu 'aṣ wuḍ 'ép múmuwali,
Something just also is flies,
Another kind of thing is also [the class] houseflies,

c hab-a 'ép ha-wúa 'é:p, hégai.
and also does to them also, that-one.
and that [kind of thing] also does it to them.

Bá:ban 'o ha-múmkicud, kómkcuḍ, cémamagǐ,
Coyotes sicken them, turtle, horned toad,
Coyotes sicken them, turtle, horned toad,

ñé:, wé:s 'ídam.
look, all of it these-ones.
look, all of these.

Dangerous objects are abstractions

In the free translation of text 1 we have attempted to convey that Gregorio is referring to kinds of things sickening kinds of people. We will now consider the evidence supporting this interpretation. There are three examples of conjoined sentences in the text:

1. *Há'icu hab wuḍ gógs c hég múmkicud g 'áli.*
   Something is dog and that-one sickens the baby.
2. *Há'icu hab wuḍ nánhagio c hég 'ep múmkicud g 'áli.*
   Something is mice that-one also sickens the baby.
3. *Há'icu 'aṣ wuḍ 'ep múmuwali c hab a 'ép ha-wúa 'é:p, hégai.*
   Something is also flies and it does it to them, that-one.

The above examples share common features: they begin with *há'icu*, "something," and the second clause of each contains the singular pronoun *hégai* – or its variant, *hég* – which refers to the subject of the first clause. It is a fact of Piman grammar that when sentences in the present tense are conjoined by *c* they have the same subjects.

These examples differ in reference to the singular or plural form of nouns. The nouns in question refer to either: (1) the animals that sicken people or (2) the people sickened by animals. In example 1, both nouns are are singular: *gógs* instead of *gógogs, 'áli* instead of *'á'al*. In example 2, mice is plural – the singular would be *náhagio* – while baby is singular. In example 3, flies is plural – the singular would be *mú:wali* – and so is the object of *múmkicud*, which is expressed as the third person plural pronoun object, *ha*.

Of the fifteen different kinds of causal agents mentioned in the text Gregorio pluralizes four. We cannot explain why he chose to pluralize some nouns and not others but the following evidence indicates that he regularly pluralized his citations of mice and not his citation of dog. The day after he spoke text 1 he referred back to it saying: ". . . *mañ 'am héki hú ṣa 'á:g, nánhagio, gógs*," ". . . as I have already told, mice, dog" (text 13).

The important point for our purposes is not about the variation in number, but instead the constant features of *há'icu* and *hég. Há'icu* and *hég* must refer to the same thing since they are subjects of clauses linked by *c*. Therefore the causal agent in these sentences is a singular noun and not flies, mice, or dogs.

Thus, Gregorio did not say: "*Há'icu hab wuḍ nángagio c hégam 'o múmkicud g 'á'al*," "Something is mice and they sicken babies." Instead he said: "Something is mice and that-one sickens the baby." This is the basis for our rendition: "Something is [the class] mice and that sickens [the class] baby." We conclude that these sentences employing *múmkicud* are not about the sickening actions of particular animals upon particular people.

In our opinion Piman discourse maintains this level of abstraction not only when the discussion concerns generalities about different kinds of sickness, but also when the shaman speaks to the patient during the actual moments of diagnosis or cure. The shaman says, for example: "*Hég 'o kĭ m-múmkicud, g gógs*," "That-one is sickening you, the dog." The reference is to the species, not to any particular dog. We will see how this interpretation reflects Piman theory and practice, namely, how diagnosis and cure are directed at species of sickening agents and not at individuals.

Parts of dangerous objects

Cloud, paint, and sun are used as subjects of sentences with *múmkicud*; however, they are not in themselves sickness-causing agents but merely "parts of," *cú'idag*, the object whose strength or way is said to cause sickness. The three examples on our list are confined to effigies and decorations used in rituals, but we assert the *cú'idag* principle holds for animal species, wind, and all the other kinds of dangerous objects.

Gregorio has said: "*Hébai g céwagĭ 'ep ha-múmkicud*," "Sometimes the cloud also sickens them" (tape 1.8). "Cloud" refers to a cloud effigy used in a ritual named *wí:gita*. It is also possible to say that the ritual sickens people: ". . . *Há'icu hab wuḍ wí:gita, 'é:p. Heg 'o 'ep múmkicud g hémajkam*," ". . . Something is *wí:gita*, also. That-one also sickens people" (text 11).

We contend the effigy may be properly referred to as *cú'idag*, or "part of," the ritual. We also maintain that the only entity which one can refer to as possessing strength or way is the ritual, as opposed to the effigy or the object the effigy represents. For example, *géwkdaj g wí:gita*, "its strength, the *wí:gita*," would be permissible usage while *géwkdaj g céwagĭ*, "its strength, the cloud," would not be permissible; likewise *wí:gita hímdag*, "*wí:gita* way," would be permissible while *céwagĭ hímdag*, "cloud way," would not be.

These speculations on Piman usage conform with the following facts: (1) the sickness resulting from misuse of the effigy is named *wí:gita* sickness rather than cloud sickness and (2) the sickness is cured by performing an abbreviated version of the entire ritual rather than by a cure directed only at clouds.

This principle – that parts of things are dangerous because they precipitate a sickness on behalf of the whole thing – is verified in reference to dangerous animal species. For example, stepping in a bear track brings on bear sickness; using the devil's things – fancy cowboy ropes – brings on devil sickness; and misusing buzzard feathers brings on buzzard sickness. Each of the above may be called the *cú'idag* of the dangerous object whose strength causes sickness.

Therefore, it should be correct to say of buzzard feathers: "*Ñúuwĭ 'á'an 'o ha-múmkicud mat hab o 'e-jú: g cú'idaj g ñú'wĭ*," "Buzzard feather sickens them if something gets done to the parts [feathers] of a buzzard." We arrive at a general scheme: a buzzard feather is to the buzzard, as a cloud effigy is to the *wí:gita* ritual, as a part of a dangerous object is to the dangerous object whose way or strength causes sickness.

Our scheme for the classification of causal agents does not distinguish between rituals and other dangerous things. This distinction has been made by Underhill (1946:265). She reported that some sicknesses result from "ceremonial lapse" and others from "the ill will of animals." We have classified rituals – for example, *wí:gita* – as causal agents with the same status as animals. We have said that a ritual artifact has the same status as the feather of a natural bird; both are parts of an abstract thing whose way or strength causes the sickness.

In defense of this merger we offer the following points.

1. Gregorio has given no Piman-language equivalent for Underhill's classification.
2. From Gregorio's point of view the ritual sickness and the natural one pose identical problems for diagnosis and cure: Both are manifest in the patient's body as strengths which may freely intermingle and which respond to the same manipulations during diagnosis or cure.
3. Underhill's distinction ignores jimsonweed, wind, ghosts, and other dangerous things which are neither rituals nor animals.

4. Since *ká:cim* sicknesses result from diverse forms of infringement upon the ways of dangerous objects they all might be said to result from a sense of "ceremonial lapse."

Granting these points, it still seems that rituals as causal agents may constitute a class distinct from the other varieties of *ká:cim* sicknesses; however, on the present evidence we can only conclude that this class is unnamed.[2]

Wandering sickness

The items of table 2 with three stars are possible subjects of sentences with *múmkicud* which fall into a distinct category. Each item is a contagious sickness which, according to Piman belief, afflicts Pimans along with all other peoples. These *'óimmeḍdam*, or wandering sicknesses are the only sicknesses which Pimans suffer in common with other races.

The nomenclature for wandering sicknesses is distinct from that of the *ká:cim* sicknesses in that the former are named with reference to the patient's symptoms rather than with reference to independently existing natural or cultural phenomena. In this respect the wandering sicknesses conform to the English pattern of nomenclature exemplified by piles and hives. These names based on symptoms, may be subjects of the verb "to sicken." This is also in conformity with English usage; for example, *híhiwdag 'o múmkicud g hémajkam*, "chicken pox sickens people." *Híhiwdag* or "sores," is descriptive of the same skin eruptions denoted by "pox." In fact, an alternate name for this sickness is the loan translation, *cúcul híwdag*, or "chicken sore."

In contrast, itchy scalp is a symptom of a *ká:cim* sickness caused by the strength or way of eagles. It is correct to say, "Eagle strength sickens a person and his scalp itches," but it is not correct to say, "Itchy scalp sickens a person."

Dangerous objects, strength, and symptoms

Underlying the differences between wandering and staying sicknesses in reference to contagion there exists a distinction concerning the operation of strength as a causal agent.

All Piman afflictions involve the strength of an entity which exists in the world. In the case of *ká:cim* sicknesses a special relationship exists between the entity (a dangerous object), the strength, and the patient's symptoms. The dangerous objects whose collective strength causes a *ká:cim* sickness are not of the same substance as any of the physical matter present in a patient's body. There are rabbits in the world, there is rabbit strength physically present in a patient suffering from rabbit sickness, and there are other substantial manifestations of rabbit sickness in the patient such as boils. We will refer to the latter as symptoms, deliberately distinguishing this category from strength. These, then, are the three relevant terms: dangerous object, strength, and symptoms. With *ká:cim* sicknesses each term refers to a different substance.

In reference to *'óimmeḍdam* sicknesses the relationship between dangerous object, strength, and symptoms differs from that for *ká:cim*. For wandering sicknesses the first and third terms seem to refer to the same substances and, consequently, strength cannot serve the logical function it does for *ká:cim*, namely the function of mediating between dangerous objects and symptoms. The lack of logical function corresponds with the lack of practical significance. Although wandering sicknesses reputedly have a strength, it is not possible – as with *ká:cim* sicknesses – for a shaman to act upon the strength and thereby effect changes in the patient's symptoms.

Each *'óimmeḍdam* sickness is an inherently virulent substance which may be considered analogous to germs, molecules, or spores. The virulent bits of such a sickness are spread by the wind, physical contact, and many other means; they are believed to be invisible to the naked eye. These sicknesses "get scattered," *'e-gántaḍ,* along the countryside, afflicting whoever crosses their path. In this manner, wandering sicknesses become manifest within the patient's body.

The different relationships between symptoms and strength are expressed in the following excerpts from tape 13.1. Gregorio contrasts heat *s-tóñ*, as a symptom of the *ká:cim* sickness, devil sickness, with heat as a manifestation of the *'óimmeḍdam* sickness, hotness or flu, *s-tóñjig.*

In the case of *ká:cim* sickness, heat is considered to be a thing "added to" or "along with," *'e-wé:nad*, the strength of the dangerous object; that is, the patient has two things in him, the strength and the heat. In the case of *'óimmeḍdam* sickness, heat is identical in substance with the agent from the outside world which has entered the patient and made him sick, namely hotness. Conceived of as an *'óimmeḍdam* sickness, the hotness is said to have its own strength and to spread throughout the countryside sickening people; however, it is not reputed to be doubly manifest in the patient – in the manner of a *ká:cim* sickness – as a symptom *plus* the strength of a different, independently existing thing, for example, a devil.

Há'icu	hab wuḍ 'ep jíawul,
Something	is also devil,

Another [dangerous] thing is the devil,

c hab a másma hab 'ep 'e-wúa,
and thus also happens,
and it [devil strength] also happens [to cause heat in the patient],

heg hékaj mo s-tóñ 'í:bdag, g káwiyu,
that-one by means of ss hot heart, the horse,
because the heart of a horse is hot,

pégi, hég 'o 'ámjeḍ 'am 'i wú:ṣk, hégai.
well, that-one from there emerges, that-one.
well, for that reason [devil strength], it [heat] becomes manifest.

Hab ṣ pi wuḍ a'i hégai mo a há'icu wud 'é:p múmkidaj,
But it is not only that-one ss something is also his sickness,
But it is not only that one [devil sickness], and he [a hypothetical patient] has some other kind of sickness [in addition],

hab a cem pi wuḍ o héma, hégai,
but not is one of them, that-one,
but it [the other sickness] is not one of them [*ká:cim* sicknesses]

c wuḍ abṣ o hégai s-tóñjig,
and is just that-one hotness,
and it [the additional sickness] is just the flu,

c 'in 'óimmeḍ,
and here wanders,
and it [the flu, as a wandering agent, causing an epidemic] is wandering around [the countryside],

hab 'ep wúa g hémajkam mo 'ep múmkicud,
also does the person ss also sickens,
it [flu] also does it to the person, it also sickens him,

ñé:, há'ap 'o géwkdag, hégai.
look, that-way is strong, that-one.
look, like that it [flu] is strong.

'Im 'i gáwul má:s, há'icu,
Here differently appears, something,
It [flu] is a different sort of thing [from *ká:cim* sicknesses],

pi 'am hú hab hí o má:sk
never on-the-other-hand will appear
it [flu] will never appear to be of the sort

mas g s-tóñ 'ab o 'e-wé:nad,
ss the heat will get with it,
that the heat will be in addition to it [the strength of the sickness],

abṣ 'am hí o múmkic.
just there on-the-other-hand will sicken it.
it [flu] will just sicken him.

One cannot contract a *ká:cim* sickness directly from a person suffering from one; something must be done to the kind of object which is governed by a *ká:cim* sickness. Thus the action of these sicknesses is constrained. They can begin only after interaction between a person and a dangerous object. The sicknesses have no life of their own in that if the objects ceased to exist or if Pimans ceased infringing upon them the sicknesses would not occur.

The actions of the *'óimmeḍdam* sicknesses are not constrained by independent events. Pimans believe these sicknesses have their own strength and they sicken people directly according to the wishes and opportunities of the sickness. They are considered to be free, individual agents. As free agents, however, they are single-minded, having no other purpose than to make people sick.

When one encounters another individual afflicted with an *'óimmeḍdam* sickness, according to Piman concepts, one should think "that sickness will get me if I let it" and then one should try to block the sickness' opportunities.* However when one encounters a case of *ká:cim* sickness it is understood that the sickness stems from the patient's past behavior toward a dangerous object such as a deer.

Texts and other information concerning the cause and cure of *'óimmeḍdam* sicknesses can be found in note 3. They establish the following:

1. *'Óimmeḍdam* sicknesses move from place to place according to their own will, whereas the *ká:cim* sicknesses "do not wander" (text 48).
2. Direct action against *'óimmeḍdam* sicknesses – sucking their strength – may not be sufficient to cure them (text 49).
3. *'Óimmeḍdam* sicknesses may be cured by inoculation, among other means (text 50).
4. Wandering sicknesses may be lied to (Russell 1908).

* Pimans do this by quarantine, inoculation, or by telling the following type of lie: "I like small pox."

Ká:cim sicknesses in Piman doctrine

Wandering sicknesses are contagious because they are endowed with an indiscriminate lust to inflict themselves on people without regard to race, age, sex, or prior actions. Each of these factors, on the other hand, is significant for *ká:cim* sicknesses. Let us now concentrate upon the first factor, race.

Text 2 explains that *ká:cim* sicknesses afflict only Pimans. A special relationship exists between the Pimans, the rules of propriety which were intended for them, and their sicknesses. Gregorio mentions the relation as if it is paradoxical. He states that the sicknesses were "given to us" during the mythical period. They may seem "wrong" but they "originate" in "propriety." Thus the *ká:cim* sicknesses were somehow destined for Pimans. The Piman notion of propriety necessitates the acceptance of these sicknesses.

Gregorio then states that the sicknesses originate only among Pimans and that they can afflict only Pimans. On these grounds they are distinct from the *'óimmeḍdam*, which originate among other races and may be transmitted from Pimans to other peoples. In summary, the *ká:cim* sicknesses, which were intended for Pimans, are implicated with the maintenance of their propriety and do not afflict any other people.

TEXT 2 (Tape 23.3)

. . .Pi hébai 'óimmeḍ,
. . .Not someplace wanders,
. . .It [ká:cim sickness] never wanders,

'í: 'o a'i 'óimmeḍ, 'í:ya,
here only wanders, here,
it only goes around here,

heg hékaj mo 'i hab cú'ig, 'í:ya
that-one by means of ss here is, here
because it is established here

matp háscu 'áb 'i t-má:,
ss whatever gave to us,
[by] whatever thing [a god] gave it [commanded the order of all things, including sicknesses] to us,

hascu 'i t-ná:to k háscu 'ab 'i t-má:.
whatever made us and whatever gave to us.
whatever made us and whatever he gave to us.

K a cem pi 'áp hab cú'ig,
And yet improper is,
And even though it [the commanded order] seems wrong,

c 'atp abṣ hab-a 'éḍa 'am wuḍ a 'áp'edag 'ámjeḍkam
but yet there is propriety from-thing
still it has its source in propriety

mo hég 'ámjeḍ 'ab ṣó:ṣon hégai hab cú'igam múmkidag
ss that-one from originates that-one kind of sickness
which is the origin of that kind of sickness

matp hé'ekia 'i há'icu 'ab 'i t-má:.
ss several something gave to us.
however many things he gave to us.

. . .Hég 'o 'áb ṣó:ṣon, 'í:ya 'o a'i,
. . .That-one originates, here only,
. . .It [ká:cim sickness] originates from that [given order] and it is only here,

. . .'ia dá:m hab 'e-wúa, hégai,
. . .here on top it happens, that-one,
. . .it [ká:cim sickness] only exists right here,

c wóho mo 'ia a'i 'óimmeḍ,
and truly ss here only wanders,
and truly it only goes around here,

'ab a'i héjel t-'áb, 'á:cim.
against-it only itself against us, us.
it only applies to us.

The special nature of the *ká:cim* sicknesses receives further elaboration in text 3. Gregorio offers examples illustrating the origin of these sicknesses from actions concerning "our food." This identification of dangerous objects with foods should be interpreted as symbolic rather than as a strict statement of fact. Not all edible species are considered dangerous and most dangerous species are not eaten. Gregorio's rhetorical purpose apparently was to give praise to the class of *ká:cim* sickness and emphasize the uselessness of the *'óimmeḍdam.* He accomplished this by connecting the notion of food with the notion of residence. Gregorio associated residence with food: certain dangerous objects are residents which live here, so to speak, for Pimans to eat them. The *'óimmeḍdam* differ on both counts in that they are not eaten and they are not considered permanent residents in the community; whatever makes them sicken people will not be clarified by the history of the patient's actions toward the sources of human nourishment.

Gregorio then mentioned an additional sense – in reference to triviality – in which the *'óimmeḍdam* sicknesses differ from the *ká:cim:* unlike the latter, the *'óimmeḍdam* are not the "consequences," *cú'ijig*, of anyone's action. The significant point is that because wandering sicknesses originate elsewhere and appear to reach Pimans through their own initiative they are not the consequences of any Piman's prior action.

TEXT 3 (Tape 23.5)

Pégi, k hémho a mat o t-múmkic,
Well, and definitely ss will sicken us,
Well, definitely it [ká:cim sickness] will sicken us,

k 'ab ha-'áb, hégam kí:kam,
and is against them, those residents,
and it is up to those residents [local animals],

heg hékaj mo há'icu wuḍ hégai mo wuḍ t-gégusig,
that-one by means of ss something is that-one ss is our food,
because something [local animal] is our food,

ñé:, m 'ant o si ṣél 'á:
look, ss I will straightly tell
look, as I will explain in detail

mo g húawĭ hab cú’ig, cú:wĭ hab cú’ig
ss the deer is, rabbit is
that the deer is, the rabbit is

mo wuḍ t-gégusig, hégam.
ss is our food, those-ones.
they are our food.

Abṣ hab-a hab ’e-wúa
But happens
But it happens

matt pi ’áp ’am hú hab o t-jú:,
ss we ever should improperly do ourselves,
if we ever should behave improperly [toward dangerous objects],

’am hég ’óidk ’am hú hás o t-jú:.
there that-one follows eventually somehow will do to us.
then later on it [sickness] will do something to us.

. . .Pégi, kc ’í:da ’óimmeḍdam múmkidag
. . .Well, and this-one wandering sickness
. . .Well, and this wandering sickness

mo hab hí má:s mo pi ’i hú hab ’e-wúa, hégai.
ss on the other hand appears ss here doesn’t happen, that-one.
as for it, it doesn’t do like that.

Pi wuḍ gégusig, hégai, háscu’i ’óimmeḍdam múmkidag,
Not food, that-one, whatever wandering sickness,
Whatever that wandering sickness is, it is not food,

k abṣ hab-a ’í:da ’atp hab cú’ig
but this-one is
but this thing is of the nature

mo wuḍ ’óimmeḍdam múmkidag.
ss is wandering sickness.
which is a wandering sickness.

’Atp hí abṣ cem hébai o hí:, hégai
ss on the other hand just anyplace will go, that-one
It can just go anyplace

matp hékid o ’e-’ái.
ss whenever will get reached.
whenever its time comes [whenever it wishes to].

Ñé:, k pi hab ’i héḍai ’ab hú wuḍ o cú’ijigk ’ab ’ámjeḍ hégai
Look, and not anybody ever will be instigator about that-one
Look, and it [wandering sickness] is not started by
[the action of] anybody

matp háscu wuḍ hégai
ss whatever is that-one
whatever it may be

matp hég ’ámjeḍ ’am ’e-náttoḍ, hégai.
ss that-one from there gets made, that-one.
which is the reason why it was made.

Pi g kí:kam.
Not the resident.
It is not a resident.

The following texts illustrate Piman doctrine connecting sicknesses and morality. We have already established that *ká:cim* sicknesses are referred to as residents, *kí:kam.* This word belongs to a family of words concerning society.[4] The maintenance of society is the purpose of the "Piman way," *’ó’odham hímdag*, which was "given" anciently. Pimans are its chosen, or fated, upholders. The stated resultants of obeying the commandments are propriety, joy, and health. Sickness comes from failure to follow the commandments of the way: failure to be careful, to remember, to believe, or to defer to things.

In text 4, Gregorio states that the Piman way was "given" at the time of creation and Pimans are not responsible for its content, which they conceive of as a conglomerate. He says it is intended to make "our society . . . stay proper" and to be "an assistance" to the life of individuals. The Piman way is dangerous if improperly used; proper use requires knowledge and remembrance.

TEXT 4 (Tape 5.1)

Héu'u,	hab 'o másma hab cú'ig,	í:da.
Yes,	thus is,	this-one.

Yes, thus it is, this [Piman way].

Ná'ags	mú'i	hía	ná:nko	másma	hab má:s	g 'ó'odham	hímdag
Well	severally	of course	variously	thus	appears	the Piman	way

Well, the Piman way is many and varied [in its parts]

mapt hékid	háscu'i	t-ná:to	'íd	dá:m	jéweḍ,
ss whenever	whatever	made us	this	on top	earth,

when whatever [god] made us here on the earth's surface,

háscu	'ab t-má:.
whatever	gave it to us.

whatever he gave to us.

Kutt hég	o hékaj,
And we that-one	will use,

And we use that [Piman way],

t hég hékaj	o s-'ap'ekad	g t-kí:dag,
that-one by means of	will stay proper	the our society,

by means of it our society will stay proper,

hég 'ámjeḍ	hab cú'ig	g hímdag,	'ápcuda
that-one from	is	the way,	thing that causes propriety

for that reason the way exists, as a way to cause propriety

mo heg hékaj	'am wuḍ a'i wé:mta	g hémajkam	dúakkuḍaj,
ss that-one by means of	there is assistance	the person	its life,

which is an assistance to the people's life,

c 'éḍa	'am a hía	'ép s-ta-'é:bidama,	'é:p
and yet	there of course	also is fearful,	also

and yet it [the way] is dangerous, too

mat pi 'am hú áp hab másma 'am o hékaj.
ss never properly thus there will use.
if one should fail to use it properly.

Mú'i ná:nko há'icu 'o hab má:s,
Severally various something appears,
Several different things are like that,

pégi, c hég 'óidk 'ab s-'e-má:c c s-'e-cégĭto,
well, and that-one follows gets known and gets remembered,
well, and it's through this it is known and remembered,

c 'ab 'á:gidas g wécij hémajkam.
and has been told the young person.
and it is told to the young people.

In text 5 we find the word *'áp'edag*, propriety, referred to in the same manner as *hímdag* in text 4, as a thing which "has been given" subject to commandments which are here said to be about "how to take care." Failure to maintain propriety is attributed to a lapse of intelligence: either disbelief or failure to remember. The resultant is sickness.

TEXT 5 (Tape 6.10)

Héu'u, há'ap 'o másma hab má:s, 'í:da.
Yes, that-way thus appears, this-one.
Yes, that's how it [Piman way] is.

No pi hab cú'ig
Because is
Because it is the case

mo wé:s há'icu 'ab má:kĭs g 'áp'edag, cíhañig 'ab 'ámjeḍ
ss every something has been given the propriety, commandment about it
That propriety has been given to everything, commandments about it

mat hás másma o 'e-ñú:kud.
ss somehow thus will get taken care of.
about how it should be taken care of.

Pégi, t ’am hú hab o ’e-jú:,
Well, ever will get done,
Well, it may happen to him [any Piman],

’am pi wóhocudk,
there won’t believe,
if he doesn’t believe it [commandments],

’o ’am hú abṣ pi o ’e-cégĭtok,
or there ever just will not remember,
or he may not remember,

’am hú hás o ’e-jú:
there ever somehow will get done
and he might do something

matp hékid háscu wuḍ o’ik,
ss whenever whatever will be,
whenever whatever thing may be there,

c ’ab o ’ábkad.
and will be against it.
and will confront him.

Hég ’o ’áb bébb’e hégai ’e-múmkidag.
That-one against it brings that-one its own sickness.
That’s where he brings on his own sickness.

The next text was collected by Herzog from the Gila River Pimans during the 1920s.[5] It is a ritual oration entitled “Elder Brother’s Prophecy.” The speech, delivered in the first person, is attributed to “Elder-brother Shaman,” *sí:s má:kai*, a mythical hero whose actions were preeminent in establishing the present-day position of the Pimans as upholders and caretakers of their own special way.

Elder-brother Shaman was the original deliverer of the oration. The audience was the Piman people and the occasion was his imminent withdrawal from participation in their affairs. Thus the oration contains a Piman sense of “commandment issuing from a god.” The oration’s spirit most nearly resembles, in Anglo-American culture, General George Washington’s Farewell Address; Elder-brother Shaman is understood to have guided the Pimans through the period when they first learned their destiny. During the time of his leadership neither he nor they knew what the final outcome of their adventures would be. The subject matter of the oration centers on the relationship between the Pimans, the world being left to them, and their propriety.

The prophetic content consists of a prediction that other people, who may be understood to be Anglo-Americans, will do that which the Pimans must not do, namely to kill the earth. The Pimans are told that they will not kill the earth. They are ordered to be "deferent," *bá:bagid*. If they are deferent they will experience propriety – enjoy health and avoid sickness – and they will live to witness the earth's death at the hands of non-Pimans.

HERZOG*

Want o hí: 'am 'ú:pam
That I will go there back again
I'm going back [away from you]

m 'añ wuḍ a hékǐ hú mú:kig.
ss I am already dead.
since I've already died.

Nt o hí: 'am 'ú:pam,
I will go there back again,
I'm going back,

kut 'am ñ-'óid c hab o 'e-wúad g ñ-kó'idag.
and there will follow me and will be doing the my corpses.
and my corpses will be doing what I have been doing.

Kumt s-bá:bagǐ,
And you will defer,
And you [Pimans] will defer to it [the world],

kut hég 'i hú wuḍ o 'em-'áp'edagk.
and down here will be your propriety.
and down here [on earth] will be your propriety.

* Reprinted, by permission, from George Herzog, Piman texts (Philadelphia: American Philosophical Society Library, Franz Boas Collection of Materials for American Linguistics), ms. 269.

[M] t o cem pi bá:bagĭ,
[If you] will not defer,
Should you not defer to it,

hég s-hó:tam o ñéi g pi 'e-'áp'edag.
that-one quickly will see the your impropriety.
quickly you will see your impropriety.

. . .Kumt pi 'á:pim o mú'ato g jéweḍ ká:cim
. . .And not you will be killing the earth staying
. . .And you will not be the ones to kill the staying earth

mant 'áb o ha-wúi dágĭto,
ss I will to them leave it,
I will leave it to them [non-Pimans],

kut 'ídam hab o jú:.
and these-ones will do.
and they will do it.

Kut 'ídam o mú'ato g jéweḍ ká:cim,
And these-ones will be killing the earth staying,
And these will kill the staying earth,

kumt 'á:pim a cem pi o há'icu má:ck,
and you even though nothing will know,
and even if you don't know anything [about it],

c abṣ s-'áp o 'e-tá:tkad,
and just pleasantly will feel,
and you will just be feeling fine,

c 'am o néi
and there will see
and you will see it

mat hékid hab o 'e-jú:.
ss whenever will happen.
when it happens.

We have found the *ká:cim* sicknesses, the foci of Piman doctrine, to be concrete expressions of impropriety and specific to the Piman people. We will continue to find that Gregorio conceives of sicknesses in moral rather than in natural, scientific, or physiological terms. The things that cause sickness are not germs, extreme temperatures, or rotten foods. Instead, the crucial topics in the explanation of cause include individual people's wishes, the commandments of propriety, and the strength that sanctions the commandments. This is not to say that Pimans know nothing about afflictions caused by rotten foods, temperature extremes, and germs, for they do, but these are not Piman sicknesses. We have seen that the Piman word *múmkidag* refers to a different range of phenomena than the English word "sickness."

3. Animal 'Sicknesses', Forebodings, and Sorcery

We will now trace the implications of the concepts presented in section 2, namely that the subject matter of *ká:cim* sicknesses concerns actions between human beings and the various nonhumans Gregorio refers to as "residents" with Pimans on the earth. The first implication is that victims of *ká:cim* sicknesses must be human. Text 6 establishes that the network of "dangerousness" between Pimans and animal species is anthropocentric in that each species sickens human beings, but no species sickens other kinds of animals. The second implication is that dangerous objects are always nonhuman or, more specifically, never a living Piman human, for ghosts and enemies are dangerous objects.

The second implication is drawn from texts dealing with two kinds of affliction, caused by humans, which are not *ká:cim* sicknesses. The first of these afflictions, called forebodings, is interesting because its causality is similar to the causality of a *ká:cim* sickness. Forebodings are caused by a parent's failure to baptize a human baby. The similar *ká:cim* sickness is caused by one's failure to baptize a newly acquired saint's image, a nonhuman dangerous object. The lengthy text contrasting forebodings and saint sickness also will introduce us to a topic pursued in later sections, namely the sense of transgression that is present in *ká:cim* sicknesses and absent in other kinds of affliction.

The second non-*ká:cim* sickness which we will discuss is sorcery. We will show that sorcery differs from *ká:cim* sicknesses in that sorcery is an act that individuals "just do" to each other. A victim of sorcery has merely a single individual operating against him, a condition shamans easily can remedy. The victim of *ká:cim* sickness suffers from the way and strength of an entire species, a situation which the shaman generally cannot remedy unaided or without the consent of the species involved.

Animals cannot contract *ká:cim* sickness

Text 6 explains why human status is a necessary precondition for being a victim of *ká:cim* sickness. The question is whether a species that sickens people can also sicken animals. It was assumed the answer would be no; we hoped that Gregorio would include in his answer the reason why this is not possible. His answer is that animals could not "get given," *'e-má:** sicknesses because sicknesses are necessarily cured by singing. "There is no evidence," *pi 'am hú táṣo*, and "it is unheard of," *pi 'am hú 'á:gas*, that animals can sing curing songs. Since one cannot contract sicknesses without having cures for them, and since curing requires singing, it is not possible for animals to become sick.

Gregorio does consider the possibility of a sort of "persons," *hémajkam*, who would combine the attributes of "being animals" and "being sickenable." He states, however, that such creatures are unknown to the Pimans. Note that these hypothetical creatures are referred to as *hémajkam* instead of *há'icu dúajkam*, animals. This confirms our interpretation that sicknesses only afflict people. According to Gregorio, if there are animals capable of becoming sick, they should be classified as "some different [from Pimans] sort of people," *há'i gáwul má:s hémajkam*, instead of true animals.

TEXT 6 (Tape 12.10)

Q

No wa wóho	mat o ha-múmkic	g há'icu dúakam,	g cémamagǐ –
Is true	ss will sicken	the animal,	the horned toad –

Is it true that the horned toad can sicken animals –

mat o múmkic,	g cémamagǐ	g gáwul má:s dúakam,	gógs,	'o g bán,
ss will sicken it,	the horned toad	the different kind of animal,	dog,	or coyote,

'o abṣ cem háscu?
or whatever?

that the horned toad can sicken other animals like the dog or coyote?

A

. . .Hab a'i má:s,
. . .Only appears,

. . .It must be [untrue],

heg hékaj	mo hégam	há'icu dúakam	hab má:s
that-one by means of	ss those-ones	animal	appears

because those animals are of a nature

* The medio-passive form.

mo gáwul má:s,
ss differently appears,
which is different,

pi hab má:s m 'in g hémajkam hab má:s.
doesn't appear ss here the person appears.
they aren't like the people around here.

C abṣ hab-a hab 'ép cú'ig
But also is
But it is also the case

matp héms há'i gáwul má:s hémajkam,
ss perhaps some differently appears person,
perhaps that certain of the different tribes [species]
of persons [animals],

'atp héms pi hab má:s 'am ha-'ámjeḍ, hégai hab cú'igam múmkidag,
perhaps does not appear there them from, that-one kind of sickness,
[well] perhaps they don't give sicknesses to each other
[across species],

'aha b 'as híg a cú'ig, nac hía ge s-má:c.
ah maybe it is on the other hand is, because of course we just don't know.
ah, but perhaps they do and we simply don't know.

. . .'Íd hí pi hab má:s
. . .This-one on the other hand does not appear
. . .However it isn't evident

mas hás másma 'e-má: g múmkidag,
ss somehow thus gets given the sickness,
how they [animals] get given [*ká:cim*] sickness,

k hás o 'e-jú:? 'O 'e-wúso?
and how will get done? Will get cured?
and then what would they do? Get cured?

Ñé:,	hég 'ám	pi 'am hú	táṣo,
Look,	that-one there	never	is clear,

Look, on that point [their ability to do curing rituals] there is no evidence,

pi 'am hú	'á:gas	hab másma,
never	has been told	thus,

it is unheard of,

'i hab a'i t-wúi,	hémajkam	wúi.
only us-towards,	people	towards.

it is only for us, people [to do ritual cures].

Hab hí	cú'ig
On the other hand	is,

It is the case [about curing rituals],

c 'am hí	há'icug	hégai	ha-ñéñ'eidalig,	hégam
and there on the other hand	is present	that-one	their songs,	those-ones

and there are the songs of those [causal agents]

matp	háscu	wuḍ	o'ik.
ss	whatever	will	be.

whatever it might be.

Né:,	heg hékaj	hab hí má:s,
Look,	that-one by means of	on the other hand appears,

Look, for that reason [knowledge of curing songs] it's like that,

c 'am há'ap	'attp hí	pi má:c
and there that-way	we on the other hand	don't know

there on the other side [as for the animals] we don't know

mas hás	másma	hab o 'e-jú:
ss somehow	thus	will get done

how it could be done

matp hab o cú'ig	'ab ha-'áb	g ha-múmkidag,	hégam
ss would be	there against them	the their sickness,	those-ones

whether they could have any [*ká:cim*] sicknesses

matp héḍai	wuḍ o'ik g há'icu	dúakam.
ss whoever	would be the something	living-thing.

whoever the animals might be.

Forebodings

The word *s-ñéijig*, forebodings, refers to the unnatural behavior of wild animals toward people – for example, if an animal approaches a person – and to accidents – for example, if a person's horse bucks him off or if he wrecks his car. They are believed to signify one of two conditions: either a newborn baby among the victim's kinsmen has not been baptized or a female relative of the victim or the victim herself has passed her first menstruation without a ritual.

The ritual which Gregorio terms "to baptize" (*Wákon*, "to wash it," applies to babies, saints' images, and everyday objects such as laundry.) has a pagan and a Christian component: *S-ñéijig* occurs when the pagan component is not performed by a shaman – he baptizes the baby and both of its parents. As part of the baptismal ritual, which must be performed in the daytime, each parent of the baby must eat a gruel which the shaman has prepared from white clay and crushed owl feathers. Then the shaman brushes their heads with an owl feather and finally he blows, spits, and presses on the top of each head. Afterwards, for at least the remainder of the day and the following night, the parents may not bathe or eat red food, salt, or fat. Red food minimally includes meat and red chili pepper, but also includes, according to some Pimans, watermelon, strawberry soda pop, and red beans. The dietary restrictions end with the next day's bath.

In the case of forebodings related to a girl among the victim's kinsmen or the victim herself passing her first menstruation without a ritual, the girl is treated with the owl feather and clay gruel in a manner resembling the baptism ritual. While in seclusion she abstains from bathing and from eating red food, salt, and fat.

Each of the rites terminates, for the parents or the girl, a state called *pi cú'ikodag:* literally, "not-free-ness"; idiomatically, "the state of a person whose actions must be constrained because they may cause sickness or *s-ñéijig* to himself, his kinsmen, or his spouse."[6]

We translate *s-ñéijig* as "forebodings" because we believe the word is built upon the root *ñeid*, "to observe it." It should be understood that certain events termed *s-ñéijig* function as warnings while other events named by the same term function as dire punishments to people who do not heed the earlier warnings. The idea is that forebodings build up until a final disaster occurs: for example, an omitted baptism may first result in small forebodings such as birds landing on the parents or their relatives; if these are unheeded someone may be injured in an accident; if this is unheeded someone may die in an accident. These events are collectively called *s-ñéijig.*

S-ñéijig differs from the *ká:cim* sicknesses in that it does not involve the way or the strength of a dangerous object. This is illustrated by text 7 in which Gregorio was asked to distinguish between *s-ñéijig* as the result of not baptizing a baby and the *ká:cim* sickness that results from not baptizing images of saints.

Gregorio stated that in the case of *s-ñéijig* no one or nothing was offended through the parents' failure to baptize. The omitted ritual is not viewed as cruelty on the part of the parents. Accordingly, *s-ñéijig* cannot be cured in the manner of a *ká:cim* sickness for, as will be seen in part IV, cures are addressed toward aggrieved parties. In reference to *s-ñéijig*, the unfortunate events are irreversible. One cannot get over, come to terms with, or be cured of forebodings. Instead it is a matter of averting future forebodings, especially the ultimate fatalities, by finally having the baptism performed.

The text states that *s-ñéijig* does not apply to saint baptisms. It asserts that "saint sickness" applies to them. According to our interpretation saints are classified among the useful but dangerous objects of the world, a category which does not include living Pimans.

Gregorio speaks of the saints' images as mere pictures which do, however, have "something strong" about them. He explained that they must be treated in the manner of human babies and, specifically, they must be "strengthened." The owner who fails to "humanize" his saint's picture – who treats it as a mere commodity – will become sick.

As with all *ká:cim* sicknesses, the action which brings on saint sickness is a human's transgression against something whose rights exist independent of human society. The notion of offense or transgression is prominent in the thinking on these sicknesses, but the transgressions always are on the part of people toward nonpeople or nature rather than between people.

Piman Indians buy pictures and statues of Catholic saints. Before they can be kept safely upon the household altar, they must be baptized. As far as we know this baptism does not involve the pagan component, *s-ñéijig*, previously discussed. The purchaser is not classified as *pi cú'ikodag.*

TEXT 7

(Tape 10.1)

Q

No a wóho mat ép o ha-'á'ahe g s-ñéijig, 'ab 'ámjeḍ
Is true ss also will reach them the forebodings, about
hégam sásanto?
those-ones saints?

Is it true that s-ñéijig afflicts people in connection with saints?

A

Héu'u, 'am o hía hás másma hab cú'ig,
Yes, there of course somehow thus is,

Yes, it is somehow,

'ab 'ámjeḍ 'í:da hab má:s hímdag, cíhañig,
about this-one appears way, commandment,

about this kind of way, these commandments,

ab 'ámjeḍ hégai 'ó'ohon, sá:nto.
about that-one picture, saint.

about the image of the saint.

B

K hí wóho mo hás 'e-wúa,
And on the other hand is true ss somehow happens,

And it's true that they [baptisms of saints] are done [similarly to infant baptisms],

abṣ hab-a gáwul másma c hía wépo másma hab 'e-wúa,
but differently thus and of course similarly thus happens,

but differently and they [practices about saints] merely resemble them,

hég hékaj mo hab másma ṣó:ṣon gḍ hú,
that-one by means of ss thus originated far-below,

because they [commandments for saints] originated far in the past,

há'icu 'ab kéli hémajkam 'ámjeḍ.
something old man person about it.
[they are] things from the ancient people.

'Atp wá:ṣ hú mé:k
Away distant
It was quite long ago

matp hékid 'i 'e-ná:to há'icu hab másma,
ss whenever got made something thus,
when the things like that [the commandments] were made,

pégi, k 'ab 'i hím k wuḍ t-má:kidag, hégai.
well, and came and is our gift, that-one.
well, and it continues until now and it is our gift.

C

Pégi, kc wóho mo hab 'e-wúa
Well, and truly ss happens
Well, and truly it [infant baptism] is done

mo hékid g 'áli 'in 'i wúṣk'e,
ss whenever the baby here emerges,
that whenever a baby is born,

k 'am o hímad c 'am o 'ái
and there is going and there reaches
and it [time] goes by and then it [time] reaches him [baby]

mat hékid hás hú 'i 'e-jú: k má:sĭ
ss when somehow ever happened and is born
whenever he happened and was born

mat o 'al 'i gé'ehogad,
ss will slightly be large,
when it will be slightly grown [not newborn],

pegi, t 'ab o hú:, hégai bíd,
well, will eat, that-one clay,
well, it will eat the clay,

k hég wuḍ wákonaḍgaj, hégai.
and that-one is its washing, that-one.
and that is his baptism.

D

Pégi, kc 'am hímk 'am hébai wuḍ 'i hímdam
Well, and there went and there sometime is later-on
Well and it [history] went on and at some point

mat 'in há'icu 'i wú:ṣ
ss here something emerged
then something [else] made its appearance

mo hab 'á'aga "sá:nto."
ss calls "saint."
called "saint."

K wuḍ wóhokam,
And is true thing,
And they are true things,

. . .géwkdag 'o hégai há'icu hab má:scu,
. . .strong is that-one something apparent-thing,
. . .that image has strength,

c 'éḍa wuḍ abṣ a cem 'ó'ohon,
and yet is just a picture,
and yet it is just a picture,

c abṣ hab-a 'éḍa géwkdag há'icu ab 'ámjeḍ.
but yet strong something about it.
and yet [there is] something strong about it.

E

Pégi,	kc hékid	hab o 'e-jú:
Well,	and whenever	will get done

Well, and whenever it happens

mat g 'ó'odham	o táccud
ss the man	will desire

that a person wants

mat o 'éñigakad	hégai	c o ñú:kudad.
ss will be owning	that-one	and will be taking care of it.

to own that [image] and take care of it.

. . .Pégi,	k hab 'e-wúa
. . .Well,	and happens

. . .Well, it happens

mat hékid	o 'i béi,	hégai,
ss whenever	will get it,	that-one,

whenever he gets it [image],

k hémho a mat 'am a hás	o jú:,
and necessarily ss there somehow	will do,

that he will have to do something,

'o o héma	má:.
or will one of them	give it to it.

or give it to somebody.

T 'am o 'i 'áp'eculidaj	hab másma	mo g 'áli,
There will cause it to be proper	thus	ss the baby,

He [the saint's padrino] will bless it like a baby,

pégi,	t hég	o hí:	wé:maj,	s-'áp	hégai.
well,	and that-one	will go	with him,	properly	that-one.

well, and it will go with him [owner], properly.

F

Pi 'im hú has o jú:,
Not ever somehow will do,
If he does nothing to it,

k s-wóhom o bék,
and believingly will take it,
and just takes it,

k 'am abṣ hí o a cem ñú:kudad,
and there just of course will try to be taking care of it,
and tries to take care of it,

natṣ cem pi 'áp o ñú:kud,
because just takes care of it,
there is no reason why he shouldn't just take care of it,

c abṣ hab-a 'éḍa hég pi o há'icugkad, hégai 'ab 'ámjeḍ
but yet that-one will not be present, that-one about it
g géwkcudaj.
the its strengthening.
but yet that thing [the baptism] will be missing about its strength.

Pégi, k hémho a maṭ 'am há'icu hás o 'e-jú:, há'icu,
Well, and necessarily ss there something somehow will get done, something,
Well, something will have to happen,

o múmkic 'ab 'ámjeḍ,
will sicken about it,
it [saint way] will sicken him,

abṣ hab-a hégai a'i
but that-one only
but only him [the owner]

mat héḍa'i o 'i béi, hégai.
ss whoever will get, that-one.
whoever will have gotten it [image].

G

Ñé:,	k pi hab má:s	mo g s-ñéijig	hab cú'ig
Look,	and it does not appear	ss the foreboding	is

Look, and it [sickness] is not the same as *s-ñéijig*

mat 'am hás	o 'e-jú:,	há'icu
ss there somehow	will get done,	something

[so] that something will happen

matp pi 'am hú	hás	o 'i 'e-jú:,
ss never	somehow	will get done,

if it [baby] doesn't have something done to it,

pégi,	t 'am hás	o 'e-jú:,	há'icu,
well,	there somehow	will get done,	something,

well, something will happen [to the baby's relatives] ,

k 'am o hímk,
and there will go,

and it will go on,

'am bá'ic	há'icu	'am hás	'ép o 'e-jú:,
there further	something	there somehow	also will get done,

and later something else will happen,

abṣ o mú'ida, hégai, 'ámai.
just will be several, that-one, there.

there will be several [misfortunes] .

H

'Íd	o hí	pi hab másma	hab 'e-wúa.
This-one	on the other hand	not thus	happens.

This one [saint sickness] doesn't happen like that.

Hab a'i másma	'ab o hí:	'ab 'áb	hégai	hémajkam
Only thus	will come	is against it	that-one	person

it only goes against that person

matp hédạị o 'i béi.
ss whoever will get it.
who got it [the saint].

Ñé:, há'ap o másma hab cú'ig, 'í:da.
Look, that-way thus is, this-one.
Look, that's how it is.

Sorcery

The word we translate as sorcery refers to the following practices of which only the last, 5, represents an affliction similar to *ká:cim* sicknesses:

1. The shaman's use of spirit helpers to spy on or incapacitate deer in advance of a deer hunt by Piman men
2. The shaman's use of spirit helpers to spy on or incapacitate enemies in advance of a raid by Piman warriors
3. The shaman's use of spirits to incapacitate the foot-racers of another Piman village in advance of a foot-race with runners from the shaman's own village
4. The use of herbal philters, purchased from shamans by Piman men, to render themselves irresistible to Piman women
5. The shaman's use of spirit helpers or philters to incapacitate his fellow Pimans.

The theme of incapacitation runs through the examples. The shaman incapacitates a victim on the behalf of a client: deer on the behalf of humans; enemies on the behalf of Pimans; another village on the behalf of his own village; women on the behalf of an individual male client, or an individual victim on the sorcerer's own behalf.[7]

We see, then, that sorcery has a public application in which the shaman helps his clients undermine their competitors. We turn now to our specific subject matter, text 8, which explains how sorcery against individual Pimans is distinct from *ká:cim* sicknesses.

Gregorio makes two distinctions between *ká:cim* sickness and sorcery: of causal agents and of cure.

1. Of causal agents. Sorcery is something that people "just do," whereas sicknesses, according to our interpretation, are caused by the way or strength of an inhuman dangerous object.

2. Of cure. The shaman can treat sorcery directly, while a ritual cure is necessary to treat a *ká:cim* sickness. Thus, in text 8, the example is given of a patient who is found upon diagnosis to have sorcery as well as a *ká:cim* sickness within him. The sorcery can be "destroyed" and "removed" at once, but the sickness must be cured at a later time and "by means of" the dangerous object whose strength is in the patient. The central concept is that the cure of *ká:cim* sickness requires the consent of the causal agent. In general, the agent's consent is attained by ritual curers rather than by shamans.

While Gregorio refers to sorcery as a sickness, *múmkidag*, he does not employ the crucial verb *múmkicud* with reference to the act of causing this kind of sickness. Instead, he says, "He [sorcerer] sorcerizes him, and then he [patient] becomes sick." Thus, "to sorcerize" *híwhoi*, is used as a coordinate term with "to cause it to sicken," *múmkicud*, although both result in a state of affairs classified as sickness.[8] Note that Gregorio uses the notion of *ká:cim* sickness to distinguish between the two varieties of sickness.

TEXT 8 (Tape 9.16)

. . .Pégi, tp hab o cú'igk
. . .Well, will be
. . .Well, if it should be the case

. . .mo 'am a wé:s ha-má'iṣṣap, hégai
. . .ss there all of it covers them, that-one
. . .that it [sorcery substance in the patient] covers up everything [the strengths of *ká:cim* sicknesses]

matp háscu wuḍ o'ik,
ss whatever will be,
whatever they may be,

c há'icu 'é:p
and something also
and the other thing [the sorcery substance]

matp hab wuḍ abṣ o ha-júñk, ha-ná:toi,
ss just will be their doing, their making,
if it's just someone's doings, someone's makings,

hég hía 'i 'ab 'á'ap'et
that-one of course is proper
then of course it is all right

mat gam hú o páḍc, hégai,
ss away will ruin, that-one,
if he [shaman] will destroy it [sorcery stuff],

gm hú o si 'i wú:ṣad, hégai.
away will remove, that-one.
he will remove it [from the patient].

Ñé:, k pi 'am hú hí há'icu wuḍ hégai,
Look, and not ever on the other hand something is that-one,
Look, and the other thing [*ká:cim* sickness] is not [the same as] that one [sorcery],

héu'u, 'o hab há'icu o 'al 'e-wé:nad,
yes, or something may slightly get with it,
yes, or there may be something with it [a sickness along with the sorcery],

tp hég 'ám hí a hékaj 'e-wúso.
that-one there of course by means of it will get cured.
and then of course he [patient] may be cured by means of it [the dangerous object whose strength causes *ká:cim* sickness].

Ñe:, há'ap 'o a'i másma hab 'ép cú'ig,
Look, that-way only thus also is,
Look, it is only like that,

c há'icu wuḍ o ká:cim múmkidag,
and something will be staying sickness,
[when] the thing is a *ká:cim* sickness,

c wuḍ abṣ o hégaik mo 'in 'óimmeḍ,
and just will be that-one ss here wanders,
and it [the *ká:cim* sicknesses] will be the kind of thing which goes around here [among Pimans only],

. . .c hég	hí'i	pi abṣ cem hékid	hab 'e-wúa,
. . .and that-one	on the other hand	just not always	happens,

. . .and the other thing [sorcery] is not always being done,

abṣ hébai	'am hab 'e-júccu
just sometimes	there gets done

it is only occasionally being done

mat ṣ g hémajkam	o ná:to	há'icu,
ss the person	will make	something,

if some person has made something [sorcery],

k 'am o wúa	g hémajkam,
and there will put it	the person,

and he will put it against a person,

pégi,	t hég 'ám	wuḍ o múmkidagk.
well,	and that-one there	will be sickness.

well, and on that basis [sorcery] he will be sick.

. . .K hab 'á'aga,	g hékĭ hú hémajkam
. . .And calls it,	the ancient person

. . .And the ancient people call it

mat héma	hab o 'e-jú:,
ss one of them	will get done,

if it happens to somebody,

m-tṣ abṣ híwhoi,
ss just sorcerized it,

he was just sorcerized,

k hab múmku.
and is sick.

and that's why he is sick.

4. Causal Relationships

Strength and way

Gregorio has said little about the mechanics of *ká:cim* sickness and much about who bears the responsibility for them. With respect to the former question there is a well-developed theory on how strengths are manifest in the patient's body, but once we leave the body we lose track of strength. Gregorio has said nothing about the origins of strength outside the body.

The lack of information on strength outside the body may not be accidental in that it may reflect something systematic in Gregorio's theory. Statements on strength are in complementary distribution with statements on way. The former refer to a physical causal agent within the patient's body while the latter refer to a spiritual agent outside the patient's body. The logic involving complementarity has not been confirmed as an explicit feature of Piman theory, but in the discussion that follows it will be treated as such.

Way refers to the authorized or commanded rights of dangerous objects. These objects were endowed with something similar to contracts at the time of creation. Thus, when way is cited as a causal agent we understand that it is not the individual object which is causing sickness but the class of dangerous objects collectively. This point is illustrated in text 9.

The text concerns a dangerous object called *kú:kpĭ*, a war trophy kept closed in a bundle. It must be fed by its owner or else he or his family will become sick. In craving food and being addressable in human speech, these objects are more like humans than most dangerous objects. Thus, it is important for us to demonstrate that it is the object's way rather than the object itself that causes sickness.

Text 9 lacks the crucial terms way and strength. It does, however, support the argument that sickness does not emanate from the individual trophy but from the collectivity of trophies, their way. Put in terms of the general theory, the line of causality is as follows: the owner violates a commandment against the way of which his trophy is a part, "enemy consequence way"; the way sickens him and the sickness ultimately is manifest as strength inside his body; when he is cured, the cure will be directed toward the way and strength of "enemies" in general – the cure will not be directed at the individual trophy he failed to feed. The textual evidence consists in the pronoun Gregorio uses to illustrate an owner addressing his trophy. It is the second person plural rather than singular. The owner addresses his trophy as a member of the collectivity rather than as an individual.

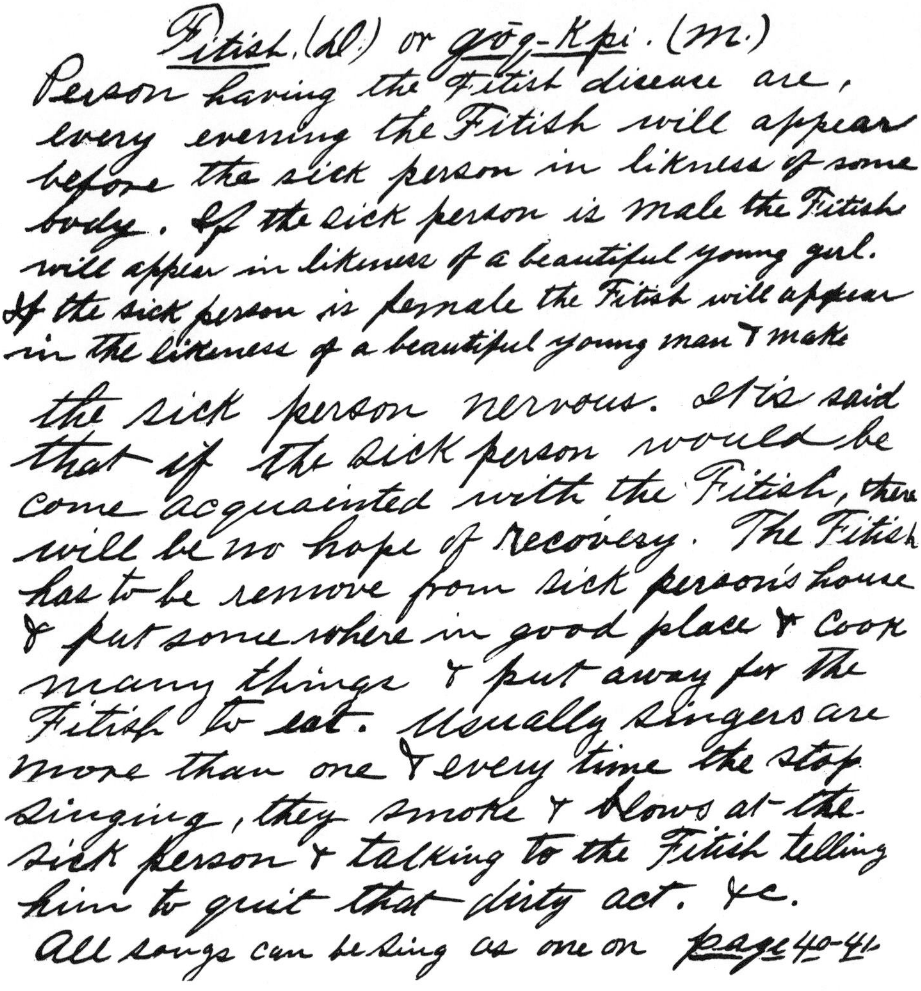

Fitish. (W.) or gōq-Kpi. (M.)
Person having the Fitish disease are, every evening the Fitish will appear before the sick person in likness of some body. If the sick person is male the Fitish will appear in likeness of a beautiful young girl. If the sick person is female the Fitish will appear in the likeness of a beautiful young man & make the sick person nervous. It is said that if the sick person would become acquainted with the Fitish, there will be no hope of recovery. The Fitish has to be remove from sick person's house & put some where in good place & cook many things & put away for the Fitish to eat. Usually singers are more than one & every time the stop singing, they smoke & blows at the sick person & talking to the Fitish telling him to quit that dirty act. &c.
All songs can be sing as one on page 40-41.

The bad consequences of not feeding a war trophy, *kú:pkĭ*. José Lewis Brennan holograph, 1897.

(*Courtesy Smithsonian Institution, J.N.B. Hewitt, Collector.*)

TEXT 9 (Tape 10.12)

. . .Hébai o hab 'e-wúa
. . .Sometimes will happen
. . .Sometimes it happens

matṣ o bíhugk.
ss will get hungry.
that it [scalp bundle spirit] will get hungry.

'Am hú hás o 'e-wúad 'am kí:kam ha-'ámjeḍ,
Eventually somehow will be happening at the family about them,
Then it [a sickness] may happen to the family,

'éḍa hég hab o 'á:gad
yet that-one will be meaning
yet it [sickness] will signify

mat bíhugim,
ss was hungry,
that it was hungry,

'o hab 'ep o 'e-jú:.
or also will happen.
or some other [wrong] thing may have been done to it.

Ñé:, mantp héms o hí:, 'á:ñi,
Look, ss I perhaps will go, I,
Look, suppose I [a bundle owner] should go somewhere,

k gm hú hébai o kí:kad,
and away someplace will be living,
off somewhere [away from home] and be staying there,

pégi b 'añ ñ-wúa hékĭ hú.
well, I did formerly.
well, that's what I used to do.

Pégi, k hab cú'ig
Well, and is
Well, and so it is

matp hékid hégai 'éñigakam –
ss whenever that-one owner –
that whenever the owner [of a fetish] –

hémho a mat 'am o ha-'á:gĭ,
necessarily ss there will tell them,
he [owner] has to tell them [the collectivity of scalp spirits],

"'Im 'ant hú o hí:.
"There I distantly will go.
"I am going off someplace.

Pi 'añ má:c mañs hékid hú o 'i jíwa,
I don't know ss I whenever will arrive,
I don't know when I will return,

k 'éḍa hab hí cú'ig 'am 'em-wé:hejeḍ
and yet on the other hand is there with respect to you [plural]
and yet as far as you are concerned

mo pi mé:k 'í:da jéweḍ,
ss not distant this-one earth,
distances are nothing,

t 'am o a'i ñ-ói."
there surely will follow me."
it [strength of your kind of thing] can surely follow me."

Hég hab 'á:g
That-one means
That means

mat 'am há'icu o wípiad,
ss there something will be remaining,
that something [food] will be left behind,

t hég 'ám o kú'aḍ,
that-one there will be eating,
it [fetish] will have it to eat,

heg hékaj	o 'áp'edag.
that-one by means of	is propriety.

therefore it is proper.

...Ñé:,	há'ap	'o másma	'e-ñú:kud	'í:da	wáṣa.
...Look,	that-way	thus	gets taken care of	this-one	bundle.

...Look, that's how to look after a bundle.

Deference to way

We will pursue the significance of way with respect to a different type of dangerous object, namely animals. Again we argue that it is not the individual that sickens people but the way operating on the animal's behalf.

Text 10 arrives at the topic of dangerous animals' "feelings" through an interpretation of the word *bá:bagid*, "to defer to it." More colloquial translations of the word are "to take it easy toward it" and "to take it slow toward it." In the first part of the text, Gregorio explains how deference is required even toward inanimate things such as the "makings" or "properties" of dangerous objects. These are the things we have defined as parts of, *cú'idag*, dangerous objects. In the case of such inanimate objects deference consists in placing an object gently, for example, as distinct from throwing it.

In part B of the text, Gregorio considers deference as it applies to animals. In this case deferent behavior consists in taking care to avoid giving an animal the sense that he is being slighted. The word *'élid* – "to think something," "to wish," "to intend" – is used to speak about such matters. Its application to the mentality of animals indicates that they, too, may suffer hurt feelings or harbor unspoken resentment because of the things they think human beings thoughtlessly do to them.

After establishing that animals do indeed possess such feelings, Gregorio then states the relationship between an animal's hurt feelings and the onset of sickness. He does not say that the offended animal retaliates by causing sickness. Instead he says that the patient's sickness will occur because of the act of indeference. This conforms to our interpretation that sickness is not caused by the ill-will of an individual dangerous object, but instead by an intervening agency, way, which is distinct from the individual animal as well as from the patient. According to this interpretation, if an animal wants to harm a human being he may bite him, but an animal cannot harm a human by using animal strength to sicken him.

TEXT 10 (Tape 17.8)

Q

Hás wuḍ 'á:ga "mat o s-bá:bagǐ," 'ab 'ámjed hégai
Somehow is means "ss it will defer to it," about it that-one
s-ta-'é:bidam há'icu?
fearful something?

What is the meaning of, "he will defer to it," [when spoken] about a dangerous object?

A

Héu'u, no pi hég 'ám hab cú'ig, hégai
Yes, because that-one there is, that-one

Yes, because it is the case

m 'an hú hab 'á:gas mo s-ta-'é:bidam,
ss already was told ss is fearful,

which has been called "dangerous,"

pégi, kc hab a'i má:s
well, and only appears

well, and it [dangerous situation] requires

mat s-bá:bagǐ 'ab hás 'ép o 'i júñhid.
ss deferently somehow also will be doing.

that he [a person] will be treating it deferently.

Pi abṣ 'am hás o si jú:
Not just there somehow will extremely do

He won't treat it excessively

matp hab o cú'ig
ss will be

if it [dangerous object] should be

matp wuḍ o há'icu'i ha-ná:toi, ha-'éñiga.
ss will be something their manufacture, their possession.

that it is something of their [dangerous species'] making, their property

Kut pi 'am hú abṣ o dá'ic,
And never just will throw,
And he [person] will never just throw it aside,

k hémho a mat o s-bá:bagĭ.
and necessarily ss will defer.
he must defer to it.

'An hébai o 'i wói
There someplace will lay
He should lay it aside someplace

matp hás o 'i másma hab hú o 'i má:sk
ss somehow thus ever will appear
if it should be like that

mat heg hékaj o s-'áp'ek.
ss that-one by means of will be proper.
and if he is to do things properly.

Pégi, 'í:d 'o hab wuḍ 'á:ga
Well, this-one means
Well, this is the meaning [of deference]

mat pi abṣ 'am hás 'am o si wúad, há'icu,
ss not just there somehow there will be doing, something,
that he won't be doing things excessively,

'ab abṣ o 'i s-bá:bagĭ 'í:da hab cú'igam há'icu.
just will defer this-one kind of something.
he will just defer to this kind of thing.

B

Pégi, k hég s-'áp'e,
Well, and that-one is right,
Well, and that's proper,

hég s-ké:gaj 'am wé:hejeḍ g hémajkam,
that-one is good there with respect to it the person,
that's good for the person,

heg hékaj mat o s-hó'ige'id,
that-one by means of ss will pity,
because then it [dangerous animal] will pity him,

c 'am o a ge hás 'élidad.
and there will somehow be thinking.
and it [animal] will feel in some [favorable] manner [toward the person].

Pi hab má:s matp héms hab o 'i 'e-'élidk,
Doesn't appear ss perhaps will get thought,
If he [person] doesn't seem so [deferent], then perhaps it [animal] will think,

"Pi 'am hú ñ-há'icu,
"Never somethings to me,
"He never considers me to be anything,

c 'am b abṣ hás 'i ñ-júñhim."
and there just somehow does to me."
and he just does anything to me."

Ñé:, b 'atp héms o má:sk 'am wé:hejeḍ, hégai
Look, perhaps will appear there with respect to it, that-one
Look, it may seem so to him [dangerous object]

matp háscu wuḍ o'ik,
ss whatever will be,
whatever it [animal] may be,

k hémho a mat hab o 'e-jú:
and necessarily ss will get done
and it [sickness] will have to happen

mat ói	hég ’ám	o ’i hí:,	múmkidaj	’ab ’ámjeḍ.
ss then	that-one there	will start,	its sickness	about it.

that then his [the person’s] sickness will begin about it.

Ñé:,	há’ap	o másma	hab wuḍ ’á:ga,
Look,	that-way	thus	means,

Look, that is the meaning [of deference],

hég ámjeḍ	’am hab s-’e-bá:bagĭ,	há’icu.
that one from	there gets deferred to,	something.

accordingly, a thing gets deferred to.

Latency of *ká:cim* sickness

We have stated that Gregorio offered no comments concerning strength beyond the boundary of the patient’s body. Way intervenes between the strength in the body and the dangerous object. By replacing the individual dangerous object as that which is offended by improper actions, the concept of way approximates the concept of a guardian of the species. In this capacity way is implicitly endowed with magical powers. Way is offended the moment an improper action is committed, but the offense is not realized until years later when the patient first feels the presence of an intrusive strength in his body.

We may speculate that in the interim period the strength was latent inside the patient’s body – an interpretation which would reduce the theoretical importance of way as a magical guardian – or that the offended way was not yet disposed to send strength to invade the patient. These two interpretations are not mutually exclusive and, in fact, Gregorio did not take an exclusive stand on this issue. The former line of thinking will be expressed in his theory of diagnosis and the latter line will be prominent in his theory of ritual cure.

The remaining texts of this section establish the long gaps across time and space which typically intervene between improper actions and the onset of sickness. It will be seen that the line of causation may bridge gaps across people as well, for many sicknesses involve a crucial distinction between the person whose behavior causes a sickness and the person who actually is afflicted. We begin with two texts that illustrate temporal and spatial gaps. The two sicknesses in question, whirlwind and jimsonweed, normally afflict adults, but their causality usually is traced to thoughtless actions which occurred in the patient's childhood.

Text 11 attributes whirlwind sickness to the patient who succumbed as a child to the normal childish urge of running inside a whirlwind. This text exemplifies the theory that childhood behavior is sufficient provocation for affliction with a sickness of latent consequences. The causal agent may not "reach," *'ái*, the victim and "sicken," *múmkic*, him until several years have passed.

Text 12 makes the same point about sicknesses which result from playing with jimsonweed. Children pick jimsonweed flowers to use for doll dresses. The sickness may not become evident for several years. We accept this as further evidence that the strength which causes the sickness has no direct connection with the physical substance of that particular flower, long since withered, with which the child played.

TEXT 11 (Tape 9.18)

. . .C hébai hab 'ép 'e-wúa é:p mo g 'á'al
. . .And sometimes also happens also ss the children
. . .And sometimes, furthermore, it happens that children

mo 'am a pi 'am hú há'icu wóho g 'é'elijc,
ss there never something true the its thoughts,
who never take things seriously,

'atp s-tá:hadkam 'élid.
pleasantly believes.
they think it will be fun [to run into the whirlwind].

T 'an o méḍad hégai síwulogĭ,
Along will be running that-one whirlwind,
A whirlwind will come along,

t 'am o méḍk,
there will run,
they will run to it,

'am o wá: 'éḍa,
there will enter inside,
and they will get into it,

'éḍa s-ta-'é:bidam.
yet is fearful.
yet it is dangerous.

'Ói a 'am 'i hímdam
Then there later
Then later on

matp s-hó:tam 'o 'ép pi o 'ói,
ss quickly or also won't follow immediately,
whether quickly or perhaps not immediately,

pégi, t o ha-'ái,
well, will reach them,
well, it will reach them,

k o ha-múmkic, hégai.
and will sicken them, that-one.
and it [wind strength] will sicken them.

TEXT 12 (Tape 1.15)

Pi 'it 'am hú hía hékaj o 'i 'ái,
Not ever of course immediately will reach it,
It [jimsonweed strength] won't reach him [child] immediately,

'am 'at o hímk,
there will go,
it will go on,

'im hú hébai háhawa ṣa'i 'ái
later sometime then reach
and sometime later it will reach him

mat 'am bá'ic o 'i gé'eda,
ss there more will be grown,
when he is more grown up,

'atp hẽms 'éḍa hú o 'i t-'áihid.
perhaps in it away will reach us.
only at that time does it reach us.

Text 13 adds the factor of gaps between people. For many sicknesses a distinction is made between the person, the patient, who "has the sickness" and the person who "has the responsibility" for causing it. In the following text the patient is a baby whose father had succumbed to temptation before the baby was born.

The "ownership" of this sickness is expressed in terms of the patient. The sickness is not said to belong to the causal agency, to the dangerous object which tempted the father, or to the careless father. It is the baby's sickness. At the end of the text Gregorio distinguishes between the person who has the sickness – the baby – and the person – the father – whose behavior caused it. The Piman word *cú'ijig* refers to the latter aspect, the relationship between a sickness and the improper action which created it. Depending on the context, we translate *cú'ijig* as 'instigation', with reference to the improper action, or 'consequence', with reference to the sickness as the material culmination of the improper action.

Like sickness, or *múmkidag, cú'ijig* can be spoken of as a thing someone can possess. For example, the possessive construction *cú'ijigaj* may be translated: '[the sickness which is caused through] his instigation', 'his [action's] consequence', or, simply, 'his fault'. The baby's sickness in text 13 could be referred to as follows: "*Hégai múmkidag wuḍ cú'ijigaj g 'ó:gaj g 'áli*," "That sickness is the fault of the father of the baby." It is thus possible for an individual's sickness to be the means by which another individual learns of his wrongful past actions.

Texts 11, 12, and 13 typify the claims commonly expressed for causal agencies with respect to time, space, and people. In reference to time, we have seen that a sickness may not appear for several years after the actions which allegedly provoked it. With respect to space, we have seen that sickness may afflict a child who was unborn at the time his father committed a fateful action. Frequently these instigating actions occur in the desert, that is, away from the home and the pregnant wife. There is no evidence that physical contagion is involved with these sicknesses. The father is not understood to

TEXT 13 (Tape 1.11)

. . .'Ó:gaj 'an abṣ o ñéidad há'icu
. . .Its father there just will be looking something
. . .His [unborn baby's] father should just look [and not interfere]

matp 'an hú a hás másma há'icu hab o cem 'e-wúad,
ss ever somehow thus something should be happening,
if some kind of [dangerous] thing is going on,

'am tá:gio hás ta-júñima o cem cú'igk.
there in the path somehow inciting to action will be.
in his path [an encounter which is] being provocative.

C abṣ hab-a hég 'ám o 'i cégĭto
But that-one there will remember
But he [father] will remember

mo hab cú'ig g wé:maj kí:kam
ss is the its with residing-thing
that there is a wife [to consider]

mat o béi g 'áli.
ss will get the baby.
that she is going to have a baby.

Hég 'at 'áb hab o 'e-jú:,
That-one against will happen,
and it [sickness] will happen to that one [the baby],

hég 'at wúi o hí:,
that-one towards will go,
it [sickness] will go to that one [the baby],

hékaj 'ab o nám g cú'ijig.
by means of will meet the consequence.
thus he [the father] will meet the consequence [of his own action].

be the physical means of transmission from the dangerous object to his unborn child.

With respect to people, we find Gregorio's warning about how one person inadvertantly can cause physical harm to another. This theme has several manifestations in Piman theory. We have already observed it in the case of forebodings where the responsible parties are adults – parents, spouses, or potential parents – and the victims are other adults – spouses, in-laws, or kinsmen. As the theme applies to sickness, usually the victims are children and the responsible parties are their parents.

5. Affliction From Contact With Noxious Objects

In this section we will compare *ká:cim* sickness with two other types of afflictions, neither of which is considered a "sickness." The first is bites of venomous animals; the second consists of ill effects attributed to "dirty stuff," *s-bí:tagi há'icu*, a substance which forms in the patient's body as the result of eating certain kinds of food. Both examples will aid our understanding of the role of strength as a causal agent.

Afflictions caused by bites

This discussion will lend additional support to our assertion that strength does not originate from individual dangerous objects. In text 14, Gregorio explains that certain local venomous pests have no connection with staying sickness: In this sense, they are not "dangerous objects," their venom is not "strength," the pains they inflict are not "sicknesses."

The question we asked Gregorio was whether three species of poisonous "bugs" – centipede, scorpion, and black widow – can be said to "sicken" people. We knew the species bite people and also that ritual cures, mentioned in section 3 as definitive of *ká:cim* sickness, are not required for the injuries suffered from these bugs. We wanted to discover if Gregorio considered the injuries to be "sicknesses." His answer indicates that afflications from bugs are outside the range of illness properly spoken of with *múmkicud*, "to sicken." He began by asserting that the species differ from other varieties of the local fauna. The difference, merely alluded to, is that the other species make Pimans sick in our established sense of *múmkicud.* Thus, the bugs are in some manner distinct from the other species on the issue of sickening.

Let us examine the words Gregorio uses to talk about sickening in text 14. First, he says the bugs "give sickness," *má: g múmkidag.* This expression is not frequent in our corpus. It is possible that he chose it simply to avoid using the word *múmkicud.* We found the same expression used in text 6, also with reference to kinds of sickening that are outside the customary usages of *múmkicud.* In text 6, Gregorio denies that either *múmkicud* or *má: g múmkidag* could be employed if the objects being sickened are animals. In the present text he grants that the bugs may "give sickness" to people, having seemingly settled on this expression as a method to denote the deviant phenomenon.

Next he uses the medio-passive form of *múmkicud, 'e-múmkic,* so as to say "[the person] will get sickened," without committing himself to the active form. In our opinion this is still another means to avoid using the crucial verb. Finally, at the end of the text he uses the crucial verb in its active form, *ha-múmkic*, only to deny that the afflications of the biting creatures are within the range of sickening denoted by this expression.

The subject matter of text 14 bears on our understanding of causal agency. Characteristically the *ká:cim* sicknesses are attributed to actions which the patient has committed and forgotten long ago. We offer this as a reason the immediately tangible, concrete transactions between biting creatures and people are not classified as cases of sickening, because such things pose no diagnostic problem.

We can now offer an explanation why strength is a necessary component of *ká:cim* sickness and why it would be superfluous as a distinct causal agent in the case of bites. Strength exists in the patient as the proxy of a class of dangerous objects, whose identity would remain unknown to the patient except for the shaman's diagnosis.

If the object that caused the sickness is known to the patient, the need for discovering its strength is obviated. The situation is analogous to that of the *'óimmeḍdam* sicknesses. In both cases, the noxious substance that enters the patient is derived from the substance of the external agent. In neither case is it necessary to posit a distinct kind of substance, the strength, which is supposed to accompany the noxious substance into the body.

In both cases, also, the noxious substance is apparent to the patient, in the sense that he does not need a shaman's diagnosis to identify the cause of his affliction. In this respect the bites and *'óimmeḍdam* sicknesses contrast with the *ká:cim*, where the causal agent is not apparent to the patient.

We conclude that the strength involved with *ká:cim* sicknesses is a cover term for a causal agent that is not apparent.

TEXT 14 (Tape 2.12)

Q

No ha-múmkicuḍ	g hémajkam,	hégam	máihogĭ	c g nákṣalĭ
Do they sicken them	the person,	those-ones	centipede	and the scorpion

c g híwcu wégĭ?
and the groin red?

Does the centipede, scorpion, or black widow sicken people?

A

Hégai	hab cú'igam	há'icu	hab hía 'e-wúa,
That-one	kind of	something	of course happens,

Of course something happens,

hía	há'icu	'ab 'ámjeḍ
of course	something	about it

about it [group of bugs]

mo hégai	pi hab má:s,
ss that-one	not appears,

but it [group of bugs] isn't of the [same] sort,

m 'in há'icu	hab hí má:s,
ss here something	on the other hand appears,

like this other kind of thing [species involved in ká:cim sickness],

. . .hímidkam,	jéweḍo	méḍdam,	'ú'uhig	dá'adam.
. . .walker,	earth-on	runner,	bird	flier.

. . .[the] walkers, runners on the earth, flying birds [which are involved with ká:cim sickness].

'Am a hás	o 'e-jú:,	há'icu,
There somehow	will get done,	something,

And something may happen [to one of the dangerous species],

k hég 'ámjeḍ	'am o í hí:.
and that-one from	there will begin.

and for that reason [infringement against a dangerous animal] it [sickness] will begin.

B

Íd	'o hía	cem hí:.
This-one	of course	merely goes.

[as for] this one [afflictions from the bugs], they just go.

Pi hab má:s.
Not appears.
They [the bugs] are not like that [to sicken people in the manner of the dangerous objects].

Hégai 'ab 'at hí a 'em-má: g múmkidag
That-one against it of course will give you the sickness
Of course they give you [a kind] of sickness

mat hékid o 'em-kéi.
ss whenever will you bite.
whenever they bite you.

Ñé:, hég 'o wuḍ a'i hégai,
Look, that-one is only that-one,
Look, that's the only thing,

'o pi hékid 'ab hú 'em-'áb hab o 'e-jú:, hégam há'akia há'icu
or never ever you against will get done, those-ones several something
or it may never ever happen to you, those several things

map 'am hab ha-'á:g, nákṣal, máihogǐ, híwcu wégǐ.
ss there you describe them, scorpion, centipede, groin red.
which you mentioned, scorpion, centipede, black widow.

C

Ñé:, 'ídam 'o pi hab má:s,
Look, these-ones do not appear,
Look, these [bugs] aren't like that [to sicken people in the manner of *ká:cim* sicknesses],

hég 'at o a'i 'e-múmkic
that-one will only get caused to sicken
that is the only manner one will get sickened [from these bugs]

mat o 'em-kéi
ss will you bite
if it bites you

mampt pi 'im hú o 'e-ñéñe'i,
ss you never will get taken care of,
if you don't take care,

t 'am hás o cú'igk,
there somehow will be,
there may be something [a bug],

c 'am hébai 'i wó'ok,
and there someplace will be lying,
and it will be lying someplace,

c 'ab o 'em-'áb céṣajk,
and onto you will climb,
and it will climb on you,

hab o 'em-jú: hab másma.
will to you do thus.
and it will do it to you like that.

Ñé:, hég 'at o a'i 'e-múmkic, hégai.
Look, that-one only will get caused to sicken, that-one.
Like that is the only method one will get sickened [from the bugs].

D

. . .Ñé:, hab a'i másma hab cú'ig, 'í:da 'ab 'ámjeḍ, hégai,
. . .Look, only thus is, this-one about, that-one,
. . .Look, that's how it has to be about this [group of bugs],

c pi hab má:s
and not appears
and it is not the case

mas 'am hú hab o cú'ig – 'am hú o 'i ge ñé'idañ.
ss there ever will be – there ever will be a singing.
in which – there would need to be a singing [in order to cure the sickness].

Pía, pi 'o hab má:s,
No, not appears,
No, it [curing bug bites] is not like that,

'o 'am hás o 'e-jú:, k hég 'ámjeḍ o ha-múmkic,
or there somehow will get done, and that-one from will sicken them,
nor does it happen that they [bugs] will sicken them [patients, as with ká:cim sickness],

pi 'o hab má:s.
not appears.
it is not like that.

Hég o a'i
That-one only
That's the only thing

mat o 'em-kéi.
ss will you bite.
when it bites you.

Afflictions caused by dirty stuff

The afflictions caused by "dirty stuff" provide us yet another basis for describing the special qualities of *ká:cim* sicknesses. These afflictions, which strike Anglo-Americans as being purely physiological, arise through the interaction of certain foods with certain things inside the patient's body. We will show how the notion of strength as elaborated for *ká:cim* sicknesses is different from and irrelevant to the cause and treatment of dirty stuff afflictions.

Dirty stuff interferes with the patient's heart, lungs, or liver. It surrounds and presses on these organs. When this condition prevails, the manifest symptom is that the patient coughs the stuff out. The phlegm coughed out by tubercular patients is classified as dirty stuff.

On the basis of its ill effects, Gregorio has classified dirty stuff as one of the kinds of causal agents which afflict the heart. In tapes 2.1 and 2.2 he mentions the following causes of affliction to the heart: dirty stuff, owl, and gopher. The latter two have *ká:cim* sicknesses, owl sickness and gopher sickness, and the causal agents which damage the heart in these cases are owl and gopher strength.

We have, then, two kinds of substance, strength and dirty stuff, spoken of in a similar manner with respect to their ill effects upon a single internal organ, the heart. Both substances are spoken of as a liquid-like, gooey substance which can "grow," *gé'eda*, or "divide," *'e-gáwolka*, within the patient's body. We know how dirty stuff looks and feels; the phlegm coughed up by tubercular patients is an example of dirty stuff. We do not know what strength looks like; probably no one except a shaman has observed or knowingly touched strength. Shamans do this routinely, for example, by sucking it from a patient's body.

Dirty stuff grows because the patient has eaten a food which engenders it. The following foods produce dirty stuff:

1. Cold food, such as soda pop, ice cream, or oranges, when drunk or eaten by menstruating women.
2. Sweet wine – for example, sweet sherry, muscatel, or tokay – when drunk in excess by anyone. (Unsweet liquors such as beer, whiskey, and tequila do not promote the growth of dirty stuff; neither does the original Piman wine made from the syrup of cactus fruit.)
3. Sweet or sticky food, when eaten to excess by anyone.

The conditions under which strength becomes active in the patient differ from the conditions governing dirty stuff in that the former are indeterminate with respect to the time, place, or tangible vehicle of entry. As Gregorio has said, strength just manages somehow to enter humans.

The notion of strength is irrelevant to the remedies for the kinds of affliction caused by dirty stuff. Gregorio has described the following methods for treatment of dirty stuff afflictions:

1. The patient may drink a purge made by boiling roots, *'á:daw* or *'é:toi*, and then he will vomit. The effects are either to "clean," *kégculid*, or to "kill," *kókda*, the dirty stuff.
2. Someone may cause the patient to vomit, in conjunction with the purge, by pressing on the patient's throat or by inserting a feather or stick into his throat.
3. The patient may be made to drink a gruel made from corn.
4. The shaman may loosen the dirty stuff by sucking out its strength, however, he cannot suck out the stuff directly. This is the major point of text 15.

TEXT 15 (Tape 15.11)

Q

Mat hékid pi o ’áp’et g hémajkam, ’ab ’ámjeḍ g s-bí:tagǐ há’icu,
ss whenever will be damaged the person, about it the dirty something,
When a person is being ill from dirty stuff,

no a wóho mat o wí:piñhu k o ’i wú:ṣad g géwkdaj,
is it true ss will suck and will remove the its strength,
g s-bí:tagǐ há’icu?
the dirty something?
is it true that he [shaman] will suck and remove the strength of the dirty stuff?

A

Héu’u, mat a wóho hab o ’e-jú:, hía,
Yes, ss truly will get done, of course,
Yes, of course it [sucking] will truly happen,

k abṣ hab-a mant ’am hab ’ep o céi, é:p
but ss I there also will vocalize, also
but as I will also say

mat hí o a ’i wú:ṣad hía, géwkdaj,
ss of course will remove of course, its strength,
that, of course he will remove its strength,

abṣ hab-a g s-bí:tagǐ há’icu gḍ hú abṣ o ’i wí’iskad.
but the dirty something deep down just will remain.
but the dirty stuff will still remain down there.

Hég a wépo másma hab o ’e-jú:
That-one similarly thus will get done
It will seem as if

mat g géwkdaj ’im hú o ’i wú:ṣañk,
ss the its strength away will emerge,
its strength will come out,

’atp héms o sa’i júṣadka ’í:da,
perhaps will slightly loosen this-one,
perhaps he will loosen it [the dirty stuff, by sucking],

k aṣ pi o sa’i ’i wú:ṣ, wé:s hégai.
but will not emerge, all of it that-one
but all of it won’t come out.

Hég ’o ’ab a’i ’áb
That-one only is against
It is only

mat o há’icu ’í:
ss will something drink
if he [patient] drinks something

matp háscu wuḍ o’ik.
ss whatever will be.
whatever [purge] it may be

Mú’i ’o ná:nko másma hab hía ’e-wúa, há’icu,
Many diversely thus of course happens, something,
There are several different methods to do it [to purge it],

abṣ hab-a hab wuḍ a ’á:ga, há’ap
but it means, that-way
but the purpose of it is

mat heg hékaj o ’i wú:ṣad g s-bí:tagĭ,
ss that-one by means of will remove the dirt,
that, by means of it, he [curer] will remove the dirty stuff,

ñé:, há’ap o a’i másma hab cú’ig.
look, that-way only thus is.
look, that’s how it is.

Pi 'it hás o ṣa'i si jú: g s-bí:tagĭ há'icu, g wí:ñhuna,
Not somehow will slightly do the dirty something, the sucking,
Sucking won't do anything to the dirty stuff,

pi 'it o ṣa'i 'i wú:ṣ.
it won't emerge.
it won't come out.

Hég a'i mat há'icu o í:,
That-one only ss something will drink it,
It is only when he drinks something,

t háhawa o 'i wú:ṣ.
then will emerge.
then it will come out.

Héu'u, géwkdaj 'at gm hú hí a 'al ha-béi,
Yes, its strength away on the other hand slightly will get some of it,
Yes, he [shaman] may get some of its strength out,

k abṣ hab-a gḍ hú o wí:, hégai.
but deep-down will remain, that-one.
but it [dirty stuff] will still remain down there.

Ñé:, há'ap.
Look, that-way.
Look, that's how it is.

Text 15 provides evidence for our interpretation that strength is irrelevant to the explanation of afflictions which are not *ká:cim* sicknesses. We have already shown this is true with respect to causal agency and diagnosis through the examples of wandering sickness and venomous bites. We will now make this point with respect to cure.

Insofar as non-*ká:cim* afflictions can be alleviated by manipulating their strengths, these manipulations are not sufficient to rid the patient of the symptoms of the affliction. There is always something remaining which is different in substance from the affliction's strength: for example, the heat of flu, the dirty stuff, the poison of venomous animals, or the stuff of sorcery.

In general, the substance that remains can be treated independently without reference to its strength.

This is not the case with *ká:cim* sicknesses. Their cure is always performed by manipulating strengths. The most direct method is the one mentioned in text 15 – the shaman sucking the strength out. This method may be insufficient to do away with the sickness, but the reason is different from one given for non-*ká:cim* afflictions. The reason is not that some other substance is present in the patient, but that the shaman's direct actions upon it are sufficient only to remove half of the strength. A ritual cure is needed to complete the task.

6. Childhood Afflictions

Our examination of childhood deformities will illustrate how sicknesses result from infringements against species of dangerous objects. There is no Piman word naming deformities as a special type of affliction. As far as we know they can only be referred to in a roundabout manner, through which we learn that they are not sicknesses but that they conform to an etiological theme similar to that of some sicknesses. Deformities, however, cannot be cured since they are not caused by strengths which can be removed by shamans or ritual curers.

Deformities result from the magical transfer of physical traits, such as the shape of external body parts or skin color, from one individual, the donor, to another, the victim. The donors are peculiar with respect to other members of their kind. In the case of human or human-like donors, the norm is the well-formed Piman Indian. Among the possible donors of deformity are crippled or oddly formed Pimans, blacks, and dolls. Blacks are peculiar with respect to the Piman norm because of their skin color. Dolls are peculiar because their faces are immobile, unlike the faces of normal Pimans.

Pimans see themselves as the ideal for all peoples. Should a Piman be overt in pointing this out, it is believed that the person, whose appearance is judged peculiar, will retaliate by transferring his trait to a Piman baby. In other words, this ethnocentrism is premised on the insulted party's awareness that physical Pimanness is regarded as the standard for the human species.

Piman theory includes a second class of potential donors in which the standard shifts from Piman humanity to the norms for animal species. These donors are individual animals who differ conspicuously from the majority of their kind. Thus a mangy dog could be a donor for manginess because mange is abnormal for dogs.

Deformities

Deformities differ from the symptoms of sicknesses in the following manner. The physical symptoms of sicknesses are drawn from what Pimans perceive to be a stock of possible afflictions characteristic of the donor species, according to the principle of magical sympathy. Thus, the symptoms, which are by definition abnormal when they appear in people, are derived from traits which are normal, or at least fitting, in reference to the donor species. Eagles give lice and bears give swollen legs. The sympathetic principle operates differently in the case of deformities since the trait transmitted is not essential to the species, being instead the very condition that marks the donor off as an anomaly from his own kind, for example, the stiff limbs or blackness of an anomalous human or the mange of an anomalous dog.

Etiologically, deformities fit a pattern typical of several kinds of sickness. They afflict babies as the result of a parent, father or mother, having teased the donor while the mother was pregnant. Like some sicknesses, the deformities are understood to be the consequence or fault, *cú'ijig*, of the parent's action.

We have two kinds of childhood disorders: one regarded as a sickness and therefore curable and the other regarded as a deformity and therefore built-in the child's body. Assuming the distinction refers to a real difference between curable and incurable afflictions among children, then, the interesting finding about Piman culture would appear to be that the same general scheme of placing the blame on the parent, has been applied to both kinds of afflictions.

In text 16, Gregorio provides an answer to the question of how actions leading to deformities differ from those leading to curable sicknesses. Wild animals sicken babies but do not deform them because, being wild, the animals stay too far away from people for their anomalies to be noticed. Also he says that the actions which generally bring sickness are hurting or killing the animal. These actions are performed under conditions opposite of those which elicit the teasing that brings deformities. Sicknesses come from the parent's failure to perceive that a dangerous animal is nearby, whereas deformities come from excessive acuity on the part of the parent.

TEXT 16 (Tape 15.1)

Q

No wa wóho	mat héma	o ná:nko	'á:gad	'o 'áṣád	mat hému
Is it true	ss one of them	will diversely	tell	or laugh at	ss presently

hás	o má:sk
somehow	will appear

Is it true that, if one [parent] will tease or laugh at how
it [donor of deformity] appears

g hémajkam	'o g háiwañ	'o abṣ cem háscu,	hégam	há'icu
the person	or the cow	or just whatever,	those-ones	something

mo s-héhemajima,
tame-ones,

a person [as donor] or cow, or just anything which is tame [not wild],

'ói a 'am 'óidk   'am hab o 'e-jú: g 'áli?
then there during   there will happen   the baby?
then, therefore, it [deformity] will happen to the baby?

Kutp 'ídam   a'i ha-'áb   hab 'e-wúa,
And these-ones   only against them   happens,
And only these [creatures] do it [give deformities],

hégam   mo wuḍ s-héhemajimakam?
those-ones   ss are tame-ones?
which are tame?

Áha no ha-áb   hab 'ep cú'ig   'ab ha-'ámjeḍ,
Perhaps against them   also is   about them,
Or is it also true about those others [that they give deformities],

hégam   s-dódajkam,   júḍum   'o bá'ag   'o abṣ cem háscu   mo wuḍ s-dúajkam?
those-ones   wild-ones,   bear   or eagle   or just whatever   ss is wild-thing?
those which are wild, bear, or eagle, or just anything which is a wild creature?

A

Héu'u,   'am o a wóho   hab másma   há'ap
Yes,   there it is true   thus   that-way
Yes, it is like that

matp há'icu   hab másma   hab o má:sk,
ss something   thus   will appear,
if something [donor of deformity] is like that [tame],

cem háscu,   cem as héms   pi wuḍ o dúakam,
just whatever,   even perhaps   not will be living-thing,
just anything [may be a donor] even if it is not alive,

c wuḍ abṣ o ha-ná:toik,
and just will be their artifact,
and it will just be an artifact [e.g., a doll],

'am a hás 'i másma.
there somehow thus.
and [odd] in some manner.

B

Pégi, k'éḍa hab cú'ig
Well, but it is
Well, but if it is the case

mat 'am hú hab o má:sk
ss there ever should appear
if one should be

mo 'am hím há'as hú'i t o béi g 'áli, g hémajkam,
ss there is going later on will get the baby, the person,
[a person] who is due to get a baby,

pégi, hég 'ám hab s-'é:bid é:p, g hékĭ hú g hémajkam.
well, that-one there fears also the ancient the person.
well, the ancient people feared that [pregnancy].

C 'atp 'an hú o a cem ñéidaḍ há'icu
And if ever should be observing something
And if one [parent] should observe something

matp hás 'i má:s,
ss somehow appeared,
how it might appear,

'am hú a cem si s-ta-'á'askima o má:s,
there ever just very laughably will appear,
it may be funny,

'o si hás ta-'ágma hab o cú'ig,
or very somehow remarkable will be,
or it may be remarkable,

pégi, pi 'am hú hás o jú: k aș 'an hí a ñéidad.
well, never somehow will do and just on the other hand observe it.
well, he shouldn't do anything except observe it.

Cem as héms 'an o ñéidad,
Perhaps there will observe it,
Perhaps he could look at it,

c pi 'am hú hás o 'á:gad,
and never somehow will address it,
but he shouldn't say anything,

kut 'am abș o 'i s-'áp'ekad.
and there just will be proper.
and everything will be all right.

C

. . .Wé:s há'icu 'o hab má:s
. . .Every something appears
. . .Everything is of a kind [not to give deformities]

. . .mo o há'icu s-dúajk,
. . .ss will be something wild,
. . .which is something wild,

c pi mía 'e-ñéid,
and not closely gets observed,
and cannot be closely observed,

kuc pi 'áp ñéid
and we do not properly observe
and we can't see very well

mas hás másma hab si má:s, 'ámai.
ss somehow thus really appears, there.
how it really is.

Kc há'icu	hab má:s
And something	appears

And [on the other hand] something appears

mo pi wuḍ a dúajkam	há'icu,
ss is not wild-thing	something,

which is not a wild creature,

c 'an a mía	'an 'e-ñéid,
and there closely	there gets observed,

and it can be observed closely,

c 'ói a hab o má:sk
and then will appear

and then it will show up

mat 'am hás	o cú'igk,	'o abṣ cem háscu,
ss there somehow	will be,	or just whatever,

whether it is any kind of [odd] thing,

pégi,	t hémho a mat 'am a hás	o 'e-jú:	g 'áli	hékid	cem má:sik.
well,	necessarily ss there somehow	will happen	the baby	whenever	will be born.

well, it [deformity] will have to happen to the baby when it is born.

D

Pégi,	kc hég	a'i mat 'am hás	o jú:
Well,	and that-one	only ss there somehow	will do

Well, that kind of thing [animal] can only do something to it [sicken a baby]

mo hab hía	cem cú'ig	mo s-dúajk.
ss of course	just is	ss wild.

if it is that it's wild.

K abṣ hab-a 'éḍa 'am a há'icu 'am wuḍ hégai
But yet there something there is that-one

But yet there is something [from wild animals]

mat 'am hás o jú:,
ss there somehow will do,

if he [parent] should do something to it,

kó'okam o jú:, 'o múa,
hurtfully will do or kill,

hurt it or kill it,

'o matp hás o 'i jú:.
or ss somehow will do.

or in whatever way he [parent] may do.

K abṣ hab-a hí pi hab má:s hab másma,
But on the other hand doesn't appear thus,

But of course it [the resulting affliction] isn't like that [deformity],

abṣ o múmkic.
just will sicken it.

it will just sicken him.

We suggest that both afflictions, curable sickness and incurable deformity, occur because the baby's parent behaved in a manner offensive to a creature who has a sense of pride or insultability. The difference between the sickness-precipitating and the deformity-precipitating action is that the latter, in pointing out the creature as a freak, effectively removes the donor from the scheme of contractual relationships between his species and humanity. The grave insult to the freak is that he is being denied valid membership in his species.

The sickness-precipitating actions are not confined to the accidental consequences of poor visibility described in text 16. The parent's action may be intentionally cruel, for example, when he wantonly kills a mouse upon learning that mouse way has been sickening his child. This type of aggression differs from the actions resulting in deformities because sickness-provoking actions are understood to be against an animal endowed with rights as a member of his species.

Other sickness-provoking actions do not involve physical contact between the parent and the dangerous animal. For example, a baby may be sickened because his parent ate food gnawed on by mouse. Leftover food should be put away at night to prevent mice from getting to it in fear that humans inadvertantly may eat from that which the mouse had eaten during the night.

As the specifics of the wrongful actions vary, the moral liability shifts between the animal and the parent. We have seen that mouse sickness may derive from dissimilar actions. The only factor common to the sickness-provoking actions is that they involve violations against dangerous-object animals which are endowed with rights with respect to humanity. (Evil spirits and inanimate objects have not been reported as dangerous objects to unborn children.) We have observed this rationale in text 10 where the following thoughts were attributed to an animal: "He never considers me to be anything, and he just does anything to me."

Because sicknesses are interpreted as sanctions following the parent's deliberate or accidental devaluation of a member of a dangerous species, deformities cannot be classified as sicknesses for they result from the parent's accurate recognition of the donor as a freak member of his species. It is the difference between saying, "You are nothing but a dog," which would cause sickness and, "You are nothing but a mangey dog," which would cause deformity. The cutting remark mentioned by Gregorio, in text 16, as being necessary for the precipitation of a deformity is of the latter kind.

Deformities, which result from identifying the donor as an illegitimate member of his species, cannot be cured in the manner of sicknesses. The cure of a sickness is attested to by the reduction or cessation of its strength. All of the Piman curing techniques aim, in one manner or another, toward the disposal of a sickness' strength.

In part IV we will show how the task of curing is divided between shamans and ritual curers and the approaches to curing are divided between the "direct" and the "prayerful." The different curing techniques can be scaled from the most direct, in which the shaman sucks the strength, to the most prayerful, in which the shaman performs what we term "the maximal level of curing." For any *ká:cim* sickness, the maximal level consists of a ritual which includes curative blowing, the use of fetishes, and the singing of songs about the way of dangerous object.

The level of curing needed to effect a cure is dependent upon the severity of the sickness. When the sickness is present in its severest form, the cure must include singing. The songs are said to be heard by something – tentatively identified with the spiritualized way of the dangerous object –

which will in turn "feel differently" toward the patient and cause the strength to subside.

The idea is that the strength must ultimately be lifted by a spiritual recipient of the song. The songs dwell upon traits unique to the species, sometimes including the same sorts of belittling things which, in the case of teasing freaks bring about childhood deformities.

In our opinion this progression of curing methods – from the extreme of human mastery, sucking out the strength, to the extreme of human supplication, singing – cannot apply to the deformities because the donor's basis for pride, his membershp in the species, was contradicted by the patient's initial action.

Our final text on deformities, text 17, complements the preceding one by comparing deformities on the issue of curability with a third type of affliction to babies, retardation. Retardations are curable, but they are not sicknesses.

Retardations

Retardations are cured by a direct kind of magic. This point sets the cures for retardation apart from the cures for *ká:cim* sicknesses. Ultimately, the sicknesses are cured prayerfully by reestablishing the patient's rapport with the kind of dangerous object whose strength causes the sickness, or as Gregorio expresses it, "by means of the thing that is sickening the person." In contrast, the magical agents used to cure retardations are treated like tools and they have no connection with the cause of the retardation.

Retardations, unlike sicknesses and deformities, have no moral implications. They are not understood to be consequences, *cú'ijig*, of the parent's ill-considered action. They are simply things that sometimes happen to babies, being subsumed under the explanatory notion of "luck," *ábamdag*, in text 17.

TEXT 17 (Tape 16.16)

Q

Nat 'am hás	másma	o béi	g 'e-'áp'edag	mat o 'áp'et	g 'áli
Will there somehow	thus	get	the its propriety	ss will improve	the baby

mat héma	hab o má:sk
ss one of them	will appear

Can he [deformed baby] somehow regain [his] propriety, will the baby get better if it should appear

mat pi o hímdagk, heg hékaj mat o ná:nko ’á:gad
ss won’t be walking-thing, that-one by means of ss will diversely tell
g gé’egeḍgaj?
the its parents?

that he can’t walk because his parents teased it [a donor of deformity] ?

A

Héu’u, b ’o hía ’e-wúa, hébai, há’icu
Yes, of course happens, sometimes, something

Yes, of course it [baby’s afflictions] may be something [deformity]

mat hab o ṣa má:sk
ss will slightly appear

if it should turn out to be

matp wuḍ o há’icu hab wuḍ o a ’ámjeḍkam.
ss will be something will be from-thing.

if something is the source [of the deformity].

. . .C pi hab hí má:s,
. . .And not on the other hand appears,

. . .And it [deformity] cannot be of the sort [to be curable],

c abṣ hab-a ’éḍa ’attp hab o a ’á: “múmkidag” ’ab ’ámjeḍ hégai
but yet we will call it “sickness” about it that-one

but yet we will call it [deformity] a “sickness”

matp hab o má:skad
ss should appear to be

if it [deformity] should be

matp g há’icu ’am ’i hímdaḍ ’éḍa g jé’ej,
ss the something there its way in the its mother,

if it [deformity] is [arises from] something in the experience of the mother,

'ó:gaj g 'áli mat koi o má:si.
its father the baby ss not yet will be born.
or father of the baby when it was not yet born.

B

. . .Pégi, ñ 'íd hab 'á:g, 'í:da.
. . .Well, I this tell, this-one.
. . .Well, I mean this [kind of curable affliction, the retardation].

'Am o hébai hab hía 'e-wúa, há'icu,
There sometimes of course it will happen, something,
Sometimes something happens,

ñé:, matp héms hab o má:sk
look, ss perhaps will appear
look, perhaps it will be

mat pi o hímdagk.
ss won't be walker.
if he [baby] won't begin to walk.

'Ab cem 'e-'á'ahe g 'áhidagk
Just get reached the year
The time [for walking] will have come

matp hékid hab o 'e-'ái,
ss whenever will get reached,
whenever it will be,

. . .pégi, k 'am abṣ o bíjim,
. . .well, and there just will pass it,
. . .well, and it [baby] will just pass it [the normal time period],

pi 'im hú hab másma hab o cú'igk.
not ever thus will be.
he [baby] won't be like that [to begin walking].

C

Pégi, kc 'am hab o cú'igk
Well, and there will be
Well, and it [affliction] will be like that

matp o s-'ábam,
ss will be lucky,
[of the sort that] he [baby] will be lucky,

pégi, t o a'i 'e-nóḍagĭ, 'ú:hum,
well, will only get turned, backwards,
well, it [retardation] will be reversed,

k o a hí: 'am hébai hímdam,
and will go there sometime later,
and he [baby] will walk, later on,

cem as 'am hú 'i gó:k 'áhid,
perhaps eventually two years,
perhaps around two years,

'o 'am 'i wúi.
or there towards.
or approximately that amount of time.

D

. . .Ñé:, hab hía másma hab 'e-wúa,
. . .Look, of course thus happens,
. . .Look, that's how it [retardation] may happen [to be overcome],

abṣ hab-a hég 'áb, hégai
but that-one against, that-one
but it [sometimes] depends on something [for a cure]

mo ’am a ṣa gáwul másma hab má:s
ss there slightly differently thus appears
which is different [from the natural recovery just described]

matp há’icu ’am wuḍ o a hégaik
ss something there will be that-one
if it [retardation] should be of that sort

mo pi hab másma ’óimmeḍ.
ss not thus moves around.
[in] which he will not begin to walk.

Pégi, k ’am o múa g háiwañ.
Well, and there will kill the cow.
Well, then [somebody] will kill a cow.

T ’am wó:kaḍ ’éḍa matp hég gm hú o ’íawua hégai
There its stomach in ss that-one away will pour that-one
Then, from inside its stomach, he [curer] will pour out

mo ’am wuḍ há’icu ’i húgij,
ss there is something its food,
the stuff it has eaten,

gm hú o ’íawua,
away will pour it,
he will dump it out,

k hég ’éḍa ’am o wá:ki,
and that-one in, there will put it,
and he [curer] will put him [baby] in it [the food from cow’s stomach],

’atp ’in húgkam, hégai ’áli.
about this much, that-one baby.
about this much [of] the baby [’s body].

Ñé:, hab a’i másma
Look, only thus
Look, this is how it is

matp hékid ’i mámsiḍ g wísilo,
ss whenever gives birth the calf,
whenever a calf is born,

cem hé’es ’al wó’okahid,
just a little while it lies,
it [calf] only lies down for a short time,

c ’ámjeḍ híhhim.
and from then is walking.
and then it begins to walk.

E

. . .É:p, mat héma pi ’ói o ñi’okĭt,
. . .Also, ss one of them not soon will begin to talk,
. . .Also one [baby] may not begin to talk soon enough,

pégi, k ’am a hás ’ép másma hab ’e-wúa, hégai.
well, and there somehow also thus happens, that-one.
well, then it is done in another manner.

Aṣ há’icu hab wuḍ ṣú:g,
Something is mocking bird,
Something is the mocking bird,

’ú’uhig mo ’in dád’e.
bird ss here flies.
a local flying bird.

Cem háscu ñí’okĭ, ha-cé’isid g ’ú’uhig,
Just whatever talks, imitates them the birds,
It does any kind of talk, it imitates the birds,

c abṣ hab-a ’éḍa ’am hab káij, s-ñíokim.
but yet there vocalizes, likes to talk.
but yet it vocalizes, it really likes to talk.

Pégi, k hég ’ep o mú’ak,
Well, and that-one also will kill it,
Well, that also is killed,

o húgc, hégai ’áli.
will make it eat it, that-one baby.
and fed to the baby.

Ñé:, k ’ói a hab ’ep o ’e-jú:
Look, and then also will happen
Look, then it will happen [to the baby]

mat o a ñío ’am ’í himdam.
ss will talk there later.
that he will soon begin to talk.

. . .Hég ’at hí pi hás másma o kégc,
. . .That-one on the other hand not somehow thus will fix it,
. . .But there is no method to fix that one [deformity],

heg hékaj hab o a má:skad, hégai.
that-one by means of will be appearing, that-one.
because of that he will [always] look like that.

Pi hab másma ’am hú o jíwa mat o wépo másmakad
Not thus there ever will settle down ss will similarly appear
It [deformed body] will never become

matp hás o cem másmakad g hémajkam, g ha-cú:kug
ss somehow ought to become the person, the their flesh
as it should be, like the flesh of [normal] people

matp hás 'i másma hab o cú'igk.
ss somehow thus will be.
if he should be like that [deformed].

. . .Pégi, pi 'at hás másma o 'áp'et, 'í:da.
. . .Well, not somehow thus will improve, this-one.
. . .Well, it [deformity] won't in any way be improved.

Ñé:, tp hab aṣ o a má:sk, 'am 'e-dúakuḍ 'am húgkam, g 'áli
Look, will appear, there its life thereafter, the baby
Look, the baby will just have to be like that for the rest of his life

matp o gé'eda.
ss will grow up.
if it grows up [deformed].

Ñé:, há'ap.
Look, that-way.
Look, that's how it is.

Concluding remarks

Three kinds of childhood afflictions have been discussed in this section: *ká:cim* sicknesses, deformities, and retardations. We have found sicknesses to be distinct from the other two afflictions on two grounds.

First, on the basis of offense to a dangerous object, we find the following distinctions:

1. SICKNESS: consequence of a parent's wrongful action against an object dangerous because it is a valid member of its species endowed with rights against human incursion
2. DEFORMITY: consequence of a parent's wrongful action against an object dangerous because it is an anomalous member of its species
3. RETARDATION: something that simply happens – through luck – to children, for which the parents cannot be blamed

Second, with regard to the possibility of curing we find the following distinctions:

1. SICKNESS: curable by appeal to the pride of the offended and legitimately different kind of thing
2. DEFORMITY: incurable because the donor has been denied its status as a legimitately different kind of thing
3. RETARDATION: curable by direct application of magic, no appeal to the causal agent being necessary

7. Piman Theory on *Ká:cim* Sicknesses

All the diverse symptoms of *ká:cim* sicknesses are explained by the presence of a single kind of intrusive substance: strength. If this substance can be removed, the symptoms will cease; the symptoms cannot be arrested without disposing of the strength.

For non-*ká:cim* afflictions we found varieties of symptoms which appear to exist in their own right as causal agents. Although it is possible to speak of a strength associated with the symptoms, it is the strength of the symptom, of hotness or of dirty stuff; it is not the strength of an independently existing class of dangerous objects.

We can summarize our theories concerning causal agency under three headings: morality, diagnosis, and cure.

MORALITY. The causal agents of *ká:cim* sicknesses contrast with those of the other varieties of affliction on the basis of origin. For each affliction which is not a *ká:cim* sickness (except forebodings) it is possible to locate a single tangible thing in the world as the point of origin of the symptoms and their associated strengths. Examples include the venom of a bug, the microscopic germs of wandering sicknesses, the concoctions made by sorcerers, and sweet wine.

We do not know the actual locality from which the strength associated with a *ká:cim* sickness originates. Wherever its point of origin, we understand that its allocation is not at the discretion of the individual inhuman creature who may have been offended by the actions of the patient. Instead, the strength appears to intervene on the creature's behalf. The offended creature is not required to take overt action.

Implicitly the source of the strength lies in some superindividual source. In terms of our own comprehension, we may equate the thing with a guardian of the way of the class of dangerous objects. More abstractly, we may suggest the Piman moral order as the source of the strength. Gregorio did not speak about either of these alternatives in a positive manner. He said that strength comes because there are ways and commandments, but he has not suggested that strength stems materially or metaphorically from these abstractions.

DIAGNOSIS. The diagnosis of non-*ká:cim* afflictions demands varying degrees of specialized knowledge on the part of the diagnostician. For example, anyone can diagnose a swollen finger as a scorpion sting, but a more profound appreciation of physiology is necessary to explain excessive phlegm as the resultant of dirty stuff.

There is a sense, however, in which all the afflictions (except sorcery) have causal agents that are apparent, as distinct from the unapparent strengths which cause *ká:cim* sicknesses. Piman doctrine maintains that a patient cannot be aware of the identity of the strengths within his body until a shaman sucks out the strengths. The Piman theory of strength in the body approximates Western European theory of the unconscious in this regard, that is, in offering a positive theory of the unknowability of strength in its undiagnosed form. Thus, in contrast to the other afflictions, the shaman's diagnosis of *ká:cim* sickness is necessary, not only because the patient is not knowledgeable enough to identify the noxious elements which have entered his body, but also because the elements, or strengths, are in principle unknowable to the Piman layman.

CURE. The Piman shaman's single great curative act consists in sucking strengths. We have seen that this is of little or no avail for afflictions which are not *ká:cim* sicknesses. We will discover that this cure succeeds only to a limited extent for the *ká:cim* sicknesses.

The curative efficacy of sucking is limited, and so is the shaman's contribution to curing in general. Sucking, however, facilitates his other major task, the identification of sicknesses. By sucking he removes the upper layers of stratified strengths, in pursuit of those which had been buried for years inside the patient's body.

It is clear that the act of sucking out the strength is the climactic moment of the nightlong shamanic session, the subject matter of part III. It is possible, however, that the climax is equally a consequence of the patient's acquisition of a sign (the strength) of his forgotten past action as it is the promise of a speedy recovery from his ailment.

The patient requires a ritual cure in order to be freed of the strength. The cures are administered by laymen, not shamans. We will characterize their method as prayerful, at least in its ultimate maximal form. The prayers are directed at a spirit which we identify with the way of the dangerous object.

[NOTE: The following rationale underlies our singular listing of forebodings and sorcery as exceptions.

Forebodings are singularly exceptional with respect to source because not even a shaman can make direct contact with the agent which "sent" them – the agent which supposedly reacted to the neglected baptism or puberty ritual and which therefore dispatched a series of forebodings. Sorcery was not included because the sorcerer is the analogue of the missing or intangible watchman-over-baptisms-and-puberty-observances and sender-of-affliction.

Sorcery is singularly exceptional with regard to apparentness of causal agency because a shaman is required to discern sorcery, just as a shaman is required to diagnose a *ká:cim* sickness. Forebodings were not included because laymen ordinarily can figure out why their accidents are occurring. Forebodings are to be considered more or less drastic proddings by an impartial source directed at laymen who reputedly will discern the message themselves. Sorcery is by definition beyond the layman's reach. It will not be apparent to him, or at any rate while he may suspect it, it remains for a shaman to pronounce it sorcery.]

PART III

THE *DÚAJIDA*

Look, that's what I mean by saying
that something is a "beneath sickness."
It is whatever sickness that arrived there first,
and got something on top of it.
Well, and only it will be observed,
because it is on top.
Look, and the lower one, he won't observe it
if it gets covered by something.
It will be worked on and then it will emerge.
Look, that's what it means.

Juan Gregorio, text 21

1. Diagnostic Function of *Dúajida*

Necessity of diagnosis

The patient's experience of his sickness begins by feeling its symptoms. They are understood as signs that a sickness is present. He needs a shaman to explain to him which sickness he has. The shaman does this in an event called *dúajida.*

Etymologically, the word means "to vitalize." As Gregorio defines it in his texts, however, the diagnostic aspect predominates over the curative. The work of the *dúajida* is said to be basically intellectual problem-solving, in which the shaman "figures out," *mámci*, the sickness.

In effect he solves the problem posed by the patient's symptoms. The patient presents him with uninterpreted physiological facts which are, before the diagnosis, in need of signification. At the conclusion of the diagnosis, which lasts all night, the shaman names the patient's sickness.

After learning the identity of his sickness, the patient must recall the occasion on which he became sick. In remembering the occasion, always an actual moment in the past, perhaps years ago, he affirms that the present sickness is his *cú'ijig*, the consequence of his earlier action.

Thus the diagnosis of his sickness moves the patient through these steps: In the beginning, he is aware of his distress but ignorant of his sickness; next the shaman identifies the sickness causing his symptoms; the patient then remembers the occasion on which he got the sickness. It is evident that the patient only discovers the reason for his sickness after a shaman has provided him with a guide for remembering.

This is the sequence of the discovery of a sickness, which moves from the present to the remembered past. We will now investigate Piman theory accounting for the reverse process, from the postulated moment of acquisition to the time of discovery. We seek the reason why a shaman is required or, in other words, the rationale for having a sickness while ignorant of its true nature.

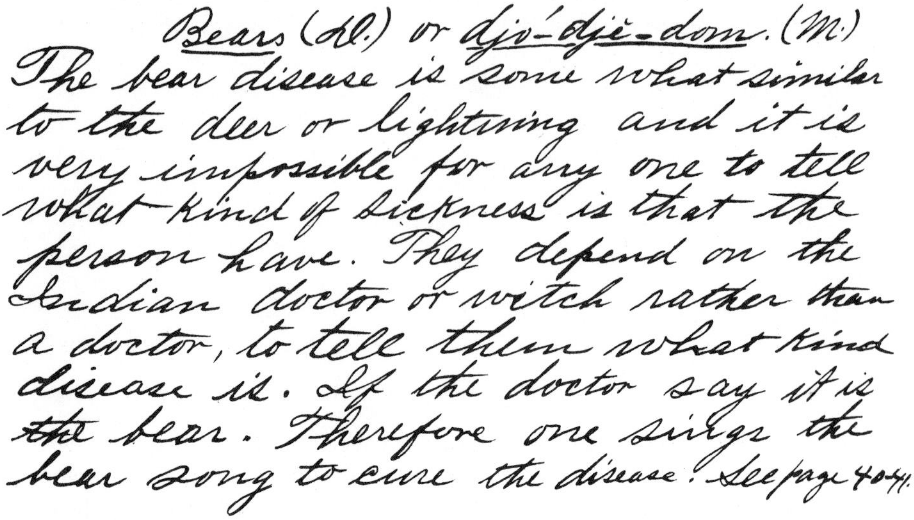

Bears (Al.) or djó-djë-dom. (M.)
The bear disease is some what similar to the deer or lightning and it is very impossible for any one to tell what kind of sickness is that the person have. They depend on the Indian doctor or witch rather than a doctor, to tell them what kind disease is. If the doctor say it is the bear. Therefore one sings the bear song to cure the disease. See page 40-41.

The necessity for a shaman's diagnosis. José Lewis Brennan holograph, 1897. (*Courtesy Smithsonian Institution, J.N.B. Hewitt, Collector.*)

Latency and permeation

Although sicknesses theoretically are dated from the moments of individual actions, they may lie dormant for long periods. We refer to this property of sicknesses as latency. Gregorio has said little about the mechanisms of latency, for example, how sicknesses enter the patient or what causes sicknesses to become active. The supposition of latency, however, is critical to our understanding of Piman etiology.

Gregorio speaks of the patient's body as the repository for a lifetime's acquisition of sicknesses, the later sicknesses being on top of the earlier ones. From the shaman's vantage point, the internal stratification of sicknesses is manifest as the strengths of the different kinds of dangerous objects which the patient has acquired through his transgressions or through the transgressions of others.

The recognized time periods for acquiring sicknesses are: (1) before the patient is born, in which case the sickness appears in an infant as the consequence of one of his parents' actions; (2) during childhood, the consequent sickness reaching one in adulthood or old age; (3) during adulthood, including old age.

People normally enter a diagnosis ignorant of the several sicknesses they have acquired. Piman diagnoses are done piecemeal, the shaman identifying his patient's sicknesses one by one during the course of his nightlong vigil.

Each sickness that he finds is sufficient to cause all of the symptoms. If the patient's symptoms persist, it is expected that the shaman, or another shaman, will keep trying until he discovers all of the strengths of all of the sicknesses within the patient. Certain symptoms are more problematical than others in that some do not exist in a one-to-one correlation with particular kinds of strength.

Unproblematical cases are those which the shaman can diagnose simply on the basis of reported symptoms. For such a diagnosis there is no need to undertake a nightlong *dúajida.* Gregorio refers to such consultations as *kúlañmada* (literally, "to apply medicine"; idiomatically, "to do an attenuated *dúajida*). He says they are brief and can be performed in the daytime.

Diagnoses are genuinely problematical for three reasons. The first and already mentioned is the presence of several sicknesses so layered that one sickness may cover the other. The second reason concerns the extent to which the sickness has "permeated" the patient, which in turn depends upon the length of time the sickness has been active and also upon an idiosyncratic factor, whether the sickness happens to be "going strongly." The permeation of any *ká:cim* sickness is complete when it reaches the patient's heart and kills him. The more permeated sicknesses are, the more difficult they are to diagnose because their strengths become intermingled. In this condition they present the classic problem in Gregorio's rendition of the *dúajida.* The shaman must dispose of the excessive strengths of the sicknesses, thereby disambiguating them and removing the immediate threat to the patient's heart.

The third reason that diagnoses are problematical is because sicknesses may try to elude the shaman by hiding from him. This aspect of shamanism, in which the shaman or his spirit helper chases after elusive evil-spirit-like things, is scantly developed in Gregorio's texts. It would be premature to suggest the importance it holds for Piman shamanism in general. It has not been reported elsewhere in the Piman literature. We will find that a definite place for this kind of action exists within the typical *dúajida* and, in fact, the provision for action between the shaman and the spirits is the feature which distinguishes the *dúajida* from the *kúlañmada.*

We can now answer the questions with which we began our discussion of latency and permeation. The shaman is required because only he can deal with these aspects of sickness. A patient can have a sickness and be ignorant of its true nature because the sickness entered him imperceptibly and was latent until it wished to make itself felt.

An inconsistency in Underhill's interpretation of the ambiguity of symptoms will be illuminated by an examination of the properties of latency and permeation. At one point she observes that the relation between symptoms and sicknesses is random:

The shaman's seeing of one of these forms of disease had nothing to do with symptoms. They were ill-defined at best, and any one of them might be attributed to any cause (1946:265).

Elsewhere she followed the established ethnographic practice (Russell, 1908; Densmore, 1929) of matching sicknesses with symptoms (1946:288-300). In her inventory there are twenty-two names, each with a distinct set of symptoms.

Her first statement fails to distinguish between simple cases, suitable for *kúlañmada*, and those which are avowedly problematical, requiring *dúajida*. This statement is false with respect to the former; with respect to the latter it requires modification: "the shaman's seeing is necessary *because* of the symptoms." We feel Gregorio would agree with her observation that any attribution is possible for almost permeated sicknesses, intermingled at the beginning of the diagnosis. Thus, Underhill's second statement can be reconciled with the first through recognition of the concepts of permeation and latency.

Concluding remarks

The shaman's task and his unique skill consist in the identification of sicknesses from signs which are ambiguous or inaccessible to the patient. The sicknesses are understood as distinct entities, each with its own causal agency – the strength or way of a class of dangerous objects – and its characteristic early symptoms. The distinct nature of his sicknesses, however, can only become apparent to the patient after the shaman has penetrated the ambiguities of the patient's manifest symptoms and enabled him to recall actions which he had forgotten. We suggest that the sicknesses are distinct in Piman culture, but that the patient's experience of them, his consciousness before and during the time he became sick, is best summarized in another manner: He is unaware. The purpose of the diagnosis is to make people aware of the sicknesses they have.

2. Events of *Dúajida*

Bahr did not witness one of the nightlong sessions called *dúajida.* Nor did Gregorio describe one from beginning to end. By way of compensation we will consider the case history of a *dúajida* published by Russell in which four shamans required a day and a night to discover a woman's horned toad sickness (1908:260-61).

> Several years ago Sala carelessly ate some weed which poisoned her and she barely had strength enough to reach home. As close relatives are not allowed to treat a patient, a neighboring medicine-man was called in.
>
> Her husband rolled a cigarette for the learned doctor, who smoked it, but however skillfully he spread the smoke cloud over the groaning patient he could not "see" the cause of the trouble. Then another Siatcokam was called in and a cigarette was rolled for him and he peered through the veil sufficiently to see "something." But he could not tell just what it was and advised sending for another medicine-man who was a specialist in intangible shapes.
>
> Sala was suffering the greatest agony in the meantime. If she moved she "felt full of pins inside." Those about her expected her to die at any moment.
>
> Number three arrived at length and smoked his cigarette, blowing the smoke across the patient from a distance to dispell the unusually heavy darkness. He said he must have his gourd rattle and magic feathers brought before he could see clearly. Meanwhile the husband had brought in a fourth medicine-man.
>
> Number four then smoked a cigarette and pronounced the verdict of death. Poor Sala had been compelled to lie quiet to avoid the torture from the "pins" but her mind was active and she understood every word that was said in her presence.

Determined to do what they could, the last two arrivals set to work singing. Number three sang four songs, followed by four more songs from number four. Then number three sang four more, and so they alternated all night. Toward morning they put ashes into a cup of water, sweeping eagle feathers over the dish meanwhile. They then announced that they would get the evil out soon. Number four sprayed water from his mouth over the patient and declared that he had found her suffering from the presence of the horn of a horned toad in her heart. Falling on his knees beside her he sucked with all his might until he had removed the offending object. As it flew into his mouth it gagged him and he hastened to withdraw it. Calling for a piece of cotton he put the hot and burning horn into it and told the brother of the patient to throw it into the river. Then two of the Siatcokam sang twice and later in the day sang twice through their set of four songs for the horned toad. This faithful treatment brought about a recovery.

Judging from Gregorio's statements on the *dúajida* this case is unusual in two respects. First, the number of unsuccessful shamans is of interest. A shaman is usually able to discover at least some of the strengths causing a patient's symptoms. Thus it would be incorrect to conclude, as the textual evidence suggests, that three out of four Piman shamans cannot make a diagnosis.

Second, only one kind of dangerous object, the horned toad, was causing the woman's sickness. We will find from Gregorio's texts that the chief difficulty in making a diagnosis is in discovering all of the kinds of strength present in the patient. We should not conclude that all Piman diagnoses are as simple as the above account from Russell.

It appears this case may have been exaggerated in the direction of burlesque. Sala was a "devout Christian" by the time Russell met her. Presumably she had been converted to Presbyterianism after her experience with horned toad sickness. Her memory of the use of shamans is perhaps unusually prodigal and their findings may be remembered as abnormally meager.

In terms of Gregorio's theory, the arrival of the fourth shaman ushered in a fundamental shift in diagnostic procedures. His predecessors had spent the daytime using the relatively limited techniques of *kúlañmada.* The fourth shaman, assisted by the third, performed a *dúajida* during the night.

In the case history of Sala the sole technique employed during the daytime – the *kúlañmada* – was a type of divination using tobacco smoke. All the other techniques were reserved for the nighttime *dúajida:* the singing, the use of magic feathers, the divining with ashes, and the climactic sucking of the horned toad's horn.

These actions can be classified according to their intended direction toward objects in one of two scenes of action: the landscape of the spirits (singing only) or the patient's body (all the other actions). It follows from this classification that the difference between *kúlañmada* and *dúajida* lies in the fact that *dúajida* operates in both scenes of action while the techniques of *kúlañmada* are confined to the scene defined by the patient's body.

The factor common to both the *kúlañmada* and *dúajida* is a concern for "illuminating," *tónlid*, sicknesses conceived of as strengths present inside the patient's body. The shaman accomplishes illumination in both cases by an act of blowing, *wústana*, onto or over the patient; this act is described by Russell. Thus, both events share one scene of action, the physical body of the patient, particularly its insides, where the strengths reside. The *dúajida* adds a second scene of action which we refer to as the landscape of the spirits.

This classification accounts for only two of the actions described by Russell: the blowing and the singing. We will show how in Gregorio's theory the use of divining crystals and feathers fall into an augmented series with blowing on one end of the continuum and singing on the other; the same interpretation would apply to the use of feathers and ashes in Russell's account.[9]

Blowing is the most direct and charismatic method to perform a divination, for it is performed by means of the shaman's heart unassisted. Singing to spirit helpers is the least charismatic method, for the burden of discovery is placed upon the spirits. The techniques in the middle of the series can be understood as orderly steps away from the naked charisma of the shaman – Gregorio calls them "accompaniments."

In addition to blowing, singing, and the various accompanying techniques, one more action is essential to the *dúajida.* This is sucking. In Russell's case history it was performed at the end of the *dúajida* to remove the horn. In fact sucking, like blowing, can also be performed during a *kúlañmada* if the shaman already has ascertained the thing he wants to suck out.

In Gregorio's texts the thing to be sucked out is always referred to as the liquid substance, strength – as opposed to solid objects such as thorns (or horns). We have no doubt that Piman shamans commonly suck out solid objects. We have not asked Gregorio to comment on this act. He did not mention it and we believe his theory is consistent without it; we will try to demonstrate this consistency.

In the sections that follow we will study the special properties of liquid strengths, for they are crucial to Gregorio's theory of the *dúajida.* In our opinion, they conform with certain of Gregorio's preoccupations about sicknesses. In fact they may be more apt vehicles for his preoccupations than would be a theory based on thorns or other solid objects. We offer three reasons for this opinion.

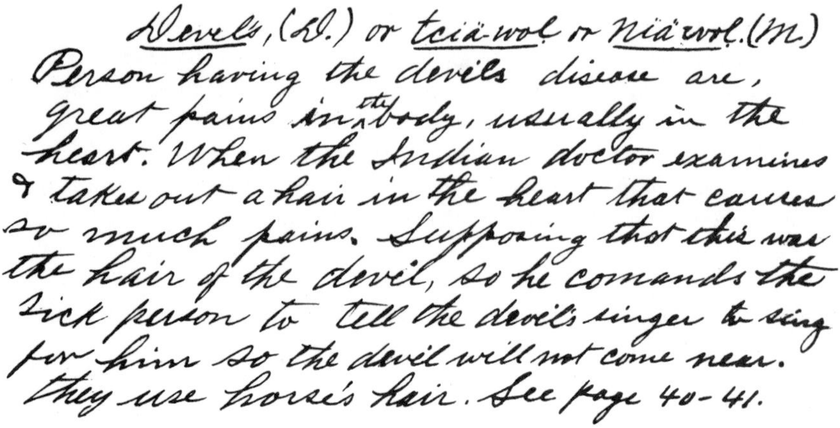

Devils, (D.) or tciä-wol or Niä'wol. (M.)
Person having the devils disease are, great pains in the body, usually in the heart. When the Indian doctor examines & takes out a hair in the heart that causes so much pains. Supposing that this was the hair of the devil, so he comands the sick person to tell the devil's singer to sing for him so the devil will not come near. they use horse's hair. See page 40-41.

An instance of the "thorn theory" of sickness. José Lewis Brennan holograph, 1897.
(Courtesy Smithsonian Institution, J.N.B. Hewitt, Collector.)

First, a shaman who found thorns would perhaps trace their origin to an individual horned toad. Gregorio does not explain sickness in this manner. We have found in part II that Gregorio does not consider the source of strength a tangible thing in nature. We have traced it to what we call a moral source: "the commandments of our society," *t-kí:dag cíhañig.*

Second, we offer the theoretical compatibility between Gregorio's notion of strength and the etiological theme mentioned in part II: the long gap in time between the sickness-provoking action and the shaman's diagnosis. This gap is one of the distinctive characteristics of *ká:cim* sickness.

Piman etiology requires a substantial or quasi-substantial substance to explain how sicknesses enter individuals without the victim perceiving the entrance of the sickness. The patient must believe that he has had a sickness for years while unconscious of its presence. Strength fulfills this. We may speculate that thorns would be a less satisfactory expression of this particular etiological persuasion for a thorn theory of sicknesses seems to imply a clearly perceptible distinction between having and not having a sickness. An individual does not have the sickness until the thorn enters his body and we assume that thorns do not enter unnoticed. Recall that Sala's sickness struck her suddenly, filling her with sensations of needles and pins inside, so she could hardly make the journey from the place where she "got" it to her home. Unfortunately we have no texts proposing thorn theory with which to confirm our speculations. The argument would be:

GREGORIO'S ETIOLOGY

1. Unperceived acquisition of sickness
2. Expressed by entry of strength

THORN THEORY ETIOLOGY

1. Definitely perceived acquisition of sickness
2. Expressed by entry of a thorn

The third point of difference concerns problematic diagnosis. For Gregorio this consists in the identification of the several kinds of strength a patient has acquired over his lifetime. The obvious causes of the patient's distress are at the top where they are readily accessible to diagnosis. In terms of strengths this indicates that the patient's body contains strata which the shaman, like the mythical earth diver, must plumb to the bottom.

In our opinion a thorn theory implies the principle of "one patient, one sickness, one causal agent." Again, unfortunately, we lack comparative evidence to confirm the argument.

GREGORIO'S DIAGNOSIS

1. Patient's distress has several causes, some less accessible than others
2. Expressed by stratification of strength

THORN THEORY DIAGNOSIS

1. Patient's distress has a single cause
2. Expressed by presence of a thorn

These three rationalizations supporting the theory of liquid strengths as causal agents of sickness are offered anticipating research on the doctrines of a shamanic theory acknowledging solid objects as causal agents. As aforementioned, we do not doubt that some Piman shamans extract thorns or similar hard, sharp objects. However, for the present we assume that Gregorio does not and, furthermore, we suggest that his theory is more congenial with the known Piman conceptions on sickness than a simple theory of thorns would be.

3. *Kúlañmada, Dúajida,* and *Wúsota*

Kúlañmada, dúajida, and *wúsota* name the events during which a patient's sickness is identified and cured. Although they were not named in Russell's account, it appears to us that all three were performed for Sala: first, a *kúlañmada*, then a *dúajida*, and finally, on the day after the thorn was extracted, a *wúsota* consisting of songs "for the horned toad."

The simplest means to differentiate these terms is to label them, respectively, limited diagnosis, extensive diagnosis, and cure. This is inaccurate, however, because a cure can be accomplished during any one of the events; for example, the treatment of a patient's sickness may be successfully concluded with a *kúlañmada.* Although the curative function is in some sense present in all three events, the diagnostic function is limited to *kúlañmada* and *dúajida.*

We will proceed with a literal and an idiomatic discussion of these terms. The idiomatic meaning refers to the manner in which Gregorio defines the events. He does so by telling what is accomplished during the event and how this is done. The literal meaning refers to our own etymological interpretation of the word's meaning based upon an analysis of the meanings of parts of the word.

Kúlañmada seems to mean literally "the application of medicine." The noun *kúlañ* – borrowed from the Spanish *curar*, "to cure" – means "medicine." The suffix *-mad* means "to apply it to something" or "to mix it with something." The final *-a* is a nominalizing suffix. Idiomatically the word means 'the minimum thing a shaman can do to discover and cure a sickness, always involving a blowing, *wústana*, to divine the nature of the sickness, and a sucking, *wí:ñhuna*, to take its strength out'.

Dúajida literally means "vitalization." The word can be analyzed into the root, *dúa* meaning "healthy" or "alive," plus the causative suffix, *-jid*, plus the monimalizer, *-a*; hence, we have *dúajid*, "to cause it to be healthy" or "to vitalize," and *dúajida*, "vitalization." Idiomatically the word means 'the maximum activities a shaman can perform to discover and cure a sickness, which always involves blowing, sucking, and singing of songs directed at spirit helpers'.

Wúsota literally means the "blowing," from *wúsot*, "to blow," plus the nominalizer. Idiomatically it means 'the curing ritual of a sickness whose identity has already been established'. There is another Piman word, *wúsosig*, also constructed from the root "to blow," whose literal and idiomatic meanings we take to be substantially the same as *wúsota*; we cannot differentiate between them.

Wúsota is performed on two levels of extensiveness, maximal and minimal. The maximal level, analogous to *dúajida*, always involves a blowing and the singing of songs directed at spiritual causal agents. The minimal level, like *kúlañmada*, involves a blowing and the application of fetishes representing the causal agent. The important thing about *wúsota* is that it involves the same kinds of action as *dúajida*/*kúlañmada*, but the actions are performed by laymen rather than shamans.

The successful completion of *kúlañmada* and *dúajida* requires an extraordinary achievement on the part of the shaman. He has privileged commerce with the substance of the sickness: seeing it, hearing about it, touching it, sucking it, or blowing on it. This is understood to be his "work" which is made possible because of his "gifts," derived from visions and dreams. His methods are obscure, utterly private, and trancelike in the sense that while he is visibly present in the room with a patient he is supposed to be in communication with things elsewhere. Thus, either in the landscape of the spirits or the patient's body, in different manners made possible by his several gifts, the shaman's perceptions and actions are keyed to objects to which ordinary people do not have access.

The *wúsota*, in contrast, involves congregational magic on the part of laymen. This complex event duplicates some of the actions of *dúajida*/*kúlañmada*, namely blowing smoke on the patient and singing toward the spirits; however, the actions are performed by ordinary people in unison. The performers of a *wúsota*, selected according to age, sex, kinship, and knowledge of curing songs, do not have the license to interact with the sickness on the privileged, individualistic grounds reserved for the shamans.

The interactions between ritual curers and sicknesses may be characterized as follows:

1. UNIDIRECTIONAL. They act toward the sickness, but they do not react to it; they do not become involved with it.
2. DISTANT. Their actions are said to be directed at some vague but distant mind, which seems to be a spiritual manifestation of the way of the dangerous object.
3. INDIRECT. Although the shaman manipulates strengths directly by seeing them, kneading them, and sucking them out, the curers never experience direct contact with strengths in the patient's body. Their actions are indirect, being mediated by spiritual entities.
4. PRAYERFUL. The curers invoke the help of a spirit.

We have noted that all three of these events – *kúlañmada, dúajida*, and *wúsota* – are considered curative and magical, although in different aspects. *Kúlañmada* and *dúajida* differ from *wúsota* in the attitudes and experiences of the people who perform them – the shamans and the ritual curers. Presently, we will concentrate on the shaman's labors in order to portray the events of *kúlañmada* and *dúajida:* what actions are performed, with what results, to what kinds of objects, and how the events conform with shamanic rationale. We will undertake an analogous task for *wúsota* in part IV.

We turn now to text 18 in which Gregorio was asked to differentiate between the three events. The resolution he provides is abstract and generalized: Both *kúlañmada* and *dúajida* may result in "figuring out" (diagnosing) or "changing" (curing) a sickness. They are said to differ on the grounds that *dúajida* is both more extensive and more intensive than *kúlañmada*; "*t 'am abṣ hé'es o 'al 'i ñéi*," "he will just observe a little bit of it," is said of *kúlañmada* and "*mat 'am o si 'i cíkp*," "when he [shaman] really works," is said of the shaman's efforts during *dúajida.*

We wished to understand how the increment in intensiveness and extensiveness characteristic of *dúajida* furthers both the curative and diagnostic purposes. The answer is foreshadowed at the end of the text 18 where Gregorio tells of the two possible results of a *dúajida.* Either the sickness will never again "show up," that is, it has been cured; or several portions of it will still "remain" and they will be the bases for ritual cures, *wúsota.* In the latter case the sickness has been diagnosed into its several components, but it has not been exterminated.

The foreshadowing consists in the word "remain." The substance which remains is the strength inside the patient's body. Most *dúajidas* succeed on precisely these grounds: They leave the patient with disambiguated strengths inside him. Thus, the shaman can complete his efforts with strengths remaining in the patient's body, apparently failing from the curative standpoint but succeeding as a diagnostician.

TEXT 18 (Tape 9.10)

Q

K hás	másma	'am gáwul	'e-wúa,	hégam	wáikk	há'icu,
Somehow	thus	differently	happens,	those-ones	three	something,

How do [the following] three things differently take place,

hégai kúlañmada mat táṣ 'éḍ hab o 'e-jú:, c hég 'é:p,
that-one medication ss daytime in will happen, and that-one also,
dúajida mat cúhugc 'éḍ hab o 'e-jú:,
vitalization ss darkness in will happen,

kúlañmada, which is done in the daytime, and dúajida,
which is done at night,

c hég 'é:p, hégai wusóta?
and that-one also, that-one blowing?

and the ritual cure?

A

Pégi, b 'o másma hab 'e-wúa, 'í:da hab cú'igam há'icu,
Well, thus happens, this-one kind of something,

Well, thus it happens, this phenomenon,

. . .hégai kúlañmada, táṣ 'éḍ.
. . .that-one medication, daytime in.

. . .the kúlañmada in the daytime.

S-'áp'e, 'o wóho'o 'am hab másma hab 'e-wúa,
Proper, true there thus happens,

Right, it really happens like that,

heg hékaj mat 'am abṣ o cécga,
that-one by means of ss there just will check,

because he [shaman] merely will check it,

k 'am hí o a ñéi,
and there of course will observe,

and he will observe him [patient],

héu'u, natṣ pi 'am hú hás o 'i cem júccu
yes, because away somehow will be trying to do
g há'icu hás tá:hadkam,
the something somehow stimulating,

yes, of course he will try to do away with
the thing [strength] that stimulates him,

pégi, k hab ’e-wúa mo abṣ cem hékid s-’áp’e,
well, and happens ss just anytime is proper,
well, and anytime it is all right [for kúlañmada],

táṣ ’éḍ, ’o héms húḍuñk.
day in, or perhaps evening.
in the day or the evening.

Pégi, t ’am o hím, k ’am o ñéi
Well, there will go, and there will observe
Well, he will go and observe it

matp si pi o ’áp’ek,
ss very not will be proper,
[and] if it [sickness] is very bad,

pégi, t ’am abṣ hé’es o ’al ’i ñéi.
well, there just few will slightly observe.
well, he will just observe a little bit of it.

Hég ’o hab ’á’aga, “kúlañmada.”
That-one calls it, “kúlañmada.”
That’s what is called “kúlañmada.”

B

C hég hab hí ’e-wúa
And that-one on the other hand happens
And on the other hand that one [dúajida] takes place

mat ’am o si ’i cíkp g ’ó’odham,
ss there will really work the man,
when he [shaman] really works,

k ’am o ’i mámci
and there will figure it out
and he will figure it out

matp hás 'i má:s, háscu wuḍ o 'ik, c hab júñhim.
ss somehow appears, whatever will be, and will be doing.
how it is, whatever the thing is that is doing it.

Pégi, k cúhugam 'óidam 'am o 'i 'ói
Well, and darkness during there will follow
Well, in the night he will concentrate on it

matp hékid o 'i dáhiwua,
ss whenever will sit down,
whenever he sits down,

k 'ámjeḍ 'am o 'i mámci há'icu.
and hence there will figure out something.
and from there he will figure things out.

Kutp 'am hú hás másma há'icu wuḍ o hégaik.
And eventually somehow thus something will be that-one.
And it [sickness] may be a certain kind of thing.

Kut 'am gáwul o cem jú:, 'am 'i 'óidk.
And there differently will try to do, there will follow.
And he will try to change it, he will concentrate on it [the patient's complex sickness].

K 'im hú gáwul másma hab 'ep o 'e-jú:,
And later differently thus also will get done,
And then he will do still another different thing,

hab o 'e-júñhim k 'e-júñhim,
will be doing and will be doing,
he will go on and on [doing different things to discover the various strengths in the patient],

k hékid o cé:mo g s-cúhugam – sí'al ké:kk,
and when will complete the darkness – dawn stands,
and when the night is finished – at dawn,

pégi, k 'atp háscu 'am o 'i wí: 'am hég 'óidk
well, and whatever there will be remaining there that-one along
well, and whatever thing [strength] will remain through
all of that [work]

mat háscu 'am o 'i 'e-cé:gǐ.
ss whatever there will get shown.
whatever [kind of strength] will have shown up.

Ñé:, 'í:da 'o hab 'á:ga,
Look, this-one calls it,
Look, this is what it is called [dúajida],

c 'aṣ 'íd hab si 'e-dúajid,
and this-one really gets vitalized,
and this [patient] really gets dúajida-ed,

"'e-kúlañmad," b 'antp másma hab 'ép o céi,
"it gets medicated," I thus also will say,
"kúlañmada-ed" is another manner of saying it,

heg hékaj mo wuḍ a wé:ngaj, hía.
that-one by means of ss is its partner, of course.
because it [kúlañmada] is its [semantic] mate.

C

Pégi, kc 'am háscu wuḍ o hégaik,
Well, and there whatever will be that-one,
Well, and whatever it [the diagnosed sickness] may be,

kutp hab o cú'igkad
and will be being
and if it should be existing

matp háscu o 'i múmkicudad,
ss whatever will be sickening it,
whatever thing is making him sick,

pégi, k há'icu 'éñiga mat abṣ cem hékid o 'e-wúso, hégai,
well, and something has the right ss just whenever will get cured, that-one,
well, and some things can be cured any time,

táṣ 'éḍa matp háscu wuḍ o 'ik,
day in ss whatever will be,
in the day, whatever it may be,

c há'icu hía mo. . . cúhugam 'éñiga.
and something of course ss. . . darkness has the right.
and some things of course have to be cured at night.

. . .Ñé:, pi 'am hú hás hí másma hab cú'ig,
. . .Look, not ever somehow on the other hand thus is,
. . .Look, it [dúajida] is not like that [not the same as a ritual cure],

hég 'o hab a'i cú'ig
that-one only is
that's the only thing [about dúajida]

mañ 'am hú hab 'á:g, "dúajida,"
ss I already told, "vitalization,"
as I have already explained, "dúajida,"

hég hí 'ámjeḍ mat 'am o cem si 'i mámci,
that-one on the other hand from ss there will try to figure-it-out,
the thing from which he [shaman] will try to figure it out,

'o o si gáwul 'i jú:.
or will very differently do.
or change it [sickness].

Pégi, k hébai hab 'e-wúa
Well, and sometimes happens
Well, and sometimes it happens

mo 'ab 'áb g 'ó'odham.
ss is against the man.
that it's up to the man [shaman].

C a wóho mo 'am há'icug,
And truly ss there it is something,
And truly there is something [sickness],

c 'im hú hab hí 'e-wúa,
and away of course gets done,
and it is done away with,

c pi 'im hú 'ep 'e-táṣogid.
and not ever again will get made apparent.
and it never reappears.

Tp hé'ekia há'icu o 'i wí:,
Several something will remain,
[however] as many things as still remain,

hég 'ám hékaj o 'e-wúso.
that-one there by means of will get cured.
he [patient] will get cured by means of them [the kinds of strength which the shaman has failed to exterminate].

Ñé:, há'ap o másma.
Look, that-way thus.
Look, that's how it is.

4. Strength

The theory of strength explains both the shaman's concern with the patient's body during the *dúajida* and the patient's ignorance of harboring *ká:cim* sickness. Text 19 introduces stratification and permeation as factors in the *dúajida.* The anchor points of this text are two phrases with the verb *'úlin* in the medio-passive, "to get held." Referring to sickness, these phrases express the goal of the diagnostic aspect of *dúajida:* to learn what a sickness is by tracing the origin of its strength.

Stratification and permeation of strength

Gregorio begins the text with the hypothetically unproblematical situation of a strength encountered in "isolated" form. The first expression with *'úlin* is: *héjelko o 'e-úl*, "alone it would get held." The text ends with the expression: *táṣo 'i 'e-úl*, "clearly it gets held." The context of the latter expression is: "And necessarily it will remain, and then it will get clearly held [isolated]. 'Look, that one apparently is sickening him'." The final line is the statement of a shaman who has performed a successful *dúajida* from the diagnostic point of view, as distinguished from the curative viewpoint. The strength remains in the patient but it has been disambiguated or "clearly isolated."

The text is divided into five parts in sequence – A, B, C, D, E, and F. A describes an unproblematical diagnostic situation of the sort that could adequately be dealt with by *kúlañmada.* In this case the strength remains isolated and unpermeated along a particular body part. It is relatively simple to know what kind of sickness a patient has, for, as mentioned in the introductory section, each kind of strength tends to originate from a different part of the body.

B introduces the first kind of problematical situation, permeation, in which the patient feels "something" (implicitly strength) "everywhere." In this text the strength's action is expressed as "to get spread out," *'e-héhemakocud.* In other texts the expression is *cé:mo*, "to permeate," "to reach saturation," "to complete a process." The patient feels sick all over because the strength has been diffused throughout his body. (See text 23 for a classic statement on permeation.)

It follows from the principle of permeation that any sickness can create generalized aches and pains. For this reason a patient who "hurts all over" cannot expect to be cured until a shaman has identified the kind of strength that permeated him.

C establishes that each strength has its source localized somewhere within the patient's body. Here Gregorio uses the word *'ámjeḍkam* to speak about strength. We translate the word as "source." The word is used to ascribe a source, producer, or origin of something; for example, a parent is the *'ámjeḍkam* of his child. In the context of diagnosis the word can be interpreted in two senses: (1) A certain body part is the *'ámjeḍkam* of strength because the strength entered and began spreading from there; (2) The commandments governing the way of a class of dangerous objects (for example, coyote) are the *'ámjeḍkam* of strength as they are the ultimate source. As mentioned above the two senses are correlated in that the strength of each kind of dangerous object tends to have a distinct origin within the patient's body.

Parts D and E repeat the sequence of first discussing the unproblematical and then moving to the problematical, but in this instance the problematical topic is stratification. D, analogous to A, states that any sickness may be unproblematically localized. If so, it (implicitly the strength) will "emerge" there. Notice that the emergence of the strength is said to be the consequence of the shaman's "work," and that the result is expressed diagnostically rather than curatively: he will "figure out," rather than "do away with," the sickness.

Gregorio's use of the word *'i wú:ṣ* "to emerge," is noncommittal not only on the issue of curative effects, but also on the question of what causes the strength to emerge. *'I wú:ṣ* is an intransitive verb. Thus, it is not clear from this text whether Gregorio intends more than figurative speech, the implication being "it all comes out right at the end." Text 20, however, presents a clear statement of the physical manipulation of strength, by massaging and sucking, for diagnostic purposes.

E introduces the problem of stratification. It is a question of a complex sickness whose different kinds of strength (for example, coyote and eagle) become piled upon each other. This produces symptoms similar to those of a single permeated strength, for the aches and pains are distributed all over the patient's body. Again the problem is phrased as a diagnostic one: the "unknowability" of the strengths.

F is the conclusion of the text, where we find the triumphant sentence with *táṣo 'i 'e-'úl,* "it will be clearly isolated," spoken of a successful night's work in separating stratified strengths.

TEXT 19 (Tape 9.11)

Q

K hás másma hab 'e-wúa mat 'an hásko hab o 'e-jú: g múmkidag?
Somehow thus happens ss there someplace will happen the sickness?
How is it, that a sickness will get someplace [in the patient's body] ?

A

Há'ap 'atp másma hab o cú'igkad,
That-way thus will be being,
That's how it will be,

no pi hégai mañ 'am hú hab káij
because that-one ss I already spoke
because of the thing which I have already mentioned

mat 'am o si 'i cíkp g 'ó'odham,
ss there will really work the man,
[about] when a man [shaman] will really work [at the dúajida],

k 'am o 'i 'ói, cúhugam 'óidam,
and there it will follow, darkness during,
and he will concentrate on it through the night,

k 'am hás 'am o wúad.
and there somehow there will be doing.
and he will be doing various things to it.

Pégi, t hab o 'e-júñhimk o 'e-júñhimk,
Well, will be getting done and getting done,
Well, he will be doing it and doing it,

hébai a wóho
sometimes truly
sometimes it is true

mat héjelko o 'e-'úl
ss alone will get held
that it [strength] will be isolated

matp háscu wuḍ o 'i hégaik.
ss whatever will be that-one.
whatever [kind of strength] it may be.

Mú'i o hía há'icu hab ha-wúa,
Several of course something does to them,
It [complex sickness] does a diversity of things to them [people],

'im háb ha-kákio 'óidk,
down there their legs along,
along their legs,

kc 'in hú ha-hón 'óidk,
and up above their body along,
or along their body,

c ha-mó'o 'óidk.
and their head along.
and along their head.

B

Kutp hab o ṣa cú'igk
And will slightly be
And if it should be the case

matp wépsko há'icu hab o 'i tá:had,
ss everyplace something will stimulate it,
that everyplace [all over his body] something
will be stimulating him,

abṣ hab-a hémho a mat o 'i 'e-héhemakojc 'am hég 'óidk, hégai
but necessarily ss will get spread out there that-one along, that-one

because it [strength] tends to get spread out along
it [the patient's body]

matp háscu wuḍ o 'ik.
ss whatever will be.

whatever [kind of strength] it may be.

C

'O há'icu hab abṣ 'ep o 'e-jú:
Or something just also will happen

Or something else may happen

matp hég wuḍ o cem 'ámjeḍkamk.
ss that-one will be from-thing.

if it [some location in the body] should be the source [of a strength].

Pégi, kc 'am abṣ o híhhimad g géwkdag,
Well, and there just will be going the strength,

Well, and the strength just goes [from there],

c abṣ hab-a hémho a mat o húhug,
but necessarily ss will terminate,

but it will have to quit [because of the shaman's actions],

k 'i hú o wí: hég 'áb, hégai
and down-there will remain that-one against, that-one

and it [strength] will remain there against it [the source in the body]

matp hég 'áb o ṣónk.
ss that-one against will begin.

where it started from.

D

Cem háscu hab 'e-wúa,
Just whatever happens,

Any kind [of sickness] does it,

cem 'im hab há'ap, kákio 'óidk.
perhaps there that-way, legs along.

perhaps it is along the legs [that the strength has its point of origin].

Há'ap o a másma hab cú'ig, 'í:da,
That-way thus is, this-one,

Thus it may be,

pégi, há'ap o másma hab 'e-wúa,
well, that-way thus happens,

well, it [strength] does it like that,

pégi, t hég 'áb, 'am o 'i wú:ṣ
well, that-one against, there will emerge

well, from that [the legs] it will emerge

mo heg hékaj 'am hab 'i cíkpan mat o mái.
ss that-one by means of there will start to work ss will learn.

which is the reason why he [shaman] works, so he can find it out.

E

Kc pi 'am hú hás 'e-wúa,
And never somehow happens,

And suppose it [strength] doesn't do anything
[it stays latent for a while],

hémho a mat abṣ 'ab o 'i ge 'e-dá:m wá:khimad, 'í:da há'icu
necessarily ss will just on-top-of-itself be entering, this-one something
hás tá:hadkam.
somehow stimulating-thing.

necessarily it [strength] will be stacked on itself, this manner of
stimulating thing [stratified strengths].

Pi 'am hú ta-má:cima hab o cú'igk,
Not ever knowable will be,
It will not be knowable,

c hía wóho mat 'im pi o 'áp'ek,
and of course truly ss there will damage,
and then of course it will hurt someplace,

c hébai pi o 'áp'ek c hébai 'é:p.
and someplace will damage and someplace else.
and someplace it will hurt and someplace else.

F

Pégi, t abṣ hab-a hékid 'am o 'i 'e-cíkpank,
Well, but whenever there will begin-to-get-worked-on,
Well, but when it [sickness] gets worked on,

'am o 'i 'e-húḍawua,
there will begin-to-get-bothered,
and it will get bothered,

k hémho a mat o wí:,
and necessarily ss will remain,
and necessarily it will remain [at its physiological point of origin],

k 'am háhawa o táṣo 'i 'e-'úl,
and there then will clearly get held,
and then it will be clearly isolated,

"Ñé:, hég 'o kĭ múmkicud,"
"Look, that-one is apparently sickening it,"
"Look, that one is sickening him,"

matp háscu wuḍ o'ik.
ss whatever will be.
whatever [kind of sickness] it will be.

Ñé:, há'ap o másma.
Look, that-way thus.

Look, that's how it is.

Depth of strength

The following texts concern the relationship between the depth of strength and that aspect of the *dúajida* by which the shaman gains access to the patient's past. The principle is that the depth of a strength expresses the length of time it has been in a patient.

We begin with text 20 in which Gregorio speaks about massaging and sucking as methods of manipulating the deep-seated strengths. In this text, as well as in following texts, the vocabulary of depth refers to the location of one kind of strength vis-à-vis other kinds of strength. The problem posed by deep-seated strengths is that they may be "obscured" or "covered up" by higher, younger ones. The shaman's pressing and sucking are discussed in terms of "causing them to show up," "gathering them," and "removing them."

Although through these actions the shaman makes contact with parts or organs within the patient's body, it is important to understand that his purpose is not said to be the protection or manipulation of the body part; rather the purpose is to gain access to the more or less deep-seated strengths. Thus, according to these texts, the shaman is interested in strength, not the welfare of the patient's internal organs.

TEXT 20 (Tape 9.15)

Q

T hás másma 'am o 'i 'e-wú:ṣad hégai géwkdag mo gḍ hú
Somehow thus there gets removed that-one strength ss distantly

si wéco hab cú'ig?
very below is?

How does he [shaman] remove a deep strength?

A

Héu'u, no pi hab 'ép cú'ig, hégai
Yes, because also is, that-one

Yes, because it is the case

matp hás 'i másma 'am o 'e-cé:gijid, hégai
ss somehow thus there will get-caused-to-be-shown, that-one
há'icu pi 'áp'edag.
something impropriety.
that somehow the improper thing [strength] is caused to show up.

Pégi, tp hab o ṣa cú'igk
Well, will slightly be
Well, if it should be the case

matp 'im hú o ṣá'i mé:kk
ss away will be slightly distant
that it will be slightly distant [deep in the body]

. . .matp 'i 'í:ya g 'í:bdaj pi o 'áp'et,
. . .ss here the its heart will be damaged,
. . .if here [for example] his [patient's] heart will be damaged
[by a deep strength],

k 'éḍa hab cú'ig
and yet is
and yet it is the case

mo gḍ hú ṣa mé:k, hégai.
ss away down slightly distant, that-one.
that it [strength] is far down [in the body].

Pégi, k hémho a mat 'á'ai o dágṣṣa, 'í:na hónḍ 'ánai,
Well, and necessarily ss on each side will press, here its body on,
Well, he [shaman] will have to press here on each side of the body,

'ab o 'i héhemapad k o 'i héhemapad.
against will be gathering and will be gathering.
he will be bunching it [strength] up and bunching it up.

Ñé:, k 'atp hé'ekio hab o 'i jú:,
Look, and several will do,
Look, and he will do it a few times,

k 'ab háhawa o cíñwua,
and against then will put-the-mouth,
and then he will put his mouth against it,

o 'i wú:ṣad g géwkdaj, gḍ hú,
will remove the its strength, away down,
he will remove its strength,

natp pi 'ab o 'i hémapadk,
because against will gather it,
because he will gather it,

gḍ hú o 'i 'úl 'ámai
away down will hold there
and he will hold it down there

mat 'ab 'ámjeḍ o wú:ṣ,
ss from will emerge,
from where it [strength] will emerge,

pégi, k s-péhegim hab 'e-wúa, hégai hab másma.
well, and easily happens, that-one thus.
well, and it is easily done in that manner.

Ñé:, há'ap o másma hab wúa
Look, that-way thus does
Look, that's how he does it

matp gḍ hú ṣa mé:k hab o cú'igk.
ss away down slightly far will be.
if it [strength] is down deep.

K hémho a mat ’ab o ’i dágĭtpa,
And necessarily ss against will press,
And he has to press it,

’ab o ṣa ’i hémapadk,
against will slightly gather,
he kind of gathers it,

k háhawa o ’i wú:ṣad.
and then will remove it.
and then he removes it.

C ha’icu ’an hía abṣ dá:m,
And something there of course just on top,
And some things may be on top,

ṣa’i mía ’al kómalk,
slightly close slightly thin,
close and slightly thin,

hí wuḍ abṣ péhegkam, hí’i.
on-the-other-hand is just easy, on the other hand.
and in that case it’s simple [to remove them].

Ñé:, há’ap ’o másma.
Look, that-way thus.
Look, that’s how it is.

Gregorio’s vocabulary on the depth of strength includes the following terms:

DEEP OR DISTANT		SHALLOW OR NEAR
(a) *gḍ hú mé:k*	vs.	(b) *’an mía*
(c) *gḍ hú wéco*	vs.	(d) *’an dá:m*

We translate the terms:

mé:k, "distant"	*mía*, "close"
wéco, "below," "beneath"	*dá:m*, "above," "on top"

We translate *gḍ hú* as "distantly," "far away," or "away down" and *'an* as "there" (at another place, as opposed to "here"). These are crude translations because they fail to discriminate between other Piman locatives (e.g., *gm hú*, "distant," and *'am*, "there").

We translate the expressions:

(a) "far down in space" or "far back in time"	(b) "close in space" or "time"
(c) "below in space"	(d) "above in space"

Examples concerning strength and sicknesses are:

(a)

K 'éḍa hab cú'ig	mo gḍ hú	sa mé:k,	hégai.
And yet is	ss away down	slightly far,	that-one.

And yet it is the case that it [strength] is far down [in the patient's body] (text 20).

(a), (b), (d)

To 'i hí:,	hégai	matp gḍ hú	ṣa mé:k	hab o cú'igk,
Will begin,	that-one	ss far away	slightly distant	will be,

It [strength] will begin [to cause symptoms] if it has been in existence for a long time,

c há'icu	'an abṣ a'i mía	mo'om ṣa'i dá:m.
and something	there just only is near	ss is just on top.

and something [another kind of strength] is just close, it is just on top of it [the more distant, longer-established strength] (tape 9.14).

(c)

C hébai	gḍ hú	háhawa	abṣ o wá:,	wéco.
And sometimes	distantly	then	just will enter,	below.

And sometimes it [strength] will have entered long ago.

An alternate translation is:

And sometimes it will enter underneath it [another strength] (tape 10.5).

(c), (d)

Há'icu	wuḍ	wéco	múmkidag,
Something	is	beneath	sickness,

Something is a "beneath sickness",

'éḍa	hégai	matp háscu'i wé:peg	'am jí jiwup,
yet	that-one	ss whatever first	there arrives,

it is whatever sickness that arrived there first,

c há'icu	'am dá:m.
and something	there on top.

and got something on top of it (text 21).

The next two texts support the interpretation of *dúajida* as an attempt to recover traces of forgotten actions. The first, text 21, was given in explanation of "beneath sickness," *wéco múmkidag:* the sicknesses, or more accurately the components of a complex sickness, which were acquired earliest in a patient's life. The text is doubly useful to us because in addition to defining the depth of sickness temporally Gregorio uses this notion as a means to distinguish between *kúlañmada* and *dúajida. Dúajida* is necessary "to cause it [the deepest sickness] to become apparent."

The text is in four parts. A defines the condition we refer to as a stratified sickness, in which a strength, already in the patient's body, has become covered by several later arrivals. Here we find an expression of latency, the phenomenon of the earliest-arriving sickness "not starting to do anything" to the patient during the time it is the only sickness present in his body. B states that *kúlañmada* suffices only for the discovery of the upper levels of a stratified sickness. C states that *dúajida* is necessary to reveal the deepest sicknesses. D defines "beneath sickness" as the component of a complex sickness which cannot be observed because, having arrived first, it has become covered by later-arriving sicknesses.

TEXT 21 (Tape 10.3)

A

. . .Pégi	kc 'atp háscu'i	wé:peg	'am hab o cú'igkad,	
. . .Well,	and whatever	first	there will be existing,	

. . .Therefore, whatever thing will be there first,

kut 'ói	a pi 'im hú	hás	o 'i 'e-jú:,
and then	never	somehow	will begin to get done,

and it won't start to do anything [it will remain latent],

kut háskojeḍ	há'icu	háhawa	abṣ 'ep o hímhid,
and someplace-from	something	then	just also will come,

and then something else [strength] comes from someplace,

c 'ab o 'áb	gé:ṣk,
and will against	strike,

and strikes against him [patient],

k hég 'ám	'ep o 'i hímk,
and that-one there	also will begin,

and it will also begin,

hébai	hé'ekia	há'icu	'ab i 'e-dá:m	gégṣa,	hégai.
sometimes	several	something	on top of itself	falls,	that-one.

sometimes several things get on top of it [the first strength].

B

Pégi,	c 'íd	'ab 'á:gas
Well,	and this-one	against has been told

Well and this is the meaning

mañ 'am hab a káij	'am hú'i	hébai,	há'icu	'ab 'ámjeḍ
ss I there said,	below	someplace,	something	about it

as I have said earlier about it

mo hás másma wuḍ kúlañmada, hégai.
ss somehow thus is kúlañmada, that-one.
[about] how a kúlañmada is.

Pégi, t 'am hí o a ñéi,
Well, there of course will observe,
Well, and of course he [shaman] will observe it,

há'as 'at hú 'am o ñéi, hégai,
a-certain-amount eventually there will observe, that-one,
to a limited extent he will observe it,

kutp héms hab o 'e-jú:
and perhaps will get done
and it may happen

matp gó:k 'am hú 'ép o 'i 'e-cé:gĭ, há'icu
ss two eventually also will get shown, something
that two things [strengths] will show up

mat hég 'ám o a 'e-hékaj, hégai.
ss that-one there will get used, that-one.
if he [shaman] will use it [two different techniques for divination?].

'Atp héms pi 'im hú o táṣok
Perhaps never will be clear
[But] perhaps it will not be apparent

mo gḍ hú si wéco, 'é:p.
ss away down very beneath, also.
that there is another [strength] far beneath it.

C

Pégi, kc hég 'áb hab 'e-wúa
Well, and that-one against happens
From that [factor of depth] it happens

. . .mat ṣ o si 'e-dúaj, cúhugam 'óidam o 'e-kúlañmad.
. . .ss will really get dúajida-ed, darkness during will get kúlañmada-ed.
. . .that he [patient] will get dúajida-ed, in the night he will get kúlañmada-ed.

Pégi, k hég 'óidam 'am o 'i 'ói, hégai
Well, and that-one during there will follow, that-one
Well, and then he [shaman] will pursue it

matp 'am hú há'icu 'ép hab 'ép o cú'igk
ss ever something also also will be
if there should be something else [undiscovered]

matp wuḍ o a'i hégaik
ss will be only that-one
if it will be only that one [the undiscovered strength]

matp háscu 'am o 'i 'e-cé:gǐ.
ss whatever there will get shown.
whatever will show up [in dúajida].

Pégi, k 'eñiga, mat 'am hás o 'i cem júccu,
Well, and it has the right, ss there somehow will try to be doing,
Well, and he [shaman] has whatever he will use [to identify strengths],

'o 'atp héms hab háhawa abṣ 'ep o 'e-jú:
or perhaps then just also will get done
or it then may happen

mat 'am háhawa abṣ há'icu 'ep o 'i 'e-má:sid, gḍ hú wéco.
ss there then just something also will get caused to appear, away down beneath.
that an additional thing will be caused to appear [from] down underneath.

D

Ñé:, hég 'añ hab 'á:gc hab káij
Look, that-one I tell and say
Look, that's what I mean by saying

mo há'icu wuḍ wéco múmkidag.
ss something is beneath sickness.
that something is a "beneath sickness."

'Éḍa hégai matp háscu'i wé:peg 'am jíjiwup,
Yet that-one ss whatever first there arrives,
It is whatever sickness that arrived there first,

c há'icu 'am dá:m.
and something there on top of it.
and got something on top of it.

Pégi, c 'am o a'i 'e-ñéi,
Well, and there will only get observed,
Well, and only it [the later one] will be observed,

heg hékaj mo 'am aṣ dá:m.
that-one by means of ss there on top of it.
because it is on top.

Ñé:, kc hég gḍ hú, pi o ñéidad
Look, and that-one away down, isn't observing
Look, and the lower one, he won't observe it

mat o 'e-má'iscid há'icukaj.
ss will get covered something-by-means-of.
if it gets covered by something.

T 'am o 'i 'e-cíkpank háhawa o'i wú:ṣ, hégai.
There will get worked and then will emerge, that-one.
It will be worked on and then it will emerge.

Ñé:, há'ap 'o másma wuḍ 'á:ga.
Look, that-way thus means.
Look, that's what it means.

In text 22 Gregorio provides us with a kind of dramatic narrative interspersed with commentary on the diagnosis of stratified sicknesses. Most of the language is familiar from the previous texts. However we find examples of two important words about feeling which need to be discussed. They are the verbs *tá:t* and *tá:had.* We translate them "to be aware" and "to stimulate," respectively.

In our opinion, *tá:t* refers to a creature's ability to feel something. Thus, the subject of *tá:t* seems always to be the recipient of a stimulation. *Tá:had*, on the other hand, refers to the thing which the creature feels and, according to our interpretation, the subject of sentences with this verb is always the thing which originates the sensations, not the perceiver himself.

We are particularly concerned with *tá:had*, which commonly appears in expressions such as *Matp hás o 'i tá:had g 'ó'odham.* According to our interpretation the translation would be 'If it [sickness] will in some manner stimulate the man', as opposed to 'If he [the man] will feel some manner'.

This interpretation may be inaccurate as Pimans frequently offer the second translation. However, we believe the first translation is at least at times accurate, discounting the latter translation on the grounds that Pimans have not been taught the English word "stimulate."

Most of the following examples conform with our interpretation. First, we compare phrases built from the two words *s-tá:hadkam há'icu* and *s-ta-tá:tkam há'icu.* The former should always and only have the sense of 'stimulative thing', 'thing that makes us feel in a certain manner'. Although it seems that the latter should always mean 'sensitive thing', 'thing which is aware', this is not always the case. The phrase may have the sense of 'stimulative thing' as well as 'sensitive thing'.

STIMULATIVE THING	SENSITIVE THING
s-tá:hadkam há'icu 'something that makes you feel in some manner'	(no examples)
s-ta-tá:tkam há'icu 'something you can feel when it comes' 'what you feel is going to happen'	*s-ta-tá:tkam há'icu* 'anything that can feel you when you are coming, like a deer or cow'

The preceding examples and their English translations were provided by Lopez. He also aided in the composition of the following sentence aimed at illustrating the senses of the two words.

Hég 'o s-cu-tá:tkam há'icu g ñ-ṣóiga,
That-one is good-at-sensing something my pet,
My pet is a sensitive thing,

heg hékaj mo ha-tá:tk, s-cem háscu
that-one by means of ss it senses them, just whatever
because he senses any [of the] things

mat 'am a hás o tá:hadag, g ñ-ṣóiga wé'hejed
ss there somehow it stimulates it, my pet with-respect-to-it.
which somehow stimulate my pet.

Text 22 uses *tá:t* and *tá:had* to explain how the individual gradually becomes aware of all the parts of his sickness. A describes the onset of a sickness. We begin with the individual "being aware" of normal feelings. He has not yet experienced the "different kind of stimulation" which will mark the onset of his sickness. B describes the situation when the individual knows he is sick but he does not know the nature of his sickness. In this hypothetical case history the individual has several sicknesses, only one of which is diagnosed on his first visit to a shaman. C explains how a partial diagnosis and cure may bring temporary relief, although, eventually, a deeper strength will become active. D describes the person's second visit to the shaman where the deeper strength, hitherto "covered up," is postulated. E states that the shaman must "bother himself" all night so that the deeper strength will emerge.

TEXT 22 (Tape 5.8)

Q

K hás	másma	hab 'e-wúa	c ha-'á'aheṣ	g múmkidag?
Somehow	thus	happens	and reaches them	the sickness?

How does it happen that a sickness reaches people?

A

Héu'u,	'am o abṣ a hía	táṣo,	'é:p,
Yes,	there just of course	is clear,	also,

Yes, it is quite clear,

no pi 'am 'e-tá:tk, 'ab 'e-hímdag 'óidk
because there gets aware, against its own way along
because he [victim] is aware during his life

matp hás 'i másma 'am hab tá:hadag.
ss somehow thus there is stimulation.
of how he [normally] feels.

Pi hékid 'am hú há'icu g gáwul másma hab tá:hadag.
Never ever something the differently thus stimulation.
He never has any different kind of stimulation.

Pégi, kc hékid mat hab o 'e-jú:
Well, and whenever ss will happen
Well, and then when it happens

matp hab hú há'icu o 'i hímad wúi,
ss ever something will begin coming towards,
that something [strength] coming to him,

c o 'á'ahe.
and will reach it.
and reaches him.

Kut 'ab a hékĭ hú hás o ṣa'i tá:had há'icu,
And already somehow will slightly stimulate something,
And already something [an earlier strength] may have stimulated him a little bit,

k wá:m mat 'am hékid o si wé:s 'ab 'áb hab o 'e-jú:.
and especially ss there whenever will really all-of-it be against will get done.
but especially when all of them will get to him [then he will really kno there is something wrong].

B

Pégi, k 'am hab 'e-wúa
Well, and there happens
Well, then it happens

mat 'am hab o 'i 'e-'él
ss there will get wished
that he will decide

mat o s-mái,
ss will know,
to find out,

"Ṣá:cu 'o hú wuḍ 'i,
"What-thing ever is it,
"What is it,

c hab ñ-tá:cud? "
and causes me to feel? "
and it stimulates me?"

No pi hía mú'i ná:nko há'icu t-múmkicud,
Because of course several diverse something sickens us,
Because many different things sicken us,

c abṣ hab-a há'icu 'am aṣ a gáwul másma,
but something there differently thus,
but the things differ,

pi hékid há'icu 'am wuḍ abṣ 'i hémako
not ever something there is just one
it is never just one thing

mas hég 'ám hás másma hab o ha-tá:hadt,
ss that-one there somehow thus will stimulate them,
that in some manner stimulates them,

c wuḍ o hégaik.
and will be that-one.
and that will be [all there is to] it.

’Am ’o a gáwul másma hab ’e-wúa,
There differently thus happens,
It happens differently,

c hébai hía há’icu cem ’alo wépo má:s,
and sometimes of course something just slightly similarly appears,
[so that] sometimes some things [a few strengths] seem to be similar,

c abṣ hab-a ’éḍa ’am wuḍ a gó’olko.
but yet there is different.
but yet they are different.

Ñé:, mo ’ab ’áb hab ’e-wúa
Look, ss is against it happens
Look, it is up to [the responsibility of] him [the patient]

matp ’am háhawa o ’i ñénhogk o ñéi
ss there then will begin to look around and will observe
that he will look around and see

matp ’an hébai o ’i dá:kad, hégai
ss there somewhere will be sitting, that-one
whether one of those [shamans] will be sitting [accessibly] someplace

matp hég o ’á:gĭ
ss that-one will tell
who could tell him [patient]

mas háscu wuḍ c hab tá:hadag.
ss whatever is and stimulates.
what the thing is that is stimulating him.

Pégi, k ’am háhawa o ’á:gĭ,
Well, and there then will tell,
Well, and then he [patient] will tell him [shaman],

t 'am háhawa o ñéidk.
and there then will observe.
and then he [shaman] will observe it [patient].

'Atp héms hab o céi,
Perhaps will say,
Perhaps he [shaman] will say,

'am hú há'icu o 'i 'á:,
there ever something will tell,
he may tell him something,

"Hég 'at kĭ m-'á'ahe.
"That-one apparently you reached.
"That one [kind of strength] seems to have caught up with you.

Hég 'at kĭ m-'ái, hégai, k m-múmkic.
That-one apparently you reached, that-one, and you sickened.
That's the one that reached you and sickened you.

Ñé:, k hab o 'e-jú:,
Look, and will get done,
Look, it will get done [to you],

k 'am o 'e-wúso.
and there will get cured.
and [you] will get cured.

T o m-'áp'et."
It will you improve."
You will be all right."

C

K hébai wóho hab 'é-wúa
And sometimes truly happens
And sometimes it truly happens

mat 'am o a'i kékiwua 'ámai, há'as hú 'ál 'i,
ss there will stand there, a-certain-amount ever a-little-bit,
that it [strength] will stop for a while,

'am hab hí a'i tá:hadkahimc.
there on the other hand has-been-stimulating.
[after] it has been stimulating him.

Hébai hab 'ep 'e-wúa mat g gḍ hú wéco,
Sometimes also happens ss the away down beneath,
And sometimes it also happens that down beneath it,

'am a hás másma hab o 'ál cú'igk, 'an hú gáwul 'i há'icu,
there somehow thus a little will be, there away different something,
there will be a little [of a] different kind [of strength],

c pi 'im hú hab másma hab 'ep o tá:hadagk.
and not ever thus also will stimulate.
and it won't stimulate him like that [as the "upper" strength had].

K hí a cem húhug,
And of course just stops,
And it [the upper strength] will just stop [having been cured],

k abṣ hab-a 'am aṣ 'al gáwul másma hab 'ép o 'e-jú:.
but there just slightly differently thus also will happen.
but then a different thing [the hitherto undetected strength] will happen.

D

Pégi, t 'am 'ép o s-mái,
Well, then also will know,
Well, then he [patient] will find out again,

"Mo kĭ 'am a há'icu 'ep ñ-'óid."
"Ss apparently there something also me follows."
"There must be something else following me."

Pégi, c wóho matp 'am 'ep o cé:, hégai
Well, and truly ss there also will find, that-one
Well, and truly he [shaman] will find it,

matp hédai 'am o 'i ñéi,
ss whoever there will observe,
whoever will observe it,

tp héms hab o céi,
perhaps will say,
perhaps he [shaman] will say,

"Héu'u, ñé:, 'íd o kǐ 'am hab 'ep cú'ig, 'í:da,
"Yes, look, this-one apparently there also exists, this-one,
"Yes, look, this [strength] is also existing,

k abṣ hab-a 'e-má'iṣc."
but got covered."
but it is covered [by the upper strength]."

E

Kc abṣ hab-a hébai hía mat ṣa mé:k o 'e-húḍawa,
But sometimes of course ss slightly distantly will get bothered,
But sometimes then, he [shaman] will bother himself with it
for a long time,

cúhugam 'óidam o 'e-húḍawa,
darkness through will get bothered,
he bothers himself all night long,

k hémho a mat o a'i wú:ṣ, hégai.
and necessarily ss will only emerge, that-one.
and it [the other strength] must come out.

Ñé:, b 'o másma hab 'e-wúa, 'í:da.
Look, thus happens, this-one.
Look, thus it happens.

5. Curative Aspect of *Dúajida*

The aspect of the *dúajida* that we have studied has been concerned with diagnosing a patient's sickness. Stratification and permeation were the crucial technical concepts, for, as dispositions of strength, they expressed the problem of knowability. Next we will consider a different, and immediately dangerous, characteristic of strength which also is expressed by permeation. If strength permeates the patient, reaching his heart, it kills him.

Let us pause to examine the following questions. How serious is the prospect of death according to Piman doctrine? How urgent are the shamans' and the ritual curers' responses to the prospect of death?

In answer to the first question, all of the *ká:cim* sicknesses can be fatal because the strength of each can permeate the patient. As far as we are aware, this is the only manner in which *ká:cim* sicknesses are fatal.

Answering the second question, it is not obligatory that the shaman take direct steps against permeation. This is established by text 26. He may observe that the permeation is complete and still do nothing to change the situation, deferring altogether to the ritual curer. Thus if the compulsion to act is a measure of urgency, the threat of death does not seem to be an urgent concern of the shaman.

Fatal permeation

Theoretically, the process of permeation conforms to a scheme analogous to "distance equals rate multiplied by time." In other words, permeation is the terminal condition of strength; the variables, length of time and speed, determine how soon permeation will be reached. The shaman's techniques are aimed at "blocking," "slowing," "stopping," or "turning back" the strength.

The theory of fatal permeation shares a common factor with the theory of stratification, namely the factor of time. In principle it is possible to arrive at an integrated account, so that the lower strength, by virtue of being the oldest, should be the first to reach the heart. This is not the case because of the following additional factors: (1) Strength is free to change its position in the pile; and (2) It is free, by the principle of latency, to become active whenever it wishes and to move toward the heart at different rates.

Owing to the idiosyncratic actions of strength, Piman theory does not predict permeation solely on the basis of stratification, or vice versa. It is for this reason that the life-saving aspect of *dúajida* is separate from the diagnostic aspect. Gregorio states, in text 23, that the two aspects are separate.

The text is in five parts. In A, Gregorio states the distinction between "on top" and "beneath" is insignificant to the dangerousness of a sickness. B reveals that strengths are dangerous only if they reach the patient's heart. At any other location in the body they are not dangerous. As Gregorio explains in C, given the fact that strengths may reach the heart, there is a corresponding preventative action: blocking the strength before it gets there. In D, Gregorio expresses the manner in which a strength becomes dangerous through permeation: The strength of a single kind of sickness "meets itself," that is, permeates the patient. E is the conclusion. It repeats that a dangerous sickness may be "anyplace" in terms of stratification.

TEXT 23 (Tape 10.4)

Q

K hébai	hab hab si 'e-wúa	hégai	mo wuḍ s-ta-'é:bidam	múmkidag,
Someplace	really happens,	that-one	ss is fearful	sickness,
dá:m	'o wéco?			
on top	or below?			

Where does a dangerous sickness occur, on top or beneath?

A

Héu'u,	'am o a wóho,	'é:p,	hégai	hab másmakaj	há'icu
Yes,	there is true,	also,	that-one	thus by means of	something

Yes, it is true also of that kind of thing [any sickness, whether on top or below]

matp háscu	wuḍ o 'i si hégaik,
ss whatever	will really be that-one,

whatever thing [kind or position] it may be,

. . .wóho'o	mo hab má:s,	in hú	abṣ hébai,
. . .truly	ss appears,	nearby	just wherever,

. . .truly it [dangerous sickness] may be anywhere [either on top or beneath],

hébai	'i hab o tá:hadt,	há'icu.
someplace	will stimulate,	something.

someplace it will stimulate him.

B

Kc hékid	matp hab o cú'igkad
And whenever	ss will be existing

And if it should be the case

matp háscu wuḍ o'ik,
ss whatever will be,

for whatever [kind of sickness] thing,

c 'ab o ṣa jíwa,	'í:bdagt	'ábai.
and will slightly arrive,	its heart	against.

and it should arrive at his [patient's] heart.

Hég	'o s-ta-'é:bidama,	'ábai,
That-one	is fearful,	against it,

That is dangerous [when it is] against it,

heg hékaj	mo hég	mélcud	g t-dúakag,	hégai.
that-one by means of	ss that-one	causes it to run	the our health,	that-one.

because it [heart] maintains our health.

C 'in hú	abṣ hébai	hásko,
And nearby	just someplace	elsewhere,

And anyplace else [where the strength may be],

pi 'o hab má:s,	hégai,
not appears,	that-one,

it is not like that [dangerous],

c hég 'ám	a'i s-ta-'é:bidama,	hégai
and that-one there	only is fearful,	that-one

and only there is it dangerous

mat hékid	g 'í:bdaj	pi o 'áp'ek.
ss whenever	the its heart	will be damaged.

whenever his heart is damaged.

C

Pégi, kc hég 'ámjeḍ hab 'e-wúa 'ídam hía há'icu
Well, and that-one from happens these-ones of course something
cíkpandam
worker

Well, and for that reason, these workers [shamans] do something

mat hémho a mat 'am a hás o 'i jú:, hégai.
ss necessarily ss there somehow will do, that-one.

that they will always do something to it [strength].

'An 'i cem kúkpa
There will try to block

He will try to block it

matp hab o cú'igk
ss will be

if it is the case

matp 'im hú abṣ gó'olko.
ss ever just is separate.

that it is separated [from the heart].

'O héms hab o cú'igk matp 'ab o 'ába'ik abṣ cem háscu,
Or perhaps will be ss will be against it just whatever,

Or it may be the case that just any kind [of strength] will be against it [heart],

cem héms g dá:m múmkidag,
perhaps the upper sickness,

perhaps the upper sickness,

. . .'o héms gḍ hú wéco.
. . .or perhaps away down below.

. . .or perhaps the lower one [will reach the heart].

D

Pégi, c abṣ hab-a hab ’e-wúa hab másma, há-ap
Well, but happens thus, that-way
Well, but here is how it happens

matp hébai há’icu o ’i pi ’áp’ek g ’ó’odham.
ss sometimes something will be wrong the man.
that sometimes there will be something wrong with a person.

Hég a wépo ’e-wúa mo wé:s ’e-nánmek, hégai,
That-one seemingly happens ss every place gets met, that-one,
’e-cé:mo,
it gets permeated,
It is as if it [strength] meets itself everyplace, it gets permeated,

wé:sko ’at o hímad, hégai géwkdaj
everyplace will be going, that-one its strength
its strength will go all over

matp háscu wuḍ o’i, hégai,
ss whatever it will be, that-one,
whatever kind of thing [sickness] it may be,

ñé:, kc hég ’ám a’i hía s-’e-ñéñe’id, hégai.
look, and that-one there only of course gets watched for, that-one.
look, and that is the only thing to look out for.

Pégi, ’o hab o cú’igkad
Well, or will be existing
Well, or it may be the case

matp ’in hú ’ép o s-kó’ok,
ss nearby also will hurt,
that it will just hurt someplace [and not all over],

t abṣ hab-a ’ab o a cem s-’áp’ek g ’í:bdaj,
but against it will just be good the its heart,
but his heart will [still] be all right,

t abṣ hab-a 'am a hás o jú:
but there somehow it will do
but he [shaman] will do something to it

. . .mat 'an o cem ṣa kú:kpad 'á'ai.
. . .ss there will try slightly to block both-sides.
. . .that he will try to close off both sides.

Hab o cem 'élidad
Will just be intending
He will just intend

mat 'in hú a héjelko,
ss nearby will be separate,
that on one side it [strength] will be separate,

c hég 'im hú a héjelko.
and that-one there beyond will be separate.
and on the other side it [heart] will be separate.

E

Ñé:, abṣ cem hásko há'ap hab cú'ig, hégai,
Look, just anywhere that-way is, that-one,
Look, it [dangerous sickness] may be just anywhere [on top or below],

ñé:, há'ap 'o a'i má:s.
look, that-way only appears.
look, that's how it has to be.

Deadly nature of horned toad sickness

We turn now to an example of horned toad sickness, illustrating how strength reaches culmination at the patient's heart. Recall that Russell's case history also involved horned toad sickness (pt. III, sec. 2). The "offending object" was said to be a [t]horn instead of the liquid-like permeating strength.

Gregorio's rendition, which does not mention thorns, indicates his concern over the length of time a sickness may remain undiagnosed. It illustrates still another characteristic of Piman sicknesses: that a single kind of strength may produce symptoms in different parts of the body, in this case the legs, arms, and two parts of the back. Finally, Gregorio's discourse shows how each of the *ká:cim* sicknesses is equally dangerous. We asked the question about horned toad sickness because its early symptoms become evident at the body's extremities. We desired to learn whether it is as serious as other sicknesses, such as enemy consequence sickness, whose initial point of attack is the heart. Gregorio's answer indicates that horned toad sickness is equally dangerous.

The horned toad discourse is contained in excerpts from three texts. Text 24 poses the question of fatality and receives an answer in terms of permeation. (Note also that twice Gregorio speaks of the collectivity of *ká:cim* sicknesses as *'óimmeḍdam t-múmkidag.*)[10]

The second excerpt, text 25, describes the progress of a neglected case of horned toad sickness from legs or hands to the small of the back, then to the upper back.

Text 26 explains what happens when the strength reaches the heart. Instead of a fatality, however, we find the shaman's statement, "You will get cured," along with the prediction that the strength will "get turned back." The word used for "cured" in this case refers to a ritual cure. The curative aspect of this *dúajida* appears to be nil. Even though strength had reached the heart, the shaman placed the entire burden of counteracting it upon the ritual cure. He did not attempt to alter the course of the sickness.

TEXT 24

(Tape 14.8)

Q

Nat o ha-múa	g hémajkam,	hégam	múmkidag,	cémamagĭ,	'o g húawĭ,
Will it kill them	the person,	those-ones	sickness,	horned toad,	or the deer,

'o g gógs	'o abṣ cem háscu?
or the dog	or just whatever?

Do these sicknesses kill people: horned toad, deer, dog, or whatever?

A

Héu'u,	b 'o másma	hab cú'ig,	'í:da
Yes,	thus	is,	this-one

Yes, thus it is [with] this [group of sicknesses]

. . .matp pi o 'óiwt,
. . .ss won't hurry,
. . .if he [patient] doesn't act quickly [to get diagnosed and cured],

pégi, t o cé:mo wé:sko g cú:kugaj
well, will permeate all over the its flesh
well, it will permeate his whole body

matp háscu wuḍ o'ik
ss whatever will be
whatever thing it is

m 'am hé'ekia há'icu wuḍ 'i 'óimmeḍdam t-múmkidag,
ss there several something is wandering thing our sickness,
of the several things which are wanderers, our sicknesses,

pégi, c 'atp háscu o 'i jíwa, 'ab 'ába'i.
well, and whatever will arrive, against it.
well, and whatever thing will arrive at it [heart].

. . .Pégi, tp pi 'im hú hás o ha-jú:, t o hímk,
. . .Well, never somehow will do to them, will go,
. . .Well, if nothing gets done to [cure] them, and they continue,

hékid o cé:mo k o múa
whenever will permeate and will kill
and then they permeate him, they kill him

matp háscu wuḍ o 'ik hégai 'óimmeḍdam t-múmkidag.
ss whatever will be that-one wandering thing our sicknèss.
whatever it may be, that wanderer, our sickness.

TEXT 25 (Tape 14.7)

. . .Matp 'am 'ói o s-má:cim,
. . .Ss there subsequently will want to know,
. . .If he [patient] then will want to know,

"K hấscu 'á:gk hab tá:hadag g ñ-káhio, 'o g ñ-nówĭ"
"And whatever means and stimulates the my leg, or the my arm"
"What is the meaning of this thing that stimulates my leg, or my arm"

matp hébai o 'i jíwa.
ss someplace will arrive.
wherever it [horned toad strength] will arrive.

Pégi, k 'íd kói o 'ái g 'í:bdaj,
Well, and this-one not yet will reach the its heart,
Well, and it hasn't yet reached his heart,

pégi, t 'am o 'e-cécga,
well, there will get checked,
well, he will get checked [by a shaman],

t 'ói a hab háhawa abṣ o 'e-jú: mo wuḍ cémamagĭ.
subsequently then just will get done ss is horned toad.
then it [diagnosis] will get done, it is horned toad.

. . .T hég hab hí o 'e-jú:
. . .That-one on the other hand will get done
. . .[or] on the other hand it might happen

. . .mat pi 'óiwt,
. . .ss doesn't hurry,
. . .if he doesn't hurry [to get checked],

t o hímk o 'ái, wé:sko 'at o wúwhakad, hégai
it will go and will reach it, all over will come out, that-one
it [strength] will go on and reach it [heart], and it will come out [be manifest] everywhere [in the body]

mat hú há'ap 'ep o wú:s, kómḍ 'án,
ss ever that-way also will emerge, its small-of-the-back on,
'o 'im hú . . .'ó'oj.
or farther . . .its upper back.
and it will be manifest at the small of his back, then higher up.

TEXT 26 (Tape 14.6)

. . .Kupt hab o céi	g 'ó'odham	má:kai,	
. . .And will say	the Indian	shaman,	

. . .And the Indian shaman will say,

"cémamagĭ	'at kĭ hab m-jú:,
"horned toad	apparently to you did,

"horned toad did it to you,

hég	m-cé:mo	kc 'ab 'ái	g m-'í:bdag,
that-one	permeated you	and reached	the your heart,

it permeated you and it reached your heart,

hab a'i má:s	mapt o 'e-wúso."
only appears	ss you will get cured."

it's necessary for you to get cured [in a ritual]."

Pégi,	ñé:,	há'ap	'o a'i másma
Well,	look,	that-way	only thus

Well, look, it is the only manner

mat hab a'i másmakaj	'ú:pam	'am o 'i 'e-nóḍagĭ.
ss only by that means	backwards	there will get turned.

only in that manner will it [strength] get turned back.

'Atp abṣ hab-a hía	s-bá:bagĭ	'ab o 'i 'áp'et,
But of course	slowly	will get better,

But he will get better slowly,

heg hékaj	mat mé:k	o a 'i hí:.
that-one by means of	ss far	will go.

because it [strength] has gone far [or for a long time].

6. Direct Action Against Advance of Strength

We will conclude our discussion of the curative aspect of *dúajida* by noting the direct countermeasures a shaman may take against permeation. Our chief concern is with the efficacy of sucking because of the essential and climactic position of this act in the performance of a *dúajida.* In addition to sucking, Gregorio has mentioned one other action which counteracts permeation: the act of putting something into the patient by means of the shaman's mouth. There exist other forms of direct intervention which Gregorio has not described, for, in text 23, he spoke of "blocking" the strength. We have no information on the techniques of blocking.

Sucking may cure a sickness if its strength is not strong.

Hémhoa mat hab o a 'e-jú:,
Necessarily ss will get done,
It will always happen,

mat o 'e-wí:ñhu.
ss will get sucked.
that it [strength] will get sucked.

Pégi,	k 'im hú	'éḍa húgkam	'im hú	o 'i jú:,	hégai	géwkdaj.
Well,	and eventually	half of it	away	will do,	that-one	its strength.

Well, and he [shaman] will do away with half of its strength.

C abṣ hab-a hébai	há'icu	hab 'e-wúa
But sometimes	something	happens

But sometimes it happens

mat koi si géwkad,
ss not yet strong,
that it [strength] is not very strong,

kut hab o ṣa 'e-jú:,
and will slightly get done,
then it will happen,

k hémho a mat abṣ o húgio, hégai.
and necessarily just will finish, that-one.
and necessarily, he [shaman] will be able to exterminate it (tape 15.12).

Next we have a similar statement in which Gregorio uses the intransitive verb *húhug*, "to stop," "to end," instead of the transitive *húgio* of tape 15.12. Correspondingly, the intransitive expression "some of it will remain" is used in place of "he will get half of it out" of tape 15.12.

. . .hab 'e-wúa mat hí o a húhug,
. . .it happens ss will stop,
. . .it happens that it will stop,

abṣ hab-a éḍa 'am o a kǐ 'al ha-wí'i.
but yet there will a little of it remain.
but yet a little of it will remain (tape 9.5).

Such is the modest claim of the efficacy of sucking: the shaman may suck and get all the strength, or he may only get half, leaving some behind, but nonetheless slowing down its progress toward the heart.

"Putting something on" or "in," *'am ṣúlig*, the patient is the other mode of curative action. Gregorio has not explained the actual objects. We may surmise that the objects are tangible because he has said that the shaman brings them to the *dúajida*, bites them, and then puts them into the patient.

On their counteractive efficacy we have the following:

Pégi, k 'am o ṣúl 'am hég 'éḍa, hégai, 'e-kégcuna
Well, and there will put there that-one inside, that-one, its own cleaner
Well, and he [shaman] puts his cleaner [the counteractive object] inside him [patient]

mat hab 'á:gk, hab o cem jú:
ss intends and will try to do
if he intends to do something

mat pi 'am hú 'ep o jíwa, hégai.
ss never again will arrive, that-one.
so that it [sickness] will never come back again.

Pégi, k wóho mo hab 'e-wúa, hébai,
Well, and truly ss happens, sometimes,
Well, and it is true that it happens sometimes,

c hébai 'atp s-géwkam o hím.
and sometimes strongly will go.
and [however] sometimes it [strength] goes strongly.

Hab o a cem 'e-jú:, hí o a 'i 'e-bá:bagid.
Will try to get done, of course will get slowed down.
It will get done [to the strength], of course it will get slowed down (tape 9.12).

The function of putting an object in the patient's body is the same as that of sucking: either preventing the sickness from returning or merely slowing it down, depending on the strength of the sickness.

7. Gregorio's Events of *Dúajida*

We conclude from the foregoing texts that the shaman's attentions to the patient's body are directed primarily at identification of the sicknesses. He can administer a cure only, as it were, at the sufferance of the strengths he undoubtedly will discover. If he finds them to be strong, the most he can do is slow them down, or, we may say, administer a kind of first aid in advance of the ritual cure.

We will now consider all the activity that takes place during a *dúajida.* We wish to place our conclusions about strengths into their total context and to identify those components of the *dúajida* which remain to be described.

Actors

The previous sections have focused on the shaman. We have said little about the patient's role, in fact, because there is little to report. The patient does not participate in the essential actions of the *dúajida.* In this respect it resembles diagnosis by an Anglo-American physician. If the patient and shaman converse at all, it is either about symptoms whose interpretation is entirely outside the patient's realm or about gossip unrelated to the task at hand. Although the *dúajida* has the psychotherapeutic consequence of making the patient learn the effect of forgotten action, the patient waits passively for the shaman to render the sign.

We complete the roster of human personnel involved in the *dúajida* by observing that the event need include no other participants than the shaman and his patient. In Russell's case history (p. 117), Sala's husband furnished the cigarettes with which the shamans divined. Such provisions or gifts from the patient's family are no longer necessary, if ever they were. The shaman now brings his own tobacco, American cigarettes, along with everything else he uses to diagnose or to cure.

Scenes of action

We have found that the shaman does the following things to strength: he sucks it out, or he puts something in the patient which will counteract it, or he massages the patient in order to separate several strengths or to gather them together. Each of these actions takes place at the end of a *dúajida* or at the ends of subparts within it, for example, sucking out one strength to clear the path for later actions toward deeper strengths. These actions occupy only a small portion of the total time spent performing a *dúajida*, perhaps ten minutes from ten hours. Gregorio states these actions take place after the identity of the strength has been established.

The remainder of the *dúajida* which we have not yet discussed, is the bulk of it, containing the actions by which the shaman identifies strengths: singing, illuminating with crystals, fanning with an eagle feather, and blowing smoke. In order to comprehend these actions, we must define a second scene of action which we call the landscape of the spirits.

In the foregoing sections, our attention has been confined to the patient's body which, in point of ethnographic fact, lies on a bed in front of the shaman. Through the introduction of a second spatial frame of reference we encompass a different territory which is literally out of doors, in the darkness. We will consider how each of these locales figures into the *dúajida*, particularly into the longest part of it when identification of the sickness is taking place.

Landscape of the spirits

The landscape of the spirits makes possible the conceptualization of soul loss, spirit flights, spirit helpers, and battles between the shaman and spiritualized causal agencies. This is the frame of reference for considering the *dúajida* an event between people and spirits occupying another world, displaced from the room containing the physical bodies of the shaman and the patient.

Piman shamans are said to differ in the extent to which they engage in activity with the landscape of the spirits. Some shamans are said to leave the patient's house in order to fight with spirits or to receive messages. This was not done in Russell's case history, nor has Gregorio spoken about it, and there are no firsthand accounts of such actions in the Piman ethnographies.

Considering the sparseness of reports on spiritual subjects, we conclude that either this aspect of shamanism is underelaborated in Piman culture or else that Pimans have been especially reluctant to speak about it. Since this spiritual aspect is one of the hallmarks of the anthropological definition of shamanism, the question arises: Is Gregorio's theory a truly shamanic one and, if so, precisely how do spirits fit into it? We will argue it is a shamanic theory.

Gregorio's texts on spirits concern two topics fundamental to Piman shamanism. First, they explain how the shaman minimizes his charisma by transferring the responsibility for diagnosis onto spirits. In Piman terms the charisma centers on the special qualities of the shaman's heart. Second, spirits are cited in explanation of the method by which a person becomes a shaman. Shamans are recruited, trained, and ordered into action by spirits.[11]

The unexpected finding, in our opinion, about Gregorio's doctrine is not simply the underelaboration of spiritual activity, but that this apparent paucity is counterbalanced by a major elaboration of the patient's body as the location of important occurrences. We have seen in the previous sections that the body is a means for gaining access to the patient's past. The question arises whether the body as a scene of action is the indispensible complement for the landscape of the spirits.

With respect to Gregorio's etiological theory discussed in pt. III, sec. 2, the patient's body seems to be a necessary complement; for example, the body is peculiarly well suited as an archival entity capable of storing the latent presences of several sicknesses. The landscape of the spirits seems to be a less suitable place to search for the proof of wrongful past actions. We may further speculate that the Piman tendency to place the blame for sickness on the patient is consistent with the elaboration of an inside-the-body method of diagnosis and inconsistent with external-evil-spirit explanations. The strength that afflicts the patient is supposed to originate without, but it is not derived from any individualized culprit other than the patient himself – except in the case of infant sicknesses, where the blame is placed on the parent. Thus it seems that the objective of the shaman's search is not an evil spirit which has entrapped the patient, but rather a commandment or a species of transgression through which the patient (or parent) has visited the disease upon himself (or upon his unborn child).

Use of spirit helpers

Our texts on the use of spirit helpers are divided between those that refer to spirits ambiguously, texts 27 and 28, and those that refer to them unambiguously, texts 29 and 30. No texts refer to them explicitly in the sense of "by name." To the extent of Bahr's knowledge, no Piman word equivalent exists for the English word "spirit."[12]

We begin with an examination of the ambiguous texts. The ambiguities involved are:

1. Tool versus spirit: whether the thing which a shaman "uses" in diagnosis is one of the tangible tools he carries with him – rattle, divining feather, divining crystal – or whether it is a spirit. According to the first reading of a statement which is ambiguous in this regard, the scene of action is the patient's body and no other intelligent agents are involved in the *dúajida* except the shaman. According to the second reading, spirits are involved. We

will find Gregorio managing the language of "use" and "having possessions" carefully and, in some instances, we will conclude that he must be referring to spirits in this manner.

2. Shaman versus spirit: whether one who "figures out" the cause of a sickness is the shaman, in which case the responsibility for the diagnosis falls on his charismatic heart, or whether it is a spirit.
3. Sickness versus spirit: whether a thing that is said to be able to move and hide of its own volition is a cause of the sickness – for example, a strength in the patient's body – or one of the shaman's spirit helpers.

We begin with text 27 which, unlike the other three texts we will consider, makes no unambiguous reference to spirits. This text only goes as far as being ambiguous, and its ambiguity is found only in the middle portion B.

Parts A and C refer to the *kúlañmada.* As we know, there is no question of spirits participating in this event. Thus, in A when Gregorio says, "I guess it's always true that there is something along with him [shaman], it is not only from his own heart," we know the extra thing is a tool, not a spirit. We know this not only from our background knowledge of the *kúlañmada/ dúajida* distinction, but also from Gregorio's use of the verb *tú'akc*, "to have a pile of something," with reference to the extra things a few lines later. This verb can only refer to the shaman's tangible tools, not to his spirit helpers.

In part B, Gregorio explicitly shifts reference to the *dúajida.* He begins with a couplet naming two typical tools of the *dúajida*, the rattle and the divining feather. The next sentence is ambiguous in reference to whether the "something" that the shaman "owns" is a spirit or a tool. The word used for "to own," *'éñiga*, in this case contrasts with *tu'akc* in that *'éñiga* is more vague and could refer to spirits. The sentence continues with a clause that explains that the ambiguous "something" "will stand against that kind of sickness." This sentence suggests the action of a spirit rather than an inanimate tool. The following two sentences of text also are ambiguous, but here the ambiguity lies between shaman and spirit. If we assume these sentences refer to the spiritual "something" of the previous sentence, then it is the spirit who "works" for the shaman and "tells" him what he has found. This reading is plausible but it is not necessary, as Gregorio could be referring to the shaman's work for the patient.

In part C, as if underscoring all he had avoided being explicit about in B, Gregorio renews his discourse on the *kúlañmada* and speaks abasively about the tools used in it. In so doing he assures us implicitly that the ambiguous things referred to in B were not mere tools.

TEXT 27 (Tape 1.7)

A

Na'ags hémho hab-a cú'ig
I guess definitely is
I guess it's always true [about the kúlañmada]

mo 'am a há'icu 'ab 'e-wé:nags,
ss there something mixes with it,
that there is something else [tool] along with him [shaman],

pi 'o wóho hégaʼi 'e-í:bdag 'ámjeḍ
its not certain that-one-only its own heart from
it [whatever is along with him] is not only from his own heart

matp hás 'i má:s
ss somehow appears
however it may be

matp háscu o 'i ñéi 'am hég 'éḍa, hégai.
ss whatever will observe there that-one in, that-one.
that he [shaman] will observe something in him [sick person].

Pégi, k hémho a mo'om a há'icu tú'akc
Well, and necessarily ss something owns
Well, and necessarily he [shaman] owns something [tool]

matp hég o hékaj, hégai,
ss that-one will use, that-one,
which he will use,

k 'am o cem ṣa gáwul 'i júccu g há'icu hás
and there will try slightly differently to do the something somehow
tá:hadkam múmkidag,
stimulating sickness,
and he will try to change it whatever kind of sickness it is,

ñé:, b 'o a'i másma hab 'e-wúa.
look, only thus happens.
look, that's about all there is to it [what the shaman does].

B

C hég hab hí cú'ig
And that-one on the other hand is
And however there is another situation,

mat ṣa cúhugam o hímk,
ss slightly through the night will go,
if it [dúajida] should go on all night,

hémho a mat g 'e-ṣáwkud o 'i mélc,
definitely ss the its rattle will begin to cause it to run,
definitely he will get his rattle going,

'e-mámcwidag hékaj o héwelhogǐ.
its finding out equipment by means of will fan.
he will fan him [patient] with his equipment for finding
things [feather].

'Atp 'am háscu o 'i cé:gk,
There whatever will find,
Whatever thing he will find,

pégi, k hab cú'ig
well, and is
well o.k., it is all set

mo 'am a 'éñiga 'atp héms há'icu
ss there owns perhaps something
that he has something [tool? spirit?]

mo háscu 'ab wúi ké:k, hégai hab cú'igam múmkidag,
ss whatever towards stands, that-one existing sickness,
whatever will stand against that kind of sickness,

pégi,	t heg hékaj	'am o cem si gáwul	'i júccu.
well,	that-one by means of	there will try very differently	to do.

well, and by means of it he [shaman? spirit?] will try to change it [sickness].

K abṣ hab-a hékid	o kú:gǐ	g 'e-cíckpan,
But whenever	will finish	the its work,

But whenever he [shaman? spirit?] finishes his work,

k 'am háhawa	o 'á:gǐ,
and there then	will tell,

and then he [spirit? shaman?] will tell him [shaman? patient?],

ñé:,	há'ap	o hí	'e-wúa,	hégai,	cúhugam	'áb.
look,	that-way	on the other hand	happens,	that-one,	darkness	against.

look, that's what happens in the night.

C

C 'í:d	abṣ cem hás	másma	'am hab 'e-júccu.
And this-one	just somehow	thus	there tries to get done.

And this other one [kúlañmada] is done in any old manner.

Cem hékid	'o 'am a há'icu,	'al 'e-hékaj
Always	there is something,	slightly gets used

There's always a little something [tool] to use

matp háscu wuḍ o'ik,
ss whatever will be,

whatever it may be,

hég 'áb	'am tóhonnoḍ	há'icu	'am wé:hejeḍ,	hégai
that-one against	there illuminates	something	there with respect to it,	that-one

it's from that [tool] that something is illuminated for him

mȧtp hédai 'am o 'i cécga.
ss whoever there will check.
whoever will check [diagnose] it.

Ñé:, há'ap o másma.
Look, that-way thus.
Look, that's how it is.

At the end of text 28, part E, we find an unambiguous reference to spirits. The earlier parts exemplify each of the three kinds of ambiguity previously listed.

Part A of text 28 is ambiguous only with regard to tool versus spirit. It is a question of which kind of thing the shaman "uses."

In part B, the tool versus spirit ambiguity continues. Here, as with the former text, there is the suggestive usage of a thing which "stands against" the sickness. In our opinion, the ambiguity is resolved in the last sentence of B through use of the word *'édagid*, "to have physical possession of." This word normally refers to tangible things such as the tools the shaman carries with him to the *dúajida.*

Part C is ambiguous concerning: (1) who – shaman or spirit – does the "finding"; (2) what – tool, spirit, or merely "the answer" that has been sought – "falls clear" due to the efforts of finding; (3) who – shaman or spirit – does the "following"; and (4) what – sickness or spirit helper – is followed.

Part D ceases the development of tool versus spirit and shaman versus spirit ambiguities to compare the effectiveness of the *kúlañmada* and *dúajida.* As before, the basis for comparison is the problem of performing a complete diagnosis. Here, however, Gregorio makes an unprecedented statement concerning difficult diagnoses: Difficulty arises when a sickness "tries to hide."

At the end of D, we know that Gregorio is referring to strengths as causal agents, for he uses the familiar language of one sickness being on top of another. Perhaps, then, the substance which tries to hide can also be interpreted as strength within the patient's body. This interpretation is not certain however. Whatever the referrent of this statement, it is notable because it is the only instance in our corpus in which Gregorio describes the shaman confronted with an intelligent causal agent.*

* In part IV we will provide Gregorio's statements concerning ritual curers dealing with intelligent spiritual causal agencies, but ritual curers are not shamans. In the next two texts, 28 and 29, we find statements concerning interaction between shamans and spirit helpers, but these are not causal agents.

Part E contains what we judge to be our first unambiguous statements about spirit helpers. Here Gregorio uses the expressions "to meet it" and "to show up for it" in a context we judge unquestionably to be a reference to spirits.

TEXT 28 (Tape 5.9)

Q

K hás	másma	hab 'e-wúa,	hégam	mo ha-dúajid?
Somehow	thus	happens,	those-ones	ss dúajids them?

How do they do it, those who dúajid them?

A

Héu'u,	b 'o másma	hab 'ép	wúa,	'ídam	hab cú:cu'igam	hémajkam
Yes,	thus	also	does,	these-ones	existing	person

Yes, thus they do it, these kinds of people [shamans]

mo héḍai	cíkpañ,	'í:da	hab cú'igam	há'icu,
ss whoever	works,	this	existing	something,

whoever works [at] this kind of thing [dúajida],

c 'am a há'icu	wuḍ hégai
and there something	is that-one

and there is something [tool? spirit?]

mo 'ab 'e-wé:nagǐs,
ss against-it gets with it,

which gets with him [shaman],

c hég 'ámjeḍ	'am hab mámcid
and that-one from	there figures it out

and because of that [tool? spirit?] he [shaman] figures it out

matp hé'ekia	há'icu	o 'i 'e-'ámic
ss several	something	will get understood

if there are many things [tools? spirits?] he is acquainted with

mat hég o hékaj, hégai,
ss that-one will use, that-one.

which he will use.

B

Ñé:, matp héms hab o cú'ig
Look, ss perhaps will be

Look, suppose it would be

matp 'am hú'i si wé:peg há'icu 'am o cem hékaj.
ss ever very first something there will try to use.

that he first tried to use something.

Kutp pi 'ab hú o 'ab kékiwua,
And never will against it stand,

And it [tool? spirit?] didn't stand against it [sickness],

'óijkam ép,
consequently also,

the following one also,

ñé:, b o 'e-júñhimk matp hé'ekia o 'i 'éḍgidad.
look, will get done ss several will have possession of.

look, he will keep on, however many [tools] he has.

C

Pégi, kc hég wé:s o ha-cé:
Well, and that-one everything will find

Well, and he [shaman? spirit?] will find all of it

matp héms 'am hú hébai o 'i táṣo géi
ss perhaps ever sometime will clearly fall

if it [tool? spirit? the answer?] falls clear eventually

mat kĭ háscu o hékaj, 'í:da,
ss apparently whatever will use, this-one,
whatever thing he uses,

'am o si 'i 'ói, hégai.
there will really follow, that-one.
he [shaman? spirit?] will really follow it [spirit? whatever spirits follow in their landscape?].

D

'Í:d, 'añ hab 'á:gc hab káij gḍ hú'i wé:peg,
This, I tell and speak down away at first,
This is what I meant when I spoke at the very first [in part B, about the shaman's successive attempts],

'am há'icu hab ṣa 'á:g mo 'am hía hás másma hab 'ép 'e-wúa,
there something slightly means ss there of course somehow thus also gets done,
I discussed something which happens somehow,

c 'íd hía 'é:p mat s-cúhugam 'óidam o 'i 'e-'ói,
and this of course also ss darkness during will get followed,
and it's this when it [cause of sickness] gets followed all night long,

k hég hab si 'e-mámci, hégai
and that-one really gets figured out that-one
and it [cause of sickness] really gets studied

mat 'am hú há'icu hab o cem cú'igk,
ss even something tries to exist,
if something happens to exist,

c o cem e-'é:sto.
and tries to get hidden.
and tries to hide.

C aṣ hab-a 'am o 'i 'e-cíkp,
But there will get worked,
But when it is worked on,

k 'am o 'i 'e-húḍawagk,
and there will get bothered,
and bothered,

k hémho a mat o a'i wú:ṣ, hégai,
and necessarily ss must emerge, that-one,
and then it will have to emerge,

ñé:, hab o másma hab 'ep 'e-wúa, 'í:da.
look, thus also happens, this-one.
look, that's how this thing [dúajida] happens.

C há'icu hab hía má:s mat abṣ hé'es 'am o 'al 'i 'e-ñéidk,
And something of course appears ss just a few there will slightly get observed,
But supposing the thing [sickness] can only be observed
for a little while,

'atp héms pi o ṣa'i 'e-táṣogi, hégai
perhaps won't slightly get caused to be clear, that-one
and then perhaps it won't get caused to be clear

matp 'am 'i hímdam 'am hí a há'icu dá:m,
ss there later there of course something on top of it,
if there should happen to be something on top of it,

k hég 'ám hí a 'e-táṣogi.
and that-one there of course will get caused to be clear.
and that one [the upper one] will get caused to be clear.

Ñé:, kc hékaj pi 'im hú hab a hí a si táṣo
Look, and thereby never of course is clear
Look, and therefore it [lower strength] is never clear

mas háscu wuḍ 'i si hégai
ss whatever is really that-one
whatever it really is

mas hég o hékaj.
which that-one will use.
[no matter] which [tool] he uses.

'Am o a s-'e-má:ck.
There will get known.
Then it [sickness] gets known.

E

Pi 'atp héḍai ṣa'i 'e-wépo másma cú'idag, hégam
Not somebody slightly like itself thus exists, those-ones
They [shamans] are not similarly constituted

matp héḍai háscu o 'i nám.
ss whoever whatever will meet.
who meet something [spirit helpers].

Pégi, k wuḍ o héma hégaik,
Well, and will be one of them that-one,
Well, and there will be one of them [spirits],

dá:m há'icu 'é:p, dá:m há'icu
on top something else, on top something
on top of that another one, and another

matp hé'ẹkia o 'i 'e-náko.
ss several will get able to do.
as many [spirits] as he can have.

'Am o 'e-cé:gijid 'am wé:hejeḍ hégai
There will get caused to show up there with respect to it that-one
They will get caused to show up for him [shaman]

mat heg hékaj o wé:mt g 'e-hájuñ. . . .
ss that-one by means of will help the its kinsman. . . .
with that he [shaman] will help his kinsmen. . . .

Our final two texts state that spirits are drawn, by means of songs, from their customary haunts inside mountains. They are drawn toward the house containing the shaman and his patient.

In these texts we lack evidence suggesting the opposing direction of action, frequently reported from other tribes, in which the shaman or his soul departs from the patient's house in search of a lost soul. Gregorio's shamanism seems remarkably sedentary. He says as much himself: ". . . *mat hab 'á:g k 'am dáhiwua k 'am ñéid, hégai*," ". . . which is the reason why he sits down and observes it, that one [the shaman]" (text 30).

As far as we are aware, songs are the only means of contact between shamans and spirits during the *dúajida*. Texts on how these songs are acquired and how people become shamans can be found in note 11. These texts state that the shaman's contact with spirits is defined by the spirits as a period of instruction and governed by them accordingly. The spirits require that the shaman put the songs to use. They do not permit people to linger on as nonpracticing students; those who do so are punished.

The result of the instruction is a collection of songs which can be addressed to the former teacher, or his way, either during *dúajida* or ritual cures. Gregorio speaks of the songs used during *dúajida* as a conglomerate resulting from the different animals or spirits a shaman has met during his life. Each song belongs uniquely to the shaman, and each will call a particular kind of spirit into action.

The plurality of the shaman's helping spirits is paralleled by the plurality of his tangible tools – rattle, feather, crystal. This facilitates the ambiguity of reference encountered above because Gregorio speaks about bringing "them" along.

We turn now to our final texts on spirits during the *dúajida*. The tool versus spirit ambiguity is no longer at issue. In text 29 the things that "get with," *'e-wé:nad*, the shaman are drawn entirely from the landscape of the spirits. The task of "figuring it out" is also attributed to the spirits. By singing his songs, the shaman "names" the spirits; Gregorio employs the word *cé:ceg*, 'to call it by name', 'to invoke it'. The shaman "brings them out" in this manner.

In text 30 we learn that each song is "connected with" one kind of spirit who will "feel happy" to hear his song. In this text the participation of the spirit is said to consist in giving an audible signal to the shaman. Gregorio uses the obscurantist medio-passive verb form in the crucial sentences; we interpret it: "Necessarily something [an audible signal] gets emitted from it [spirit], it [the spirit] is its [signal's] source, whatever thing [the signal? the cause of sickness?] will be found."

All that is clear is that the spirits communicate something about the cause of the sickness. It is not clear whether the shaman's spirits are mediators between him and the cause of the sickness, or whether they are linked with the cause of the sickness. If the latter were the case, then among the shaman's *dúajida* songs may be the horned toad song, which elicits a signal from a horned toad spirit in case the patient has his type of sickness. We have not questioned Gregorio on this point. Judging from the *dúajida* songs collected by Russell and Underhill, the spirits must at least sometimes be confined to mediating roles, because some of the songs are addressed to kinds of objects which are not known to cause sickness.

TEXT 29 (Tape 22.8)

Q

Hás	másma	'am wuḍ ñéidalig	'ab 'ámjeḍ	g dúajida?
Somehow	thus	there is attributes-of-singing	about it	the dúajida?

What are the songs of the dúajida like?

A

Héu'u,	no pi hab a'i hía má:s
Yes,	because only of course appears

Yes, because it seems

mo 'ab a'i 'áb	hégai
ss only is against	that-one

that it is entirely up to him [shaman]

matp héḍai	'am o 'i ñéi,	héḍai 'am o 'i dúaj
ss whoever	there will observe,	whoever there will dúajid

whoever will observe it, whoever will dúajid it

matp hás	'i káidam	ñéñ'ei
ss somehow	sounding	songs

how the songs sound

'matp háscu   wuḍ o 'i hégaik.
ss whatever   will be that-one.
whatever they will be.

Pégi,   k hab má:s
Well,   and appears
Well, and it seems

mat hég 'óidk   'am o hí:
ss that-one during   there will go
that throughout that [dúajida] it [shaman's voice] will go

m 'in cú:c   g dó:dag,
ss there stand   the mountains,
where the mountains are standing,

c hég 'é'eḍa   'an há'icu   'an hab má:s,
and that-one inside   there something   there appears,
and inside of them there is something [spirit],

'o g há'icu   méḍdam
or the something   running thing
or some [kind of] thing that runs around

matp hás   'i má:s,
ss somehow   appears,
however it will be,

c 'am o 'e-cé:gĭ.
and there gets caused to show up.
and gets caused to show up.

Pégi,   t hémho a matp hég 'óidk   'am o 'i hímhi,   hégai,
Well,   necessarily ss that-one during   there will be going,   that-one,
Well and necessarily that thing [song] will go through there [landscape of spirits],

k hég 'ám o 'i ha-wú:ṣadad.
and that-one there will remove them.
and it [song?] draws them [spirits] out.

Kc pi hab cú'ig mas 'am hú wuḍ a'i hémako,
And not is ss there ever is only one,
And it is not that there is only one of them [songs],

'o hé'ekia 'am ṣél wáwañ,
or several there straightly stretch,
or that [only] several are straightly stretched,

t abṣ wé:sko há'icu o 'i cé:c
just everywhere something will name
he'll name [invoke] everything

matp hab o cú'ig
ss will be
if it is the case

matp 'am há'icu hab o 'i má:sk.
ss there something will appear.
if something [song? spirit?] will appear.

Pégi, mat heg hékaj 'ab o 'e-wé:nad,
Well, ss that-one by means of against it will get with it,
Well, therefore they [spirits] get with him [shaman],

c 'am hab o mámcid, hégam
and there will figure it out, those-ones
and they [spirits] will figure it out

matp háscu wuḍ o 'ik hégai.
ss whatever will be that-one.
whatever [sickness] it may be.

Ñé:, há’ap ’o másma hab cú’ig, ’í:da.
Look, that-way thus is, this-one.
Look, that’s how it is.

TEXT 30 (Tape 22.9)

. . .Pégi, t hémho a mat ’am o ’á: g ñé’i
. . .Well, and necessarily ss there will tell the song
. . .Well, and necessarily he [shaman] will tell the song [by singing it]

mat hég ’áb o ṣa ’e-géwṣṣapad, hégai
ss that-one against will slightly get connected, that-one
if it [song] will be connected with it [spirit]

mo háscu wuḍ hégai.
ss whatever is that-one.
whatever it [spirit] is.

Pégi, t hémho a mat o si – hég a wépo
Well, necessarily ss will – that-one is like
Well, necessarily, it is as if

matp o si s-’áp ’i ’e-tá:t.
ss will very well get to be aware.
it [spirit] will feel happy.

Hémho a mat ’áb o káijid, há’icu,
Necessarily ss against it will get vocalized, something,
Necessarily, something [an audible signal] will get
emitted from it [spirit],

hég wuḍ ’ámjeḍkam
that-one is from-thing
it [spirit] is its [signal’s] source

mat háscu 'am o 'i 'e-cé:, hégai.
ss whatever there will get found, that-one.
whatever thing [the signal? the cause of sickness?] will be found.

Pégi, k wépo másma hab 'e-wúa
Well, and similarly thus happens
Well, and it seems to happen

mo heg hékaj 'im hú hab 'i júccu
ss that-one by means of away does
that with that [assistance] he does away with it

mat hab 'á:gk 'am dáhiwuak 'am ñéi, hégai
ss means and there sits down and there observes, that-one
which is the reason why he [shaman] sits down and observes it

matp hás 'i másma wuḍ o há'icuk.
ss somehow thus will be something.
how something [sickness] will be.

Mú'i o há'icu hab cú'ig, 'í:da.
Many something is, this-one.
Many things [spirits] are like that.

Ñé:, há'ap o másma 'ab 'i 'e-wéhhemat, 'í:da.
Look, that-way thus gets accompanied, this-one.
Look, that's how he [shaman] gets accompanied.

8. Shaman's Charisma

According to our interpretation, the allusion to spirit helpers in the *dúajida* displaces magical responsibility away from the shaman. We will now study the action that is based on his charisma, *wústana*, "the blowing." In the context of the *dúajida*, the word denotes a physical act of blowing by which the shaman illuminates the sickness and is able to figure out its cause: a divination.

We have stated that blowing and sucking are the basic actions of the *dúajida.* Everything else, including the use of tools to illuminate the strengths and the singing of songs to call on the spirits, is supplemental. Functionally, blowing discovers the sickness and sucking removes its strength.

We also stated that Piman doctrine transfers the task of curing from the shaman to the ritual curers. The shaman is the only person who sucks, but the curative function of sucking has been diminished by a doctrine which entrusts the final extermination of strength to lay curers. A different accommodation has been achieved between the shamans and the curers for the act of blowing. The shamans retain monopoly over the diagnostic function, but they share the act of blowing with the ritual curers. For this reason we will delineate two doctrines of blowing, one in the context of *dúajida* and the other in the context of ritual cure. Our immediate concern is with the former, however, we will pause to sketch the total scheme which will be fully elaborated in part IV.

Meaning of blowing

A comparison of the different meanings of blowing as expressed by three verbs and three nouns will be useful. The verbs are *wústan, wústad*, and *wúsot*; the nouns are *wústana, wúsota*, and *wúsosig.*

1. THE VERBS. Presumably *wústan, wústad*, and *wúsot* are different forms of the same verb stem. Mathiot has found that the final *-n* and the final *-d* mark categories of "actor event number" (1968:210). The two categories are:

   -n, semelfactive: "to do it once, to do it on one occasion"
   -d, recursive: "to do it at regular intervals"

   We have not employed this distinction in translating the three verbs of blowing. Rather than the semelfactive versus recursive distinction, our analysis concentrates on whether or not the verbs denote concrete acts of blowing. We find that each of the three verbs may denote concrete acts of blowing, but two of them may denote other things as well, namely, the diverse acts of divination or of ritual curing. Furthermore, when the verbs do denote acts of blowing, these actions take on different significance depending on whether the blower is a shaman or a ritual curer.

2. THE NOUNS. Of the three nouns, one, *wústana*, denotes the concrete act of blowing. The other two nouns, *wúsota* and *wúsosig*, denote a complex event which we call the ritual cure. During these events, the concrete acts of blowing, *wústana*, take place, but ritual cures include many other actions other than acts of blowing, for example, singing, dancing, and pressing fetishes on the patient's body.

Wústana, the act of blowing, when performed by a shaman has the divinatory purposes "to illuminate something," *tónlid*, or "to figure something out," *mámci.*

The rationale for the shaman's acts of blowing centers around his charisma because the action depends upon the special nature of his "heart," *'í:bdag*, or his "breath," *'í:bhei.* We will refer to this action of *wústana*-by-means-of-the-shaman's-breath as the "basic sense" of the shaman's *wústana.* We will show how the charismatic act of blowing generally is augmented through the use of certain inanimate tools, such as tobacco, crystals, and divining feathers, and how the shaman's breath and his breath's augmentation ultimately are superseded through the agency of spirit helpers.

We find two stages of augmentation. In the first stage, the shaman's breath is augmented by tobacco smoke which he blows over the patient's body. In the second stage of augmentation, the shaman's act of blowing over the patient's body is performed in conjunction with other actions which he directs toward the patient's body. We know of two such actions: (1) fanning the body with an eagle feather; and (2) using a divining crystal, in an undescribed manner, to illuminate strengths within the patient's body.

Finally, the shaman employs the ultimate of his divining techniques and appeals with songs for the help of spirits. At this stage the scene of action shifts away from the patient's body into the landscape of the spirits. Furthermore, at this stage the special properties of the shaman's heart or breath are no longer cited as the means by which the divinatory purpose is accomplished. For this reason we state that the shaman's charisma has been superseded.

The linguistic evidence for our analysis consists in sentences with verbal forms of *wústana* where the subject is shaman rather than ritual curer, and where another noun, breath, tobacco, smoke, crystal, or feather, is said to be the "means" of the act of *wústana.* In Piman, the suffix *-kaj* indicates things that are the "means."

In our texts the basic sense – by means of the shaman's breath – and the first stage of augmentation – by means of tobacco smoke – are clearly documented. The second stage of augmentation – by means of a feather or a crystal – is scantly documented. In accord with our hypothesis, there are no cases in which spirits or songs directed to spirits are spoken of as the means for doing the *wústana.* According to the hypothesis the absence of such usages is understandable because at this stage the shaman's charismatic blowing has been superseded by a different divinatory agency, the spirit.

The following examples show how *wústana* is spoken about in its various stages of augmentation.

1. The basic sense

'E-'i:bdagkaj 'at o 'i wústan, g mákai.

Its-own-heart by means of it will blow, the shaman.

The shaman will blow by means of his own heart [or breath].

2. The first stage of augmentation

. . .Kú:ps, jé:jena mat heg hékaj, 'ab o si wústanad.

. . .Smoke, smoking ss that-one by means of, against-it it will really blow.

. . . with smoke, [or] smoking [of tobacco], using that he will blow on him.

3. The second stage of augmentation

k 'ab o 'i wústan, 'e-mámcwidagkaj.

and against-it it blows, his-own-figuring-out-thing by means of

and he blows [divines?] against it [cloud?], by means of his divining feather.

4. The ultimate stage

We believe it is incorrect to speak of the shaman's *wústana* as being accomplished by means of the spirits. We have no examples of such usage. Examples would be: "Coyote song by means of, he [shaman] will blow" or "Coyote spirit by means of, he [shaman] will blow."

In our opinion these examples would be incorrect usages of *wústana* as they would credit the shaman for action accomplished by the coyote. When coyotes are invoked during the *dúajida*, their skills supersede those of the shaman. The coyote works within the landscape of the spirits. The shaman does nothing except wait patiently for the coyote's communication. We doubt the word *wústana* has been extended to encompass this situation, in which the shaman blows, or divines, by means of a mind or spirit which exists independently of his own heart, *'í:bdag* or "breathing thing."[13]

We conclude that the basic ingredient of the shaman's *wústana* is within his own physical nature and this is our basis for terming the act of blowing a charismatic action. We have seen how the stages of augmentation supplement or conceal this charismatic fact of the shaman's nature by substituting external means to accomplish the divinatory function.

The divination is charismatic in a broader sense even in the ultimate stage because the tools and helpers are said to be peculiar to each shaman. Thus the results of each *dúajida* are, in principle, unreplicable by any other shaman. However, when it is a question of the spirit helpers of the ultimate stage, the success of the divination no longer derives from an "inherent property," *cú'idag*, of the shaman. His own charisma is explicitly subordinated to the skills of the external agents, the spirits.

We turn briefly to the meaning of the act of blowing, *wústana*, within the context of the curing rituals. The act has the generalized curative purpose: "to do away with the sickness," *gam hú hab 'i wúa g múmkidag.*

The rationale is prayerful rather than charismatic in that the blowing is intended to persuade a spiritual causal agent "to do away with the sickness." The efficacy of the blowing does not depend on any special qualities of the blower's heart or breath; it depends on the response of the spirit.

Contrasting the two contexts of *wústana*

Text 31 is in four parts. Part A affirms that *wústana*, in one of its senses, takes place during ritual cures: *Wuḍ a cem hégai mat o 'e-wúso*, "It is simply that-one when one gets cured." In part B, Gregorio shifts into the other context: *C abṣ hab-a 'éḍa 'am aṣ a gáwol másma hab 'ep 'e-'á'aga*, "But yet there is a different meaning." This is the context of *dúajida*, when the shaman "checks" and "observes." Part C refers back again to the ritual cure, when the act of blowing results in "doing away with the sickness."

Note the following parallel between parts B and C which displays the two contexts and purposes of *wústana.*

(B) *Matp g má:kai 'am o cécga, 'am o 'i wústan k o ñei.*
That the shaman will check it [sickness], he will blow on him, and observe it [strength].

(C) *Mo 'am 'i wúsot, c 'am hab wústan, c gam hú hab 'i wúa, hégai.*
That he [curer] cures him, and he blows on him, and does away with it [strength].

Cécga, "to check," identifies the diagnostic function of the *dúajida*. *Wúsot*, "to cure," carrying the special meaning "to perform a ritual cure," identifies the curative task of the ritual cure. Thus text 31 states: In B, the shaman may "check" by the action of *wústana* and this means that he "observes" something; in C, the curer may "cure" by the action of *wústana* and this means that he "does away with" something, presumably the strength.

Part D returns to the shaman's use of *wústana* during *dúajida*, but perhaps as a carry-over from C, Gregorio speaks of an effect which appears to be curative. He says that the shaman "does away with it" and that the sickness "clearly comes out." This is the only example of the shaman's *wústana* being spoken of as a curative action in our corpus of texts. The curative effect is only alluded to by the expression, "to do away with it," which in other contexts has been used with reference to strengths. This usage mystifies us. The remaining texts on the shaman's *wústana* attest only to the divinatory purpose of this action.

TEXT 31 (Tape 9.6)

Q

Ṣa: o má:s	hégai	mo hab 'á'aga	"wústana"?
How appears	that-one	ss calls it	"wústana"?

What kind of thing is that which is called "wústana"?

A

Hab o másma	hab 'á:g,
Thus	means,

Its meaning is thus,

c 'am hab 'e-wústan
and there gets blown

that he [patient] gets blown

mo cem háscu	'o hab 'e-'á'aga	'ab 'ámjeḍ	hégai,
ss just whatever	gets called	about	that-one,

so that just anything [any kind of ritual cure] is referred to by that [word],

k wuḍ a cem hía	hégai
and is just of course	that-one

and it is simply that one [ritual cure]

mat o 'e-wúso,
ss will get cured,
when one [patient] gets cured,

hég o hí wuḍ a cem.
that-one on the one hand is.
that's what it [wústana] means on the one hand
[in the context of ritual curing].

B

C abṣ hab-a 'éḍa 'am aṣ a gáwul másma hab 'ép 'e-'á'aga.
But yet there differently thus also gets meant.
But yet there is a different meaning.

Ñé:, matp héms hab o má:sk
Look, ss perhaps will appear
Look, if it should be the case

matp g má:kai 'am o cécga, hégai,
ss the shaman there will check, that-one,
if the shaman checks [diagnoses] him [patient],

'am o 'i wústan k o ñéi
there will blow and will observe
there he will blow and observe

matp háscu wuḍ o'ik hégai.
ss whatever will be that-one.
whatever thing [sickness] it will be.

C

Pégi, k 'í:da hab wuḍ wústana, 'éḍa hab wuḍ abṣ a cem 'á:ga
Well, and this-one is wústana, yet just means
Well, and then there is wústana [in the context of ritual curing]
and yet it just simply means

mo 'am 'i wúsot,
ss there cures,
that he [curer] cures him,

c 'am hab wústan, hégai,
and there blows, that-one,
and he [curer] blows on him,

c gam hú hab 'i wúa, hégai
and far away does, that-one
and he does away with it [strength]

matp háscu wuḍ 'i pi 'áp'edag.
ss whatever was impropriety.
whatever [the strength of] the impropriety may be.

D

Ñé:, hégai hab másma, hégai
Look, that-one thus, that-one
Look, that [other] one [shaman's wústana] works like that

mañ 'am hú hab 'á:g
ss I there already explained
as I have already explained

mat g má:kai o hékaj.
ss the shaman will use.
when the shaman does it.

'Am o 'i wústan,
There will blow,
He will blow,

k gam hú hab o 'i jú:cu
and far away will be doing
and he does away with it [strength]

matp 'am há'icu hab o 'e-jú:,
ss there something will get done,
if something happens,

'am táṣo o 'i wú:ṣ
there clearly will emerge
then it will emerge clearly

matp háscu wuḍ o 'ik,
ss whatever will be,
whatever [strength] it may be,

c o múmkic.
and will sicken it.
that sickens him.

Ñé:, hég hab wuḍ "wústana," hégai.
Look, that-one is "wústana," that-one.
Look, that's [the meaning of] "wústana."

Wústana as a method for divination

Blowing during *dúajida* enables the shaman to "figure out" the cause of the sickness by "illuminating" it. This is the diagnostic task, a kind of divination in which the shaman is the diviner and the patient's body is the object into which the shaman divines.

Our presentation will be in two parts. The first piece of evidence is an excerpt from tape 10.8, where we find the word *cécga*, "to check it," used in connection with *tóhonlid*, 'to cause it to shine', 'to illuminate it'.

C 'í:da hab má:s há'icu
And this-one it appears something
And this kind of thing [dúajida]
mat hí abṣ o 'e-cécga,
ss on-the-one-hand just it will get checked,
when it will get checked,
héu'u, nats hí pi 'am o tóhonlid.
Yes, because on-the-other-hand there it will illuminate it.
Yes, because he will illuminate it.

'Am hab o s-mái.
There it will learn.
He will learn (tape 10.8).

Our next evidence is text 32 where *wústana* is said to be the method for illumination.

TEXT 32 (Tape 16.5)

Q

Hás wuḍ 'á:ga hégai "mat o tóhonlidad há'icu
Somehow is meaning that-one "ss will illuminate something
mat hékid o kúlañmad"?
ss whenever will kúlañmad"?
What is the meaning of "he [shaman] will illuminate something when he does the kúlañmada"?

A

Héu'u, mo a wóho
Yes, ss truly
Yes, it is true

mo hab 'á'aga, hégai
ss means, that-one
that they call it [shaman's action during kúlañmada]

mo tóhonlid,
ss illuminates,
illumination,

'éḍa wuḍ abṣ a cem 'á:ga
yet just means
yet it just means

mo wústan k 'am o 'i mámci, hégai.
ss blows and there will figure it out, that-one.
that he blows and figures it out.

B

Hég ’atp hab ’e-’á’aga
That-one gets meant
That one [act of blowing] is meant

mat ’am o ’i tónlid,
ss there will illuminate,
when [it is said that] he illuminates it,

’am o mámci
there will figure it out
he figures it out

matp háscu wuḍ o ’ik.
ss whatever will be.
whatever it [sickness] will be.

Hab wuḍ a cem ’á:ga, hégai,
Just means, that-one,
And that’s just what it means,

c abṣ hab-a hab ge káidam hab ’e-’á’aga,
but just soundingly gets told,
but it is just called in this manner [one says “illuminate”
and he means “blowing”],

c ’éḍa wuḍ a cem hégai
and yet is just that-one
and yet it is just that [concrete action of blowing]

mat ’am o ’i wústan,
ss there will blow,
that he will blow,

k ’am o ’i mámci.
and there will figure it out.
and there he will figure it out.

Ñé:, há’ap o a’i másma hab cú’ig.
Look, that-way only thus is.
Look, that’s how it is.

First stage of augmentation

The texts which follow, 33 and 34, deal with the shaman’s use of tobacco smoke to augment his (or her) heart. These texts establish that the divinatory blowing may be accomplished without the help of smoke, solely by means of the shaman’s heart. Smoke is said to be the shaman’s “helper.”

TEXT 33 (Tape 16.6)

Pégi, hémho a mat ’am o ’ó:wick,
Well, and necessarily ss there will roll a cigarette,
Well, and necessarily he will roll a cigarette,

’am o wústan c ’am o mámcid, hégai,
there will blow and there will figure it out, that-one,
and blow and figure it out,

c hég ’ám tóhonlid
and that-one there illuminates
and [in so doing] he illuminates it

matp háscu wuḍ o ’i hégai.
ss whatever will be that-one.
whatever it may be.

Pégi, ñé:, há’ap o másma hab cú’ig, ’í:da,
Well, look, that-way thus is, this-one,
Well, look, that’s how it [the method of illumination] is,

c wuḍ a hégai,
and is that-one,
and it is that [wústana by means of breath],

no pi g 'e-'í:bdag 'ámjeḍ 'i – 'am 'i tóhonlid, 'í:da,
because the its own heart from – there illuminates, this one,
because he illuminates it from his own heart,

k wé:maj tóhonoḍ
and with it shines
and it [his heart or breath] shines with it [strength of sickness]

matp háscu wuḍ o 'i tónligajk, géwkdajk,
ss whatever will be its light, its strength,
whatever it may be, its light, its strength,

b 'ant hí k abṣ 'ep o 'á: 'é:p.
I may on the other hand just also tell also.
as I may also call it.

TEXT 34 (Tape 16.3)

. . .Pégi, tp hab o cú'igkad,
. . .Well, if should be,
. . .Well, it may be the case,

abṣ cem heḍai, 'ab hía ha-'áb.
just whomever, of course against them.
it [qualification to do wústana] is just up to anybody.

'Óks, t o a 'e-náko
Old woman, will be able to do
[Even] an old woman can do it

mat hab o a wústan.
ss will blow.
if she will blow.

Kutp ’éḍa héms hab o cú’igk
And yet perhaps will be
And yet it may be the case

mat pi o jé:ñid, hégai ’ó’odham, ’o g ’óks.
ss won’t smoke, that-one man or the old woman.
that he [or she] won’t smoke, the man or old woman.

Pi ’it hás o ’e-jú:,
Not somehow will get done,
It doesn’t make any difference,

no pi hég wuḍ a wé:nagaj, kú:ps, jé:jena
because that-one is its helper, smoke, smoking
because smoke, or smoking is only his [or her] helper,

mat heg hékaj ’ab o si wústanad,
ss that-one by means of against it will surely blow,
so that thereby he can surely blow against him [patient],

’ab i hóhowogk.
against it puffs.
he can puff on him.

. . .Pégi, pi ’it hás o ’e-jú:,
. . .Well, not somehow will get done,
. . .Well, it doesn’t matter [if there is no smoke],

t abṣ o g ’e-’í:bdagkaj ’am o wústan, hégai.
just will the its own heart by means of there will blow, that-one,
he will just blow by means of his own heart.

Second stage of augmentation

The additional items of the shaman's tool kit are, like tobacco smoke, augmentations for his heart. The tools are the magic crystals and the eagle feather.* First we will examine Gregorio's statements concerning the use of the tools, then, we will turn to his statements about tools in general.

1. THE DIVINING CRYSTAL. Our corpus, unfortunately, lacks texts on the use of crystals. We do know, from enthnographic studies, that the crystals are sources of illumination for they are referred to as *má:kai tóndam hódai*, "shaman's shining stone." Underhill reports that the crystals grow inside a shaman's heart (1946). Russell was told that they are given to shamans by anthropomorphic spirit helpers and that they embody the spirit of the donors (1908). Pilcher relates that they are alive (1967). We have no information on these points, except the observation in text 36 that Gregorio speaks of the stone as an alienable possession. This category of possession is expressed by the suffix *-ga* in possessive constructions. Inalienable body parts, such as the heart, are not spoken of with *-ga* in possessive constructions. Thus, this use of the suffix *-ga* suggests that magic crystals are not native to the shaman's physical substance.

2. THE EAGLE FEATHER. The following text, obtained by Hale from Sam Angelo, refers to the use of feathers which are called *mámcwidag*, literally, "figuring-out things," "problem-solving devices." The text refers to a type of divination which is outside our subject matter, namely the prediction of rain. We include it because it is our sole evidence of a feather being referred to as the "means" for *wústana*. The text indicates that the physical act of blowing is not necessarily denoted in some usages of *wústana*. Instead the word may have a special, extended sense best translated as "divination." It seems that the physical act of blowing is altogether absent from the divination referred to in this text.

K'ab o 'i wústan, 'e-mámcwidagkaj
And against it it blows [divines?], his own figuring out thing by means of,
and against it [clouds?] he blows [divines?] with his divining feather,
hékaj 'am mámci g jú:ki.
by means of it there it figures out the rain.
thereby to figure out the rain.

* As far as we know the shaman's rattle is not considered a tool for *wústana*. Like his voice, the rattle is directed at spirits rather than at the patient's body.

SHAMAN'S

Tobacco pouch

F. *Russell*, The Pima Indians, *1908*

Crystals

TOOLS

Department of Anthropology Museum, Arizona State University

Eagle feathers

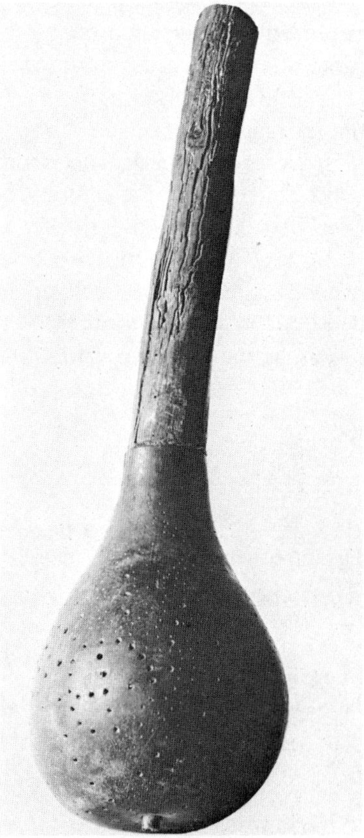

F. Russell, The Pima Indians, 1908

Rattle

The hypothesis that *wústana*, at the second stage of augmentation, has an extended sense is supported by the grammar of the text because the suffix *-kaj* identifies *mámcwidag* as the means by which the blowing was performed. Our hypothesis is also supported by prior knowledge about the physical setting of rain divination. In divining the rain, the shaman stands alone in an open space at quite a distance from the clouds which are the object of his inquiry. Thus, unlike the physical setting of sickness divination, there is no physical body close for him to blow against.

In text 35 Gregorio speaks at length on the use of feathers during the *dúajida.* He does not, however, speak of them as a means for the *wústana.* Rather, he makes a distinction between the shaman's blowing – here expressed by the verb *wústanad* – and his act of "moving the feather."

TEXT 35 (Tape 18.7)

A

. . .Hab hí	másma	hékaj,	hégai	má:kai
. . .On the other hand	thus	uses,	that-one	shaman

. . .Thus the shaman uses it [feather]

mat heg hékaj	g gm hú	hab o 'i cem wúad
ss that-one by means of	that-one away	will try to do

by means of it, he tries to do away with it

matp háscu wuḍ o'ik
ss whatever will be

whatever it may be

matp hég 'ám	pi o 'áp'et.
ss that-one there	will damage it.

that is hurting him [patient].

B

Pégi,	k hég	hab 'e-wúa,	hégai,
Well,	and that-one	happens,	that-one,

Well, and that's what happens,

'á'ai	hás	'am júñcug,
back and forth	somehow	there does,

he makes it move back and forth,

gm hú 'i cem híhimicud,
away tries to push,
he tries to push it [strength] away,

'am jégko 'i cem 'úliṣ, hégai
there in the open tries to hold, that-one
he tries to free it

mas háscu hú wuḍ 'i hégai.
ss whatever ever is that-one.
whatever it may be.

C

Héu'u, natṣ pi 'am o wústanad
Yes, because there will be blowing
Yes, of course he will be blowing on it

mat o wústanad hí a, 'é:p,
ss will be blowing of course, also,
of course he will be blowing, too [in addition to using the feather],

k abṣ hab-a hég 'ám o hékaj, hégai,
but that-one there will use, that-one,
but as for that [feather], he will use it,

ñé:, k hab o júñhim,
look, and will be doing it,
look, and he will be doing it,

k a wóho mat hébai 'im o táṣo 'i wú:ṣ, hégai
and truly ss sometimes there will clearly emerge, that-one
and truly, sometimes it [strength] will really come out

mo kǐ háscu wuḍ,
ss apparently whatever is,
whatever it is,

c pi 'áp'et, hégai.
and damages it, that-one.
that damages him.

Concluding remarks on the stages of augmentation

Text 35 treats the virtues of feathers as tools for the manipulation of strengths in the patient's body. The evidence that we have examined on the use of smoke and divining crystals indicates that these, too, are rationalized in terms of the patient's body as the scene of action. They are useful to the shaman as bridges or connecting links between him and the strengths that are in the patient.

The smoke, according to text 33, induces strength "to shine." The divining crystals also seem to promote vision. The scattered information we have about them indicates that crystals, like smoke, assist the shaman's *'í:bdag*, the Piman word that means at once "heart" and "breathing-thing." The virtue of the eagle feather lies not in extending the shaman's vision, but in extending his powers of manipulation. By fanning the patient, he "pushes" the strength and tries "to free" it.

We have designated smoke as the first stage of augmentation (1) because it is the nearest thing to the shaman's breath, literally mingling with it, and (2) because smoke is the only thing that Gregorio has spoken of as a "means" for the *wúhstana*. We have designated the crystal and the feather together a step removed from the *wúhstana* on the evidence that, while being directed at the patient's body, they are physically dissociated from the shaman's breath.

We conclude our discussion of the media of the *dúajida* by noting the means by which the shaman gains access to spirits: This is the sound produced by his voice and his rattle. Thus, the media complement each other, vision and touch being directed solely at strengths, and sound solely at spirits.

Relationship between the shaman's tools and his heart

Whereas we learned in texts 33 and 34 that, in principle, the shaman may accomplish divination by means of his heart alone, we find in the next two texts, 36 and 37, that, in general, the *dúajida* is not performed in this manner. This is the main point of "It is not true that he only uses his heart" (text 36). We learn that *dúajida* is always performed with excess equipment. Each of the shaman's different tools seems sufficient to execute the task which could have been accomplished by his heart alone.

These two texts complete our discussion of the *dúajida*. Text 37 consists of Gregorio's response to the blunt question, "How is the shaman's heart, which gives him the right to suck or to blow? " The critical sentence of his answer is, "None of us ever sees inside his heart." The relationship between the shaman's charismatic heart and his tools seems, in Gregorio's opinion, obscure and the "gifts" (text 36) of each shaman are, in point of doctrine, incomparable.

TEXT 36 (Tape 16.8)

A

. . .Pégi,	t hémho a matp hé'ekia'i		o 'éñigak,	hégai	má:kai
. . .Well,	necessarily ss several	something	will possess,	that-one	shaman

. . .Well, there are always many kinds of things that the shaman has

mat hég 'áb	o 'e-náko,
ss that-one against	will get enabled to do it,

with which he can do it [dúajida],

heg hékaj	o s-'e-'ámic.
that-one by means of	will get understood.

by means of which he understands.

Pégi,	k a wóho	mat 'am o hékaj	hégai	hás	i má:s,	'e-hódaiga.
Well,	and truly	ss there will use	that-one	somehow	appears,	its own stone.

Well, truly, he will use his whatever-kind-of-crystal.

Pégi,	'am 'i ná:nko	há'icu,	'é:p
Well,	there diverse	something,	also

Well, there are diverse other things

matp hédai	hé'ekia	há'icuk	'ab o' s-'e-'ámicudad.
ss whoever	several	something	against-it will get understood.

if he will understand several things.

B

Pégi,	kutp 'éda	'am o héma	há'icukad	g hás
Well,	and yet	there will one of them	be present	the somehow
	'i cú'idaj	há'icu		
	its possession	something		

Well, and yet one of his various possessions will be present

mat heg hékaj o a mái, 'atp héms,
ss that-one by means of will learn, perhaps,
which is the means by which he will learn, perhaps,

pégi, t 'am 'ep o 'i wú:ṣad,
well, there also will remove it,
well, he will take it out,

k hég o hékaj, hégai.
and that-one will use, that-one.
and he will use it.

T hás 'e-júñk,
Somehow gets done,
It just might happen,

k hab háhawa abṣ o 'e-jú:
and then just will get done
that it will get done

mat 'am háhawa abṣ ge táṣo o 'i wú:ṣ,
ss there then just clearly will emerge,
that then it [strength] will clearly emerge,

"A héu'u, ñé:, 'á:pi 'ap kĭ s hab 'e-wúa, hab másma,"
"Yes, look, you apparently happen, thus,"
"Ah, yes, look, you [sickness] are doing it,"

b 'atp o 'i 'él, 'í:da.
will think, this-one.
he will think.

C

Kc wóho mo hab hí a ha-'á'aga,
And truly ss it of course calls them,
And truly, they [the public] call them,

mo wuḍ "má:kai."
ss is "shaman."
"shaman."

'Atp 'am a hía hás má:s g 'í:bdaj,
There of course somehow it appears its heart,
Of course his heart appears to be somehow [special],

pi wóho mas hég a'i hékaj 'e-'í:bdag,
not truly ss that-one only uses its-own-heart,
[but] it is not true that he only uses his heart,

b 'o há'icu 'e-wépenad, hégai
something gets with it, that-one
there is something [else] with it

matp háscu o 'i s-má:ck,
ss whatever will know,
whatever thing he will know,

háscu o 'i hékaj,
whatever will use,
whatever thing he will use,

k wuḍ má:kidagaj.
and is its gift.
and it is his gift.

Hab wuḍ 'á:ga mat heg hékaj o mámci g múmkidag,
Is meaning ss that-one by means of will figure it out the sickness,
It means that it [the gift] is the means by which he figures out the sickness,

'o heg hékaj 'am o 'i wé:mt
or that-one by means of there will help
or it's the means to help [the patient]

mat ’im hú hab o ’i cem jú:, hégai múmkidag.
ss away will try to do, that-one sickness.

if he will try to do away with the sickness.

D

Ñé:, há’ap o másma ’á:gk hab ’e-wúa, ’í:da.
Look, that-way thus means and happens, this one.

Look, that’s what it means and how he does it.

Pi ’at wóho hég a’i hékia ’e-’í:bdagkaj,
Not truly that-one only unaccompanied its own heart by means of
’am hab o ’e-jú:.
there will get done.

It’s not true that he does it by his heart alone.

Ñé:, há’ap.
Look, that-way.

Look, like that.

TEXT 37

(Tape 16.9)

Q

K hás másma hab cú’ig g ’í:bdaj g má:kai
Somehow thus is the its heart the shaman

How is the shaman’s heart

mo ’éñiga mat o wí:piñhu, ’o mat o wústan?
ss has the right ss will suck, or ss will blow?

which gives him the right to suck or to blow?

A

Héu’u, no pi wuḍ ’í:da, hí a
Yes, because is this, of course

Yes, it is this [kind of person]

mac hab hí a ha-'á'aga "mámakai,"
ss we of course call them "shamans,"
which we call "shamans,"

pégi, wóho'o matp hab má:s,
well, truly ss appeared,
well, it's true that he seems [to be something special],

heg hékaj mo 'am a há'icu – 'atp 'am a s-'ámicuḍ,
that-one by means of ss there is something – there understood,
because he understands something,

k wuḍ héjel 'éñigaj,
and is himself his possession,
and it is his own right,

kuc pi 'am hú héḍai ñéid g 'í:bdaj 'éḍa
and we never anybody observes the his heart inside
and none of us ever sees inside his heart

mas hás má:s, hé'ekia há'icukaj 'i 'e-'ámicud.
ss somehow appears, several something by means of gets understood.
how the several things are by means of which he understands.

Pégi, kuc hab hía ha-'á'aga mo wuḍ "mámakai,"
Well, and we of course call them ss is "shamans,"
Well, and we call them "shamans,"

'éḍa pi 'e-wépoḍag,
yet not like itself,
yet they are not the same,

héma 'o hé'ekia 'am s-'e-'ámicud,
one of them several there gets understood,
one of them will understand several [things],

gó:k, wáikk, gí'ik, 'atp hab hía cú'ig
two, three four, may of course be
two, three, four, there may be

matp hég ṣa ha-dá:m hab má:s, hégai,
ss that-one slightly on top of them appears, that-one,
if he is rather superior,

pégi, mo hég 'ámjeḍ heg hékaj, hégai.
well, ss that-one from that-one by means of, that-one.
well, it is from that [number of things that he knows] and because of

B

Kuc pi héḍai má:c,
And we nobody knows,
And none of us knows,

sá:cu 'o hú'i k 'ab s-'e-'ámicud.
which-thing ever and against-it gets understood.
what the thing is which he understands.

Héma 'ép 'o hé'ekia
One of them also or several
One [tool] or several more

matp hé'ekia 'i há'icukaj,
ss several are present,
if there are several,

pi héḍai má:c.
nobody knows.
nobody knows.

K 'ab a'i héjel ába'i
And only himself up to it
And it is only up to him

matp hás 'i másm̥a 'am há'icu o ñéidad, o tónlidad,
ss somehow thus there something will observe, will illuminate,
how he will observe something, he will illuminate it,

k 'am o mámci, 'o o mái
and there will figure it out, or learn
and figure it out, or learn

matp hás o 'i má:sk.
ss somehow will appear.
how it will be.

C

Pégi, 'atp hab o cú'igk
Well, will be
Well, it may be the case

matp hab o 'ábk
ss will be up to him
if it will be up to him

mat o 'e-náko
ss will get enabled
if he can do it

mat g gn hú o 'i ha-béi, 'í:da.
ss that-one away will get some of it, this-one.
if he will take some of it [strength] away.

Pégi, k hémho a mat o wí:ñhu,
Well, and necessarily ss will suck,
Well, and necessarily he will suck it,

k 'im hú hab o 'i jú:,
and away will do,
and he will do away with it,

’o ’am há’icu o ṣúl
or there something will put in
or he will put something into him [patient]

mat heg hékaj ’im hú hab o ’i ’e-jú:.
ss that-one by means of away will get done.
by means of which it [strength] will get done away with.

Ñé:, há’ap ’atp másma hab cú’ig, ’í:da,
Look, that-way thus is, this-one,
Look, that’s how it is,

pi wé:s ’e-wépo má:s.
not everything like itself appears.
they are not the same.

D

. . .Pégi, pi ’ac má:c,
. . .Well, we don’t know,
. . .Well, we don’t know,

ṣá: ’o hú’i másma s-’e-’ámicud,
what thing ever thus gets understood,
in what manner he understands,

kuttp héma o kák’ed.
and we one-of-them may be asking.
and we may ask one of them.

B’o a’i héjel ’áb, hégai.
Only himself against, that-one.
It is only up to him.

Tp ’am o s-’e-’á:gam,
There may want-to-tell,
He may want to tell it [to the public],

k 'am o 'e-'á:,
and there may get told,
and he may tell,

"Há'akia 'ant kĭ 'áb."
"Several I had apparently against it."
"I have several of them."

Tp héms pi 'am hú o 'e-'á:,
Perhaps never will get told,
Perhaps it will never be told,

heg hékaj 'am o a ge hás 'e-'élidad, hégai,
that-one by means of there will somehow get thought, that-one
because something may be thought about it [by him],

k 'ab a'i héjel 'áb, hégai.
and only himself against, that-one.
and it is only up to him.

Hía s-'e-má:c mo ha-kúlañmad,
Of course gets known ss medicates them,
Of course it is known that he does kúlañmada to them,

pégi, k abṣ hab-a g má:cigaj,
well, but the its knowledge,
well, but his knowledge,

pi má:c, 'í:da
doesn't know, this-one
this one doesn't know

mas háscu – hé'ekia há'icu 'i s-má:c.
ss whatever – several something knows.
what it is – the several things he knows.

Ñé:, há'ap o 'ep má:s.
Look, that-way also appears.
Look, that's how it is.

PART IV

THE RITUAL CURE

Is it true that the animals like it
when they hear their songs?
Yes, it is the case,
they probably are pleasant stimulations for them,
when something gets pronounced
how it appears, how it does things.
Well, if they are clearly told,
then it will feel very pleasantly,
when it hears its song
which is true, how it is told,
and pronounced,
as it vocalizes.

Juan Gregorio, text 40

1. Theory of Ritual Curing

Superficially, the ritual cure duplicates the actions of *kúlañmada* and *dúajida* and, therefore, the main concepts underlying our interpretation of ritual curing were introduced in part III. As with the acts of shamans, the acts of ritual curers are divided between the scenes of action defined by the patient's body and the landscape of the spirits. The cures differ, however, in purpose – to expel the sickness rather than to divine it – and in the reasons for success. Briefly, the cures are rationalized as prayers. They do not succeed because of any special potency vested in the curers, but because a spiritual causal agent responds to the curer's actions and rids the patient of his symptoms. This fact has implications for our interpretation of the act *wústana*, blowing, as manifest in both *dúajida* and ritual curing and for our interpretation of the roles of spirits in *dúajida* versus ritual curing.

Tables 3 and 4 delineate the sequence of actions common both to *kúlañmada* and *dúajida* and to the minimal and maximal levels of ritual curing.

Following the notation of tables 3 and 4, *kúlañmada* and the minimal level of *wúsota* consist of actions 2 and 3, performed once. *Dúajida* and the maximal level of *wúsota* consist of repeated performance of the entire sequence. Repetition in the case of *wúsota* begins with singing a different song directed toward the same kind of spirit, while repetition in *dúajida* begins with singing a different song addressed to another of the shaman's spirit helpers.

Just as *kúlañmada* and *dúajida* are distinct from one another on the basis of involving only one or two scenes of action, respectively, there is a gradation with respect to the methods for curing a given *ká:cim* sickness in the curing ritual. The minimal form is confined to actions directed toward the patient's body; the maximal form involves the landscape of the spirits in addition to the patient's body. As far as we know the two levels of curing do not have separate names. We refer to both as *wúsota.*[14] Even though it is not specified, we will show that the distinction between levels of curing is significant in the sense that maximal cures specifically are required in order to cure difficult cases of sickness.

TABLE 3
SEQUENCE OF ACTION FOR *KÚLAÑMADA/DÚAJIDA*

Actions Directed Toward Objects in Landscape of Spirits	1. Act of singing to spirit helper	4. Act of singing to another spirit helper
Actions Directed Toward Objects in Patient's Body	2. Act of blowing for divination	5. Act of blowing for divination
	3. Act of sucking strength from patient to diagnose, alleviate, or exterminate the sickness and to clear the path for work on deeper strengths; or act of putting medicine in/on the patient	6. Act of sucking strength from patient to diagnose, alleviate, or exterminate the sickness and to clear the path for work on deeper strengths; or act of putting medicine in/on the patient

TABLE 4
SEQUENCE OF ACTION FOR CURING RITUAL

Actions Directed Towards Objects in Landscape of Spirits	1. Act of singing to persuade a spirit to stop causing sickness	4. Act of singing a different song to persuade same spirit to stop causing sickness
Actions Directed Toward Patient's Body	2. Act of blowing to persuade a spirit to stop causing sickness or to introduce breath into the patient's body, thus curing sickness	5. Act of blowing to persuade a spirit to stop causing sickness or to introduce breath into the patient's body, thus curing sickness
	3. Act of putting a fetish on the patient to persuade a spirit to stop causing sickness or to introduce curative strength of fetish into the patient's body, thus curing sickness	6. Act of putting a fetish on the patient to persuade a spirit to stop causing sickness or to introduce curative strength of fetish into the patient's body, thus curing sickness

2. Carry-overs From *Kúlañmada/Dúajida* to *Wúsota*

In studying the *dúajida* we were concerned with a small number of concrete actions. We offered the analysis of a standard event, the *dúajida*, which positioned each kind of concrete action in a single scheme. The actions were understood as graded means for the divination or the cure of any *ká:cim* sickness. We cannot speak about a standardized *wúsota* in this manner, for many of the ritual cures when performed at the maximal level, require actions which are idiosyncratic to particular sicknesses. One group of cures, for example, deer or rabbit sicknesses, includes a feast consisting of the flesh of the dangerous object; the ritual for another sickness requires sand painting and another requires orations.

This difference between the ritual cures and the *dúajida* may be understood in the following manner. All ritual cures have, among their concrete actions, certain carry-overs from the *dúajida* including singing, *wústana*, and the putting of objects on the patient. Ritual cures do not contain certain actions found in the *dúajida*, namely sucking and the supplemental techniques of the divinatory *wústana*, that is, the use of the crystal, the feather, or the ash as a means of divination (Russell 1908). Finally, ritual cures may contain certain actions characteristic of cures alone. We will ignore the latter group, attributing them to the particularities of the curing cults of each recognized dangerous object. (See Appendix B for a list.)

The following explanation will clarify the distinction between the standard *dúajida* and the specialized ritual cures. Each shaman has a standard *dúajida*, suitable for use on any *ká:cim* sickness, and each sickness has a standard ritual cure, suitable for use by any curer. The reason for variation among *dúajidas* is found in the unique endowment of the shaman, not in the sickness for which he performs the *dúajida*. The variation in ritual cures is traced to the unique way of each class of dangerous objects, not to the special properties of the individuals who perform the cures.

Let us pause to justify our approach to the problem of variation and similarity. Why do we stress the carry-overs and ignore the differences? First, we are following the pattern of Gregorio's thinking as evidenced in discourse. Second, it is interesting to note that all the ritual cures have certain common actions and, furthermore, that these are precisely the actions shared with the *dúajida*. These common actions suggest that the cures, although clearly not shamanic in their rationale, still are not far removed from a shamanic prototype. No attempt will be made in this study to reconstruct an historic differentiation between Piman shamanism and ritual curing. We will devote ourselves instead to showing how the shamans and the curers presently accomplish different objectives, albeit through similar actions. Specifically we will deal with the shaman's charisma, the curer's prayerfulness, and Piman concepts concerning spirits.

Third, and reminiscent of a point made in part II, we are skeptical of Underhill's distinction between the cures performed for ritual sicknesses – which require an abbreviated performance of the relevant ritual – and the cures of an implicitly nonritual kind. According to our interpretation, the minimal levels of curing exist even for Underhill's ritual sicknesses,* and the maximal level of curing for any *ká:cim* sicknesses may accurately be termed a ritual. Thus, in stressing the carry-overs from *dúajida* to *wúsota* and in underplaying the differences among *wúsotas*, we continue to champion the point of view maintaining that Piman sicknesses have common factors.

Finally, we admit a loss as to how to examine the variations or idiosyncrasies, other than by listing them as we have in the Appendix. The present study lacks an analysis of the content of the way connected with the cure of each *ká:cim* sickness. Instead of comparing the songs used for different kinds of sickness, or relating the content of each kind of song to the rest of the actions done in ritual cures, we are presently confined to noting their position in an abstract framework of actions and purposes.

* This point has not yet been confirmed.

3. Act of *Wústana*

The shaman blows to divine and nothing is said about curative effects of his blowing; the curer blows to cure and nothing is said about divinatory effects. We found the shaman's charismatic blowing to be the basic act of divination. The different tools of the *dúajida* augment his breath and they may be spoken of, up to a certain point, as means for accomplishing the act of *wústana.* The progression runs:

1. *Wústana* by means of the shaman's breath
2. *Wústana* by means of tobacco smoke, the first level of augmentation
3. *Wústana* by means of feathers and crystals, the second level of augmentation for which we have scant evidence

In the final step of the progression, spirit helpers supersede the shaman's heart and tools.

Now we will consider the language and doctrines concerning *wústana* in the context of ritual curing. This act of curative blowing is not based on anything inherent in the blower. The curative *wústana* is based on the dangerous object whose way and strength have caused the sickness; that is, the things spoken of as means for the *wústana* are properties of the dangerous object, rather than properties or possessions of the person who performs the blowing.

Wústana in *dúajida* and *wúsota*

SUBJECTS. The subjects of the verb forms of *wústana* – *wústaḍ, wústan*, and *wúsot* – are always human beings. In the context of *dúajida*, the blower is always identified as a shaman, *má:kai*. In the context of ritual curing, the blower is always identified as a "disposed-to-be-blowing-man," *s-wúsos 'ó'odham.* We freely render this term as ritual curer.

OBJECTS. The object of a verbal form of *wústana* is always identified as a "sick person," *múmkudam*. We render this term as "patient."[15] According to our interpretation, the sick persons are objects only in the sense of being the physical things against which the blower's breath or smoke collides. There is another set of objects, invisible to the naked eye, against which the *wústana* is really directed. These are: (a) for divination, strengths inside the patient's body and (b) for ritual curing, either spiritualized representatives of the way of a dangerous object or, perhaps, strengths inside the patient's body.

MEANS. The things spoken of as means (nouns, plus *-kaj*) in sentences with verbal forms of *wústana* are:

1. In the context of divination either breath, tobacco smoke, crystal, or feather. Examples are given in pt. III, sec. 8.
2. In the context of ritual curing either the name of a dangerous object, the name of a kind of curing song, or a fetish, *'íagta*, specific to the kind of dangerous object and defined as inherent property, *cú'idag*, of the dangerous object. For example:

   a. *Háiwañkaj,o 'e-wúso.*
   Cow by means of, he [patient] will get cured.

   b. *Cúkud né'i hékaj o 'e-wúso.*
   Owl song by means of he [patient] will get cured.

   c. *'Íagtakaj, o 'e-wúso.*
   Fetish by means of, he [patient] will get cured.

Note the presence of songs among the means for curative *wústana.* We have argued that songs could not be means for the divinatory *wústana.* Absent from the curing list are tobacco smoke and breath; shortly we will argue that breath should never be mentioned during the ritual cure. We think smoke could be mentioned with the qualification that smoke is never the sole means for accomplishing a cure.

The three attested examples of curative *wústana* identify the means as properties or parts of the dangerous object. It is apparent that curers literally do not blow by means of cows, songs, or fetishes. Therefore, in all these cases we translate the verb as "to cure" rather than "to blow," with the understanding that "cure" is a shorthand term for "to free a person from his sickness." The word "cure" is used because it is non-committal as to the concrete actions that bring about the desired result.

The problem in the texts on ritual cures involves deciding when to translate a word as "blow." As aforementioned, we have no sentences where smoke or breath is specified as the means; that is, we have no sentences which unquestionably demand a translation of "blow." On the basis of the narrative context, however, we decided that two of the three verbal forms – *wústan* and *wústaḍ* – should always be translated as "blow." In these instances we believe the concrete act of blowing is the referant. The third verbal form – *wúsot* – has been translated both as "blow" and "cure," the latter form being used whenever a name of a dangerous object, song, or fetish is specified as the means by which the act was accomplished.

We have observed that Gregorio's texts lack any mention of breath or smoke as the means for curative blowing. Why is this? Ritual curers never blow on patients solely by means of their own breath. They always blow smoke. Therefore breath should not be specified as a means because such events never occur. This is in contrast with the shamanic blowing described in text 34. A further constraint upon curative blowing is that the blowing of smoke is only performed in conjunction with an action that involves a property or part of the dangerous object: either putting a fetish on the patient or singing (or orating) or both. Curative blowing, unlike divinatory, cannot be dissociated from the use of an accompaniment which has no intrinsic connection with breath. Whereas the shaman's blowing is based upon his charismatic nature, the curer's blowing never occurs unaccompanied by an ingredient drawn from the dangerous object.

We regard the presence of song among the means for curing as a permissible usage because the curer's blowing has no charismatic basis. There is nothing inherent to the curer which could affect a cure unaided; if there were, he would be a shaman not a ritual curer.

Ingredients of the curer's *wústana*

The ingredients of curative *wústana* consist in blowing plus using a fetish, which corresponds with the minimal level of curing. Since the curer has no charisma, we cannot outline stages of augmentation such as exist for shamanic blowing. One can maintain either that the curer's breath is always augmented or that he has no charismatic breath to augment. The means of curing are graded, but the grading consists in the nature of the things which, as parts of the dangerous object, are external to the curer's breath. The grading is exemplified in the following excerpt from tape 16.2.

Kutp hab o cú'igkad
And it will be
And if it should be the case

mat pi 'in hú o míakad, hégai
ss never it will be nearby, that-one
if he [a ritual curer who knows the appropriate songs]
should not be accessible

matp o s-má:c.
ss it will know it.
who knows it [the songs needed for the maximal level of curing].

Kutp wuḍ abṣ o hémakc,
And just it will be anybody,
And he [the person who will attempt the wústana] will be just anybody,

pégi, kc 'am a 'ep o hékaj dágitpa, hégai 'íagta
well, and there it also will by means of it press it, that-one fetish
well, and he [curer who is just anybody] will press him [patient] with the fetish

matp háscu wuḍ o 'ik.
ss whatever it will be.
whatever kind of thing it [fetish] will be.

Pégi, k 'am hab o a 'ep wústaḍ, é:p.
Well, and there it will also blow, also.
Well, and he will blow, too.

The point of this text is that anyone – not necessarily a shaman or a ritual curer, defined in the strictest sense as a person who knows the songs necessary for the maximal level of curing – may be able to perform a curative *wústana* simply by blowing (tobacco smoke, presumably) on the patient in conjunction with pressing the fetish onto his body. In fact, the democratization of curing goes a step further – although we have no texts on this point – in that Pimans sometimes use fetishes in the manner of charms, without blowing; that is, sicknesses may be cured by the fetish alone. This constitutes the minimal form of curing, or, we may say, subminimal, because it does not include the act of *wústana*. It is not clear whether these "unblown" pressings can be referred to by verbal forms of *wústana*. We assume that they cannot – that the person who merely puts a fetish on a patient cannot be said to have "blown" or "cured" him. Table 5 summarizes our knowledge concerning the place of *wústana* within the doctrines of divination and ritual curing.

TABLE 5
SENSES OF *WÚSTANA*

	Context of *kúlañmada/ dúajida*	Context of *wúsota*
Actions which cannot be referred to by verbal forms of *wústana* as they supersede it	singing	none
Special translations of verb forms of *wústana*	Divining, without actually blowing	Curing, used with reference to ritual cures, maximal or minimal
Concrete acts of blowing:		
With breath, smoke, and another accompaniment	The second stage of augmentation	The basic sense of curative *wústana*
With breath and smoke	The first stage of augmentation	Never performed alone
With breath alone	The basic sense of divinatory *wústana*	Never performed
Actions which cannot be referred to by verbal forms of *wústana* as they undercut it	none	Putting a fetish on the patient without blowing on him

Department of Anthropology Museum, Arizona State University

Horse tail

F. Russell, The Pima Indians, *1908*

Horned toads

F. Russell, The Pima Indians, *1908*

Lizard

FETISHES

4. Spirits

Our texts on *kúlañmada/dúajida* found the shaman's action divided between two kinds of objects: spirits and strengths. The former were only slightly elaborated, while the latter were discussed in considerable detail as they constitute that which was manipulated by the blowing and sucking.

In our texts on ritual cures we find a reversal in the relative emphasis between the two fields of action. Strengths within the patient's body are scarcely mentioned because the curers do not act upon them directly. Although the curers direct some of their actions toward the patient's body, they do not do what the shaman does, namely observe, suck, or in any other manner manipulate the strengths within the body. Instead, their actions upon the patient's body, as well as their singing, are primarily intended to persuade a spiritual causal agency, which is not a strength, to cease sickening the patient. The spirit accommodates the curers by causing the strength to diminish.

Table 6 summarizes our findings concerning those manifestations of sickness which are spoken of as objects for shamans' or curers' actions.

We distinguish between spirits and things on the grounds of subjective mentality. The subjectivity of spirits consists in their disposition to like or dislike an individual's behavior toward them; for example, they like to hear their songs and they dislike being whipped.

A relationship which we define as prayerful exists between humans and spirits, both in *kúlañmada/dúajida* and in ritual cures. A task exists – divining or expelling strengths – which cannot be accomplished by people unaided. Spirits are uniquely capable of helping people, but their requirements must be met before they will lend themselves to the task. As the last resort, people must sing songs which the spirits like to hear. Then, upon hearing the songs, the spirit brings his own uniquely sufficient skill to bear on the task.

We describe the relationship between people – either shamans or curers – and spirits as prayerful because the spirits are invoked as a last resort. They are appealed to when lesser methods have proven inadequate. Further justification for terming the relationship prayerful lies in the fact that final appeal is directed toward an object which has a mind. We note, however, that the prayed-to entities are not considered capable of refusing to answer the prayers. Instead, the theory maintains that the spirits withhold their assistance just as long as people try to use lesser means than prayers to accomplish the task. It is as if the divination or cure ends with a surrender by the people involved. They begin by trying to accomplish the task on their own and, finally, they reach the point of delivering the task into the hands of the spirits who, upon hearing the songs, comply automatically.

On the present evidence, the shaman appears to be as prayerful as the curers. We have found that his performance of *wústana* is, in general, insufficient to accomplish divination. This means that his own powers are inadequate in the long run. Thus, in addition to being "sedentary" (pt. III, sec. 7), we should characterize Gregorio's rendition of shamanism as "humble."

In addition, the shaman's actions are not in any obvious manner more magical or powerful than those performed by the ritual curers. Both petition the spirits. We will establish grounds for our contention that the shaman's contacts with spirits and sicknesses are more intimate than those of the curer. We should not conclude, however, that he has any more power over the manifestations of sickness.

TABLE 6
SPIRITS AND STRENGTHS INVOLVED
IN *DÚAJIDA* AND RITUAL CURE

Spirits (endowed with subjective mentality)		**Things** (not endowed with subjective mentality)
Within the Landscape of the Spirits	*Within the Patient's Body*	*Within the Patient's Body*
"Women of the darkness," respond to curing songs Shaman's spirit helpers, respond to *dúajida* songs		Strengths, manipulated by shamans
Spiritualized things associated with the way of each kind of dangerous object, respond to curing songs, curative *wústana*, and the pressing of fetishes	Spiritualized things associated with the way of each kind of dangerous object, respond to curing songs, curative *wústana*, and the pressing of fetishes	

We distinguish strength from the spiritual manifestations of sickness because strength is not spoken of as a conscious entity (with one possible exception, noted in pt. III, sec. 7). They are said to be the substance upon which both people and spirits act. In diagnosis the shaman needs his spirit helper to illuminate the strength, and in curing the shaman or curer must finally appeal to spirits to expell the strength.

Since direct action upon strength is almost entirely absent from the curer's part of the *wúsota*, we conclude that the curer's approach to sickness is basically prayerful. He is concerned with asking for help on the patient's behalf rather than with grappling with the sickness directly.*

In contrast, the shaman's approach is more direct and intimate. Correspondingly, the *kúlañmada/dúajida* differs in emotional tone from the ritual cure. The climax of the former occurs when the shaman sucks out the strength. This is a direct, intimate act: one individual has finally ejected the substance that is sickening another. On the other hand, in *wúsota* the curers maintain an indirect, distant relationship between themselves and the substance of the patient's sickness.

We turn now to the varieties of spirits. We define them as objects with subjective mentality who are located in the landscape of the spirits. As table 6 shows, only two varieties of spirits are spoken of in exactly this manner, while a third variety is ambiguous on the criterion of location. The two clear-cut varieties are the shaman's spirit helpers and an uncanny variety of women. The third, ambiguously located variety of spirit will be identified as the spirit of the way of the dangerous object.

Briefly, the first two varieties of spirits readily submit to such English categorizations as visions, apparitions, or supernatural entities. A portion of the real world is set aside for them: inside mountains or the darkness outside the patient's house. They are understood to be similar to living people in the sense of being enduring, individualized entities which may be encountered in the world. They can be seen and heard. Pimans know where to go and what to do if they wish to meet them.

The third variety of spiritual entity – the spirit of the way – seems to exist outside the realm of individualized objects. These spirits are appealed to during the *wúsota* and it is understood that their compliance is necessary in order for strength to be expelled. But apart from being responsible for the recession (and perhaps the onset) of strength, these spirits give no clues as to

---

* The only qualification is a rationale for curing characteristic of the minimal level of *wúsota* in which the act of *wústana* or the application of a fetish, is said to work directly upon the strengths inside the patient's body. This nonprayerful method will be discussed in pt. IV, sec. 7.

their existence. We identify them with the abstractly conceptualized way discussed in part II.

According to Piman theory, no one knows or cares where these spiritualized entities are located. Curers make appeals to them by means of singing, by *wústana*, and by pressing fetishes onto the patient's body. Hence, according to our scheme, they seem to be residents of the landscape of the spirits as well as the patient's body. So far as we know, the shaman's actions are not addressed to them.

The spiritual entities of way are distinct from the more precisely defined spiritual women whom we will discuss in sec. 6. The former are more important than the spiritual women because the final appeal of any cure is directed toward these entities. Having thus identified them with the way of the dangerous object, we conclude that the cure of sickness, along with the cause, can be traced ultimately to a moral source, external to any individual whether person, animal, or spirit, outside the domain of physical matter, and authorized as binding upon Pimans at the time of creation.

5. Songs Within Maximal Level Cure

In pt. III, we have shown that singing is the ultimate resort of shamans attempting to divine an unknowable sickness. Our next two texts, 38 and 39, make an analogous point about curing songs. Text 38 concerns songs and sicknesses generally. It deals with three sets of variables as they apply to all sicknesses: (1) the seriousness of the patient's infringement upon the rights of a dangerous object; (2) the severity of the resulting sickness; and (3) the level of curing necessary in order to relieve the sickness.

Text 38 is in two parts, A and B. A deals with the seriousness of the patient's infringement, distinguishing between an action which is physically damaging to an animal – hurting or killing him – and an action which is damaging to or disrespectful of his property, *cú'idag* – stepping on a bear track or eating a coyote's food. The former seems to be the more serious and the resulting sickness more severe: "more painfully it reaches him [the patient]." Part B relates the levels of curing, maximal and minimal, to the other sets of variables. The relationship seems to be that any severe sickness demands a maximal cure. Severe sicknesses, however, may also result from minor types of infringements. This formulation is reminiscent of our theory of the permeation of strengths as a function of time (pt. III, sec. 4). The freedom of action accorded to causal agents keeps the theory from being mechanically systematic. In text 38 the causal agent – presumably the spiritualized way of the dangerous object – is free to produce a serious sickness though the patient's infringement did not seem to warrant it.

In this text, the minimal level of curing is expressed by the application of a fetish to the patient's body. The return of the symptoms after a short period of relief – several weeks or months – serves as proof that a more extensive cure will be needed.

The text has two sentences employing the verb *wúsot.* We translate each as "cure." The first refers to the minimal level of curing – that level which includes pressing the fetish but not singing. The second occurrence of *wúsot* refers to the maximal level. Unfortunately, the distinction is not clearly drawn in this text, and we must turn to text 39 for an explicit statement.

Text 39 concerns songs and a specific sickness, gopher sickness. It is divided into three parts: A, B, and C. Part A states that all cures are followed by a cessation of symptoms and then considers the possibility, discussed in the previous text, that after a certain amount of time the symptoms may reoccur. The reason given for the relapse is that the causal agent "wishes," *'élidad,* to cause it. Thus, Gregorio speaks of the subjective mentality of the causal agency. Abundant examples of this mode of expression are evident throughout our texts on ritual cure. We found only one instance of this mode of expression in the texts on *dúajida* – in which the causal agent was said to "try to hide" – and we found no instance of it in the texts concerning the origins of *ká:cim* sicknesses in part II.

According to our interpretation, the reference from text 39 is to the spiritualized way of the dangerous object (gopher). Gregorio refers to the causal agent in the singular but he does not give it a name. Thus it is only by inference that we identify the agent with the way. We do not believe that Gregorio is referring to any particular gopher; nor do we believe that Gregorio refers to gopher strength. For reasons that will accumulate in the following sections, we suggest way as the most probable reference.

Part B offers ethnographic detail on gopher fetishes in the process of describing one of the precautions patients normally take against the recurrence of sickness. They save fetishes.[16]

Part C indicates that the causal agent may not be satisfied with a cure consisting of no more than the use of fetishes. It will continue to sicken (here expressed as *tá:had,* "to stimulate") the patient because "it wants to hear its song." At this point the maximal cure is required.

The patient must find singers who can perform the entire cure. The cure is not simply a matter of singing, for as Gregorio explains the singers will also use fetishes. In addition the singers will blow, although Gregorio does not mention this fact. Thus, the maximal level of cure requires the services of experts – *s-wúsos 'ó'odham*, ritual curers – who know the ritual, whether simple or complex, appropriate for the patient's sickness.

TEXT 38 (Tape 24.8)

. . .Mat hémho a mat o ha-múmkic
. . .ss necessarily ss will sicken them
. . .[if people do something wrong] then necessarily it will sicken them

mat 'am hú hás o 'e-jú:.
ss there ever somehow will get done.
if anything gets done to it [dangerous object].

'O cem as a pi hás o jú:,
Or perhaps doesn't somehow do,
Or perhaps even if he [person] doesn't do anything to it [to the dangerous animal],

k abṣ hab-a hab 'e-wúa
but happens
but [still] it happens

matp háscu wuḍ o 'ik g ha-cú'idag
ss whatever will be the their parts
whatever their [animals'] parts [inherent properties] are

mam hé'ekia há'icu wuḍ 'i hégai,
ss several something is that-one,
how many things there are [e.g., feathers, tracks, etc.],

t 'am hú hás o jú:,
there ever somehow will do,
and he [person] might do something to them,

'aha nat hab o 'élidad,
then if will be intending,
or should he [person] think,

"Natṣ hí g o ñ-'á'ahe,"
[literal meaning unknown],
"Maybe it won't reach me,"

t 'ói a o 'ái 'am 'i hímdam,
then will reach later on,
and then eventually it [sickness] will reach him later on,

wá:m hégai matp há'icu wuḍ o dúakamk.
especially that-one ss something will be living-thing.
and especially if it [dangerous object] is an animal.

'Am o a cem s-má:cid mat o múmkic,
There should know ss will sicken it,
He should know that it will sicken him,

pégi, 't 'am hú hás o jú:, 'o omúa,
well, there ever somehow will do, or kill,
well, if he [person] should do something [bad] to it, or kill it,

pégi, bá'ic 'at 'i skó'okam o 'ái, hégai.
well, additionally painfully will reach it, that-one.
well, all the more painfully it [sickness] will reach him.

B

C hébai há'icu wuḍ abṣ 'o 'ámjeḍkamk,
And sometimes something just will be from-thing,
And sometimes something [minor kind of wrong action] is the source [of a sickness],

pi 'am hú hab si másma –
not ever thus –
and it [the action] isn't really like that [the bad action such as killing] –

k abṣ hab-a 'éḍa 'am a pi o 'áp'et.
but yet there will damage it.
but still it will damage him [patient].

Ñé:, kc hégai a mat o 'e-wúso.
Look, and that-one ss will get cured.
Look, and therefore [because sickness isn't serious] he will get cured [at the minimal level].

'O 'am hía hé'es 'o 'al 'i –
Or there of course a few a little bit –
Or perhaps for just a little while [the sickness will seem cured] –

mat abṣ g 'íagtakaj o'e-dágĭtpa
ss just the fetish by means of will get pressed
if he [patient] will just get pressed with a fetish

matp háscu wuḍ o 'ik.
ss whatever will be.
whatever it may be.

Ñé:, hég 'o táccu mat o 'e-wúso.
Look, that-one wants it ss will get cured.
Look, it's required that he [patient] will get cured
[with a complete ritual].

TEXT 39 (Tape 24.7)

A

. . .Matp wuḍ o hégaik g jéwho múmkidag,
. . .ss will be that-one the gopher sickness,
. . .if it should be gopher sickness,

pégi, k hab 'e-wúa mat o 'e-wúso,
well, and happens ss will get cured,
well, and he [patient] will get cured,

pégi, k hémho a mat 'im hú hab o 'i 'e-jú: 'am hé'es'i.
well, and necessarily ss away will get done there a little bit.
Well, it [sickness] will always get done away for a while.

Tp hab o 'élidad
May be intending
[But] it [sickness] may wish

matp 'am hab o si 'élidad
ss there will really intend
if it really wishes

mat o múmkic,
ss will sicken it,
to sicken [patient],

pégi, k ’atp héms ’am ’i hímdam hab ’ép o jú:, ’é:p.
well, and perhaps there later will do, again.
well, and perhaps it will do it to him [patient] again.

B

. . .Pégi, t hab o jú:,
. . .Well, will do,
. . .Well, it [sickness] will do it,

k ’an o a cékjcid hég ’ámjeḍ
and there will keep it that-one from
and so he [patient] will keep it [fetish] because

matp ’am hú hab ’ep o ’e-jú:
ss ever again will get done
it [sickness] may happen again

mo ge ’al wágt, “mú’adaj,” bac ’á’aga
ss a-little-bit digs out, “its expelled dirt,” we call it
[so] he [patient] will dig out some of its diggings

mat ’am o ’i wú:ṣ, gḍ hú wágaḍ ’eḍ, g jéwho.
ss there will emerge, down-away its hole in, the gopher.
which will emerge from the gopher’s burrow.

. . .’Am o ge ’al “ñépodga,” bac ’á’aga, o gakic,
. . .There will slightly “make it oval shaped,” we call it, will cause it to dry,
. . .He [patient] will shape it into an oval, he will dry it,

’an o cékjc,
there will keep it,
there he will keep it,

t o s-káwkam gákṣ, hégai.
will hard-ly dry, that-one.
it will dry hard.

Tp 'am hú hab o 'e-júñhog,
There ever will get done,
And if it [gopher way] should do it [sicken him again],

t hékaj abṣ o 'e-dágĭtpa, hégai.
that by means of just will get pressed, that-one.
then he [patient] will get pressed with it [fetish].

Ñé:, k 'am a 'ep s-wóhocud, hégai, o héwaj
Look, and there again causes-it-to-believe, that-one, will lessen
Look, and it [gopher way] is convinced by that [fetish], it [sickness] will lessen

matp háscu 'an o 'i pi 'áp'et.
ss whatever there will be damaging.
whatever thing is hurting him.

C

K abṣ hab-a hébai hab 'ep 'e-wúa,
But sometimes also happens,
But sometimes it also happens,

k hab 'ep 'á'aga, 'é:p, g kékelbaḍ hékĭ hú hémajkam
and also tells it, also, the dead-old-ones, former person
and the old people who have died, the ancient people, tell it

mat pi 'im hú o 'áp'et,
ss not ever will fix it,
that he [patient] may not get better,

k 'am hab abṣ o a 'i tá:hadagk,
and there just will stimulate it,
and it [gopher way] will just stimulate him,

'o 'am hú hía hé'es o ṣa'i 'áp'et.
or eventually of course a-little-bit will slightly fix it.
or perhaps he will just get a little bit better.

T hab o 'á:,
Will mean,
They [ancient people] call it,

"S-'e 'o kǐ káimk,
"Apparently wants to hear,
"Apparently it [causal agent] wants to hear it,

'e-ñé'i s-káim."
its own song wants to hear."
it wants to hear its own song."

Pégi, t 'am háhawa o ñé'iculidk
Well, there then will sing for it
Well, then he [curer] will sing for it [causal agent]

matp hédai o 'i s-má:ck,
ss whoever will know,
whoever [curer] will know it [songs],

'an o 'i gá: mat hédai o s-má:ck g jéwho ñé'i.
there will look-for ss whoever will know the gopher song.
then he [patient] will look for him, whoever knows the gopher songs.

C abṣ hab-a hég o a hékaj, hégai.
But that-one will use, that-one.
But he [ritual curer] will use it [fetish, along with the singing].

S-wúsos 'ó'dham, ritual curers

Curing songs are said to originate in visionary encounters similar to those which produce *dúajida* songs. The two types of songs have different purposes: one a request for termination of sickness and the other a request for assistance in diagnosis. We know little about whether or how the two forms of the songs, *dúajida* and curing, differ in content. Gregorio distinguishes between them terminologically – *dúajida ñé'i, dúajida* song vs. *wúsosig ñé'i,* curing song – and he implies that *dúajida* songs are earmarked as such by the spirits who teach these songs to shamans (see note 12). On the other hand, Underhill found certain songs being used for *dúajida* as well as for curing (1946:275).

Dúajida songs do differ in that they are personal to the shaman who has been given them in a vision or dream, while curing songs are public property. Spirits who listen to curing songs seem to prefer a male chorus consisting of the largest possible number of singers. Thus Pimans are encouraged to learn curing songs from each other, enabling them to sing at each other's ritual cures. The result is an indefinitely large group of people who have become ritual curers simply because they like to learn and do rituals. Although the learning of curing songs is not regulated, there are rules governing who can sing at particular cures. In general, the singers must be men who are not close relatives of the patient and they must have been invited by the patient's family to sing a cure, which is normally performed at the patient's house. The patient or his family is responsible for gathering together the complement of curers for any particular ritual. There is an air of "by invitation only" about them because most cures are performed at night when Pimans are supposed to stay inside their houses minding their own business. The curers bring everything to be used in a cure, including rattles to accompany their singing, cigarettes for *wústana*, and fetishes.

We conclude that curers sing songs which were conceived in shamanic visions, but the curers do not invoke any visionary connections with the source of their songs. Neither need the singers have suffered from or been cured of the sickness in question. Furthermore, people who have been cured of a sickness do not necessarily become ritual curers for that sickness. Thus, Piman society maintains the following independent statuses:

1. Person who has been taught a song by a spirit: We believe that Gregorio would refer to any such person as a shaman, *má:kai*, for he defines "shaman" as anyone to whom "something has been imparted by [a spirit's] instruction." This definition refers to any kind of visionary instruction including the acquisition of curing songs.
2. Person who performs ritual cures for people: *S-wúsos 'ó'odham.*
3. Person who has been cured of a sickness: We are not aware of a special name for this status.

Rationale for singing

Our next two texts, 40 and 41, provide a rationale for curing songs about dangerous objects, specifically animals. The songs describe the way of

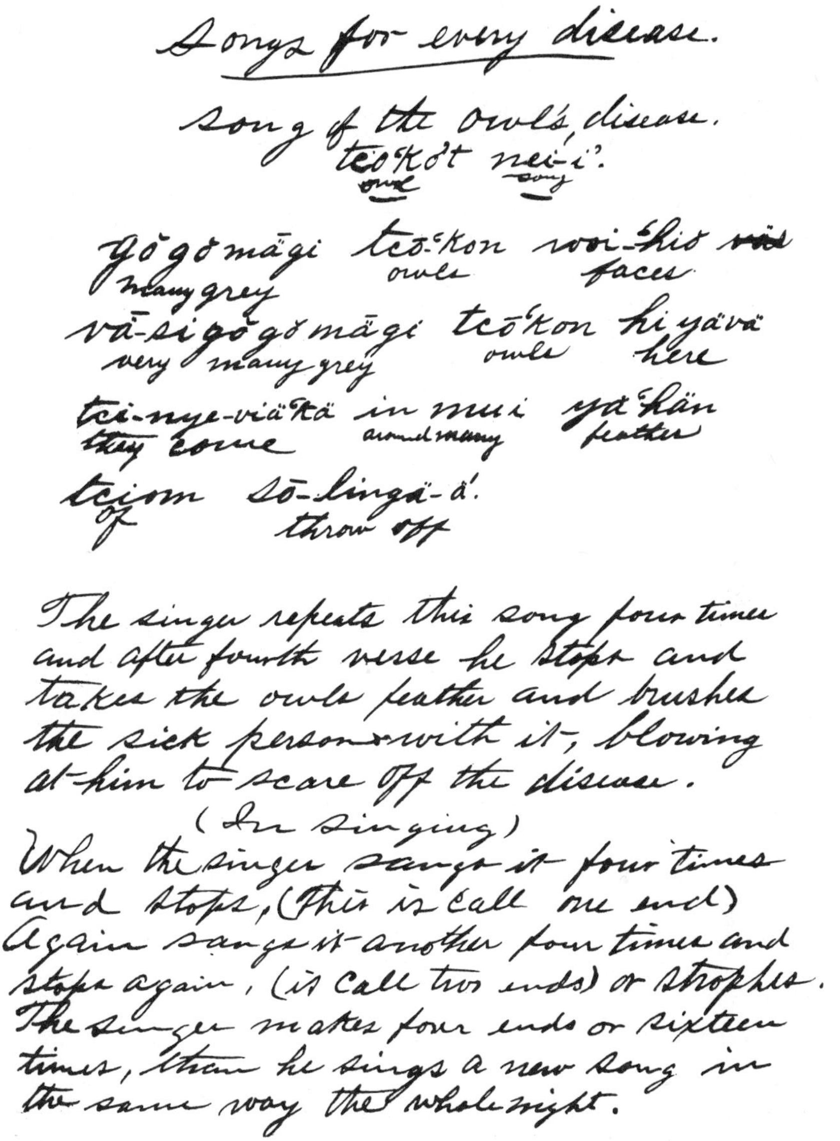
Songs for every disease.

song of the owls disease.
tcökot neei-i:
owl song

yõgõmägi tcö:kon vooi-:kiö
many grey owls faces
vä-sigõgõmägi tcö:kon hiyävä
very many grey owls here
tci-nye-viäkä in mui yä:hän
they come around many feather
tcim sõ-lingä-ä.
of throw off

The singer repeats this song four times and after fourth verse he stops and takes the owls feather and brushes the sick person with it, blowing at him to scare off the disease.

(In singing)
When the singer sangs it four times and stops, (This is call one end) Again sangs it another four times and stops again, (is call two ends) or strophes. The singer makes four ends or sixteen times, than he sings a new song in the same way the whole night.

The maximal level of cure and the nature of curing songs. José Lewis Brennan holograph, 1897.

(Courtesy Smithsonian Institution, J.N.B. Hewitt, Collector.)

the animal, which reputedly takes pleasure in hearing the songs and thus expels the sickness. In text 41, Gregorio explains one of the factors which makes the songs pleasing: their humor. The songs dwell on quirks of the species involved.[17]

We observe the attribution of subjective mentality to causal agencies in text 40. Songs are spoken of as "pleasant stimulations," *s-'áp tá:hadkam*, for the spiritualized entities who hear them. The spirit "feels well," *s-'áp 'i 'e-tá:t*, upon hearing them. (See pt. III, sec. 4 for a discussion of these verbs of "feeling.")

Text 40 also provides evidence for differentiation between the spiritualized causal agency and the manifest substance of the sickness: "They [spiritualized causal agents] will quickly do away with it." It is not clear to what the "it," which is done away with, refers. It could be strength or it could be the stimulation spoken of in the previous line of the text. In either case, the text demonstrates that sicknesses are cured through the mediation of spiritualized hearers of the songs.

TEXT 40 (Tape 15.4)

Q

No a wóho mo s-hó:ho'id hégam há'icu 'óimmeḍdam
Is true ss enjoy those-ones something wandering-thing
Is it true that the animals [or their ways] like it

mat o ká: g 'e-ñé'i?
ss will hear the its song?
when they hear their songs?

A

Héu'u, b 'o cú'ig,
Yes, it is,
Yes, it is the case,

ḍ 'atp hú'i si s-'áp tá:hadkam 'am ha-wé:hejeḍ
is perhaps very well stimulating there with respect to them
they [songs] probably are pleasant stimulations for
them [animals or spiritualized ways]

mat há'icu 'am si táṣo háb o 'e-káijid
ss something there very clearly will get pronounced
when something [song] gets plainly pronounced [by singers]

mo hás 'i má:s, hás 'e-júñhim há'icu.
ss somehow appears, somehow getting done something.
[about] how it [animal's way] appears, how it [animal] does things.

Pégi, t 'am si táṣo 'am o 'á:gask,
Well, there very clearly there will have been explained,
Well, if they [things about the way] are clearly told [by singing],

kutp hú o 'i si s-'áp 'i 'e-tá:t,
and ever will very well get felt,
and then it [animal or its way] will feel very pleasantly,

'am o káiok hégai 'e-ñé'i
there will hear that-one its song
when it hears its song

mo a wóho mo hás másma 'am hab 'á:gas,
ss is true ss somehow thus there is explained,
which is true, how it [way] is told [sung],

c 'am hab cé'is,
and there has been pronounced,
and pronounced,

'am hab káidagc.
there pronounces.
as it vocalizes.

Pégi, k 'atp héms hégai wuḍ há'icu hás tá:hadkam,
Well, and perhaps that-one is something somehow stimulating,
Well, and perhaps it [sickness] is some kind of stimulating thing,

gm hú si s-hó:tam 'im hú hab o 'i jú:, hégam,
away very quickly away will do, those-ones,
they [spiritualized causal agents] will quickly do away with
it [strength? stimulations?],

heg hékaj mo s-'áp 'am hab cé'is
that-one by means of ss properly there has been pronounced
because it [song] has been accurately pronounced

mo hás másma wuḍ hímdaj.
ss somehow thus is its way.
how its [animal's] way is.

T hég óidk 'am hab o 'e-jú:.
That-one during there will get done.
Accordingly it will happen [that the sickness will stop].

Ñé:, há'ap.
Look, that-way.
Look, that's how it is.

TEXT 41 (Tape 15.3)

Q

No a wóho mo s-ta-'á'askima hab cú'ig, hégam há'icu 'óimmeḍdam
Is it true ss funny is, those-ones something wandering thing
wúsosig ñéñ'ei?
ritual curing songs?
Is it true that the curing songs about animals are funny?

Ṣa: 'o másma s-ta-'á'askima, hégam ñéñ'ei?
How thus is funny, those-ones songs?
How are those songs funny?

A

Héu'u, no pi hab má:s
Yes, because appears
Yes, because they [songs] are of the sort

matp hás 'i má:s wuḍ o há'icuk,
ss somehow appears will be something,
[about] how a thing will be,

c ’am hég ’é’eḍa, hégai hímdaj
and there that-one in it, that-one its way
and be in its [animal’s] way

matp hás ’i másma ’am hab o ’e-júñhid.
ss somehow thus there will be getting done.
if it does things in some [notable] manner.

Hébai hab má:s
Sometimes appears
Sometimes it [song] is of the sort

mat ’am si hás másma hab o ’á:gask
ss there really somehow thus will have been meant
if it really has been stated in some manner

mat hab ’e-jú: hégai há’icu dúakam,
ss got done that-one something living thing,
that it [something interesting] got done to the animal,

’o matp háscu wuḍ o ’ik,
or ss whatever will be,
or whatever [kind of dangerous object] it may be,

k hég ’ám s-ta-’á’askima, hégai
and that-one there is funny, that-one
and that [event which happened to the animal] is what is funny

mat hég ’ámjeḍ ’am hab o céi
ss that-one from there will vocalize
so for that reason one will speak about it [the reason why songs are funny]

matp ’ep hab o cú’igk,
ss also will be,
if it should be like that,

mantp – 'á:ñi 'am o hí: 'am hú hébai.
ss I – I there may go away someplace.
if I [for example] should happen to go someplace.

Kutp 'in hú há'i gáhijeḍ 'am o ñ-ñéidad
And away some of them sideways there will be at me looking
And some people [at a distance] will be watching me through the corners of their eyes

mantp hás 'i másma 'am i hímad.
ss I somehow thus there will be going.
as I am walking in some manner.

'Ói a 'am hú hás o 'i ñ-jú:,
Then ever somehow will to me do,
Then I just might do something,

'ói a o 'i cem géi
then will almost fall
then I might almost fall

mantp hás o 'i ñ-jú:,
ss I somehow will myself do,
whatever I do,

t 'i hú o si ñ-'á'asi, hégam,
here away will really at me laugh, those-ones,
then they [onlookers] will really laugh at me,

'im hú abṣ gáhijeḍ 'am ñ-ñéijc.
there away just sideways there me observes.
watching me through the corners of their eyes.

Ñé:, wépo másma hab cú'ig, 'í:da
Look, similarly thus is, this-one
Look, this is similar

mo g ñé'i 'am hab a cú'ig
ss the song there is
to the songs

matp hás 'i káidam 'am o 'á:gask,
ss somehow audibly there will have been meant,
if the meaning will be expressed somehow,

'am o hás 'e-júñhim hímdagk,
there somehow will be doing way
how the way will be done,

k hég hab 'á'aga hégai hab másma,
and that-one means that-one thus,
and that is what is meant,

s-ta-'áskima ñéñ'ei.
funny songs.
funny songs.

Ñé:, há'ap.
Look, that-way.
Look, that's how it is.

6. Other Spiritual Appeals Within Maximal Level Cure

According to our interpretation of Piman theory, the maximal level of curing includes singing as the ultimate appeal to the sensibility of a spirit which we identify with the way that sickens the patient. The spirit will "do away with" the patient's sickness upon hearing his songs. We now will present additional textual discourse concerning other spiritual appeals during cure.

Our first discussion, concerning songs, will establish that the audience of curing songs is not confined to spiritualized representatives of the way of the dangerous object. Another variety of spirit responds at least to some kinds of songs; Gregorio refers to this other variety as "women," *'ú'uwǐ.* He scrupulously distinguishes between these female spirits and living Piman females. The voices of the female spirits – the women of the darkness – are heard in accompaniment to the following kinds of curing songs, which, in curing, are only sung by men: scalp bundle (*kú:kpǐ*), ocean, devil, and owl (or ghost).

Women of the darkness

The following three texts, 42, 43, and 44, will elucidate Gregorio's conception of the women of the darkness; the texts contain his most explicit statements concerning communication between a human singer and a spirit. They stand as examples of the expository precision which Gregorio could easily attain when speaking about spiritual topics.

His texts on communication with the spirits during *dúajida* are comparatively pale and inexact. We suggest the acceptance of those texts as expressions of a vagueness which actually exists in the doctrine on spirits in the *dúajida.* We would expect this aspect of spiritualism to be vague insofar as it is incompatible with Gregorio's theory of strength in the patient's body.

Text 42 serves as our introduction to the spiritual women. Here we find the first of several statements on the behavior of these spirits. They "come running" when scalp bundle songs are sung. This expression suggests an eagerness that is absent from the texts on the movement of spirits during *dúajida*, texts 29 and 30. These texts contain the following usages:

a. *'E-cé:gǐ*, "to get caused to show up." This refers to the "running things" or "whatever" which appear when the shaman sings, however, it is not clear how or where they appear; specifically, it is not clear whether they approach the house where the *dúajida* is taking place.

b. *Ha-wúṣadad,* 'to remove them', 'to draw them out'. The shaman, by singing, draws the spirits out from their haunts in the mountains.

c. *Ṣél wáwañ*, "to stretch straightly." The shaman's song stretches to the spirits.

d. *É-géwṣṣapad*, "to get connected." The shaman's songs get connected to the spirits, that is, each song is associated with one of his spirit helpers.

The vocabulary Gregorio employs referring to spirits during *dúajida* suggests the spirits being "tied" to the shaman's magic in such a manner that he must extract them from their customary haunts and pull them in toward the task at hand.

Eager though the spiritual women may be, they do, however, stop short of entering the scene where the cure takes place. Toward the end of text 42 – and in greater detail in texts 43 and 44 – we are told that they remain "someplace in the darkness"; by our definition "someplace" would be located within the landscape of the spirits. The women of the darkness are heard but not seen by the singers.

TEXT 42 (Tape 12.3)

K 'am há'icu hab si cú'ig, é:p
And there something really is, also

And there surely exists one kind of thing [curing ritual when spiritual women become manifest]

mant 'am hab o céi,
ss I there will speak,

which I will mention,

há'icu aṣ hab wuḍ kú:kpĭ,
something is enclosed-thing,

something is the scalp bundle,

c wuḍ 'ó:b ha-'ámjeḍkam.
and is Apache their from-thing.

and it is produced from Apaches.

Pégi, c hab másma hab ’ep ’é-wúa
Well, and thus also happens
Well, and it [cure of kú:kpĭ sickness] happens like this

mat hékid ’am o ’e-’á: g ñé’ij,
ss whenever there will get told the its song,
whenever it’s [ku:kpĭ’s] song gets pronounced,

k ’am hébai ’i hímdam t o wó’i, hégam,
and there someplace later will arrive running, those-ones,
and then eventually they [spiritual women] will come running,

s-káimk g ’e-ñé’i.
wants to hear the its song.
wanting to hear their song.

“’Ú’uwĭ,” b ’o hía ha-’á’aga,
“Women,” of course calls them,
“Women,” one calls them,

pi ’am hú hékid “cécoj” ha-’á’aga,
not ever “men” calls them,
one never calls them “men,”

hégam a’i ’ú’uwĭ ’am wó’ipoḍ.
those-ones only women there arrive running.
only women come running there.

K wóho mat ’an hab o káijid ’an hébai s-cúhugamk ’éḍ,
And truly ss there will be vocalizing there someplace darkness in,
And it’s true that they will be emitting sounds someplace
in the darkness,

ha-wé:majk.
will be with them.
they [women] will join in with them [the real singers].

Ñé:, hég 'áb 'ep táṣo
Look, that-one at also clear
Look, from that it is also true

mo wóho mo wuḍ kú:kpĭ,
ss truly ss is enclosed thing,
that it's truly the scalp bundle,

c múmkicud.
and sickens it.
which sickens him [patient].

Text 43, in which our female spirits are further examined, is in four parts. Part A introduces the problem of the "reality status" of the women, a topic which Gregorio pursues throughout the text. He says that their singing is heard only intermittently and he attributes this fact to "the darkness." The term darkness, *s-cúhugam*, is analogous to the English uncanny, supernatural, or spiritual. Darkness is used to explain odd but 'real' or 'true' sensations; we translate the word *wóho* either as 'real' or 'true'.[18]

Gregorio refers to the women as products of darkness: "It's just the darkness that does it." Yet the sounds they emit do not merely come from the darkness in the sense of "That is nothing but the darkness, a figment of your imagination." Rather the idea is that the sounds come from definite, nonimaginary, uncanny spirits. The sounds are "their doings," *ha-cú'ijig.*

Part B specifies two types of cures during which the women are heard – the cures for devil way and ocean way. These cures are spoken of as if they are independent of the spiritualized women. Therefore, the women appear to be additional or idiosyncratic spiritual factors who just happen to make their appearances during the performance of certain kinds of ritual cures. Thus far we have established that the women are associated with a specific group of sicknesses – *kú:kpĭ*, ocean, devil, and owl; these sicknesses are cured by songs whose subject matter is the way of each class of dangerous objects; and the spiritualized way of each class of sickness responds to the songs.* In addition to this standard kind of spiritual response, however, the aforementioned four kinds of songs induce the spiritual women to chime in, in an uncanny manner. We are not told about the relationship between the women and the four kinds of sickness. We know that the curing songs are for the different

* Evidence for this claim is given in text 45 on devil sickness.

kinds of sickness. For instance, they are named "owl songs," not "nighttime women songs." Gregorio says in part B, ". . . Owl songs, Well and by means of them [songs], he [patient] will get cured." He did not say, "Women songs, by means of which the patient will get cured." We conclude that the patient is being cured of – or as Gregorio puts it "cured by means of" – owl sickness, not "woman sickness."[19]

In part C, Gregorio renews his discussion of the real but uncanny status of women as singers. He undertakes an explanation of how situations in which living women singing curing songs differ from situations in which spiritual women perform their singing. He selects the songs of ocean way for his example. These songs are sung on two different occasions: (1) during cures for ocean sickness and (2) during rituals intended to purify salt brought from the ocean and to purify the men who have brought salt.[20]

Gregorio clearly shows that under the latter circumstances women may join in the singing of ocean consequence songs and that this occurs during the night. These, however, are living women, namely the wives of men who have brought the salt. In contrast, when the same songs are sung during a ritual cure for the benefit of a sick person, no living women are permitted to join in. In this case the audible female voices originate from the landscape of the spirits, not from the group of living people assembled for the cure.

In part D another example of a cure is given, the cure of enemy consequence sickness in which scalp bundle songs are sung. Here Gregorio identifies the women as "scalp bundle women," implying that each of the four cures has its own variety of spiritual women.

TEXT 43 (Tape 12.4)

A

. . .Pégi, mé:k o ṣa hímk,
. . .Well, distantly will go,
. . .Well, it [singing by spiritual women] goes on for a while,

k háhawa pi o ha-céi.
and then not will be vocalizing them.
and then they stop making sounds.

'O hab 'ep o má:sk mat há'icu o ṣa 'e-wé:nad,
Or also will appear ss something will slightly get with it,
Or it may seem that something [sounds from the women] will kind of mix in [with the sounds from the men],

pégi, t hémho a mat há'as hú 'am hab o 'al 'i cé'i,
well, necessarily ss a-little-bit ever there will slightly vocalize,
well, they [women] always make sounds for a little while,

k 'am hú hébai t o hí:.
and away someplace will go.
and then it goes away.

D abṣ s-cúhugam, c hab 'e-wúa,
Is just darkness, and happens,
It's just darkness that does it,

c abṣ hab-a s-má:c 'atp
but knows
but they [real singers] know

matp hab má:s hégai, a wóho 'ab ha-'ámjeḍ, ha-cú'ijig.
ss appears that-one, truly about them, their consequence.
that it [singing] truly comes from them [women], [it's] their doing.

B

Pégi, ñé:, k hab má:s
Well, look, and appears
Well, look, and it [a kind of curing ritual] is like that

mant hab hía másma hab o céi. . . cúkuḍ.
which I of course thus will vocalize. . . owl.
which I will mention in this respect, the owl.

B 'o a másma g cúkuḍ ñé'i
Is thus the owl song
it is like this with owl songs

mañ hab 'á:g,
ss I explain,
as I explained,

b 'at a másma hab o céi
thus will vocalize
they [real singers] will vocalize

matp wuḍ o wóho hégaik, cúkuḍ ñé'i,
ss will be truly that-one, owl song,
if it will really be owl songs,

pégi, k hékaj o 'e-wúso.
well, and by means of will get cured.
well, and by means of them [songs] he [patient] will get cured.

Pégi, t hab o a wó'i 'atp hébaijeḍ hí o a hégai,
Well, will arrive running from someplace of course that-one,
Well, they [women] will come running from somewhere of course,

ḍ aṣ o s-cúhugam c hab o káijid.
will be darkness and will vocalize.
it is the darkness making sounds.

Jíawul hímdag,
Devil way,
Devil way,

b 'o a másma hab 'ep 'e-wúa, hégai,
thus also happens, that-one,
it also does like that,

hégam 'at 'am o a 'ep ñé'ed ha-wé:m hégam 'ó'odham.
those-ones there will also sing with them those-ones men.
those [women] will also sing [devil songs] with the men.

C

. . .Pégi, c 'am há'icu 'é:p
. . .Well, and there something else
. . .Well, and there is something [a kind of cure] else

mo hab ’e-wúa, ’é:p,
ss happens, also,
which is also like that,

sú:dagĭ cú’ijig
water consequence
ocean consequence

m ’in hú wó’o
ss there lies
which [the ocean] lies there

mo hébai ép ha-múmkicud,
ss sometimes also sickens them,
which also sometimes sickens them,

c abṣ hab-a hég hí táṣo
but that-one on the other hand clearly
but of course it is obvious

mo hab ’e-wúa
ss happens
that it [purification rite] happens

mat hékí ’án o béi g ’ón, k o dáda.
ss already there will get the salt, and will arrive.
when they [salt getters] have gotten the salt and arrived
[back at the village].

Pi abṣ ’am o ’i hú:
Not just there will eat
They can’t just eat it

mat o ’ip kĭ wúso hégai ’e-’ónga.
ss until will purify that-one their own salt.
until their salt is purified.

Ñé:, gam hú o 'e-kégcudk sí'alim
Look, distantly will get cleaned at dawn
Look, finally it will be purified at dawn

mat 'an háhawa 'al 'i ha-mámkahi
ss there then a little be giving to them
then they will be giving it away to them [people]

matp hé'ekia 'am o 'i 'e-hémapa.
ss several there will get gathered.
to as many [people] as will be assembled.

Ñé:, 'am o si táṣo hab 'e-wúa, hí a,
Look, there very clearly happens, of course,
Look, then obviously it happens [that living women will sing],

hí wuḍ s-dódakam,
however are living-ones,
but of course they [women] are alive,

(tp hég hí háscu wuḍ o 'ik).
(that-one on the other hand whatever may be).
(as opposed to the other kind of women, whatever they may be).

'An o 'i dáihhi g ha-wé'ewem kí:kam,
There will start sitting the their-with-ones living-things,
Their [salt getters] wives will be sitting around,

. . .pégi, hémho a no pi g 'ón táccu, gé'e s-béhim.
. . .well, necessarily because the salt desires, big amount wants to get.
. . .necessarily they will, because they want the salt, they want to get a lot of it.

Wé:s hab o 'e-jú:
Everything will get done
They will all do that [the ritual]

mapt hé'ekia o 'i dáḍhaiwua, hégam ñé'edam
ss several will sit down, those-ones singers
the many singers that will be seated there

mat 'am o ha-wúso.
ss there will purify them.
who purify them [salt getters and their salt].

Ñé:, k hab o káijid,
Look, and will vocalize,
Look, and they [wives] will vocalize,

o ha-wé:m 'á'agad hégai ñé'i,
will with them be telling it that-one song,
they will join in the singing,

ṣú:dagĭ cú'ijig ñé'i.
water consequence song.
ocean consequence song.

Ñé:, hég hí táṣo,
Look, that-one on the one hand is clear,
Look, in that case it's obvious [that living women may join
in the singing],

c abṣ hab-a hébai abṣ o 'e-wúso
but sometimes just will get cured
but sometimes one [patient] will just get cured

mat wuḍ aṣ o múmkudam,
ss will be sick-one,
if he is a sick person,

c 'am o 'e-wúso.
and there will get cured.
and he will get cured.

Pi 'am hú cem há'i wuḍ o 'ú'uwĭk,
Not ever just any of them will be women,

None of them [ritual singers] will be women,

c abṣ hab-a 'éḍa 'am hab o 'e-káijid ha-húgid 'am, hégai,
but yet there will get vocalized beside them there, that-one,

but yet, it [the sound of women] will be heard alongside of them [the songs sung by men],

c hab-a hég 'ámjeḍ heg hékaj mo wuḍ wóhokam
but that-one from that-one by means of ss is true-thing

but it is from that [spiritual women] because it is a real thing

matp hég múmkicud, hégai,
ss that-one sickens, that-one,

when it [ocean way] sickens him,

pégi, t hab o káijjid.
well, will vocalize.

well, they make sounds.

D

C háicu wuḍ 'ép kú:kpĭ
And something is also enclosed-thing

And another example is the scalp bundle

mañ 'am hékĭ hú hab 'ép káij,
ss I there already also vocalize,

which I have already mentioned,

'ab 'ó:b 'ámjeḍ, 'ó:b cú'ijig 'ámjeḍ.
enemy about, enemy consequence about.

about the enemy, about the enemy's doings.

Pégi, k hab 'ep céce, 'é:p, hégai,
Well, and also vocalizes, also, that-one,
Well, and they [women] also make sounds then,

hab wuḍ o a 'ep 'ú'uwĭk,
is also women,
it is also women,

pi o hékid g cécoj 'am hú wó'iopad.
not ever the men ever arrive running.
it is never men that come running.

Ḍ 'at o a 'ú'uwĭk, c 'am o wó'i,
Will be women, and there will arrive running,
It is always women and they come running,

t hégam 'am hí o a ñé'ed hía, 'ó'odham.
those-ones there of course will be singing of course, men.
of course the men are there singing.

Pégi, t abṣ hab-a 'an hú hébai 'atp hás o cú'igk, g s-cúhugam,
Well, but ever sometimes somehow will be, the darkness,
Well, sometimes it may [merely] be the darkness,

'éḍa hébai 'im o ha-cé:cegad, hégam.
yet sometimes there will naming them, those-ones.
yet sometimes they [singers] will be invoking them [by songs].

Hég 'o 'am a'i si 'e-cé:ceg 'ú'uwĭ,
That-one there only really gets named women,
the women must get invoked,

ñé:, kú:kpĭ 'ú'uwĭ.
look, enclosed thing women.
look, scalp bundle women.

Text 44 explains why the women join in the singing. They do so because they like to hear the songs of the four ways, *kú:kpĭ*, ocean, devil, and owl. This is the same disposition we found attributed to the spiritual ways of animals. Furthermore their pleasure has precisely the same consequence, the cessation of the patient's symptoms. The text is ambiguous, however, on the role the women play in causing the cure. We are told they enjoy the songs of the ways and we are told that it or they – either reading is possible – will stimulate the patient differently, that is, expel his sickness.

TEXT 44

(Tape 12.6)

. . .Há'icu hab si táṣo hab má:s
. . .Something very clearly appears
. . .One thing [about spiritual women] is quite clear

mañ 'am hú hékĭ hú hab 'á:g
ss I before already told
as I have already explained

mo hég 'ámjeḍ hab 'e-wúa, 'am kákk'ej g 'e-né'i
ss that-one from happens, there hears the its own song
which is the reason why when they [women] hear their song

mat o wó'i,
ss will arrive running,
that they come running,

k hémho a mat o há-wé:mt.
and necessarily ss will join them.
and they will always join in with them [the singers].

Ñé:, hab másma hab cú'ig, 'í:da,
Look, thus is, this-one,
Look, this is how it is [why they do that],

c táccu, s-hó:ho'id, s-káimmuk
and desires, enjoys, wants to hear
and they [women] desire [the songs], enjoy them, like to hear them

mo wóho mo heg 'ámjeḍ 'am hab pi 'á'ap'et, há'icu,
ss truly ss that-one from there is improper, something,
[all of] which is true but there is something wrong with it,

c 'in 'i g há'icu, gáwul má:s há'icu hab má:s
and here is something, differently appearing something appears
[because] there are things, various things of this kind

mo hía cem pi hab má:s, mas ñéñok,
ss of course does not appear, ss is talking,
and of course it is not [the same kind of thing] as
[when an ordinary person is] talking,

c abṣ hab-a 'éḍa hég 'ámjeḍ 'am hab cú'ig,
but yet that-one from there is,
but yet in this case [of spirits],

hab má:s mo 'am hab-a káij.
appears ss there vocalizes.
it appears that it [spirit] emits sounds.

K abṣ hab-a pi hab 'e-wúa,
But does not happen,
But they don't do it [make sounds in the manner of living people],

'am a hás 'e-wúa 'atp, 'í:da,
there somehow happens, this-one,
they do however behave [communicate] in some manner,

c hég 'ámjeḍ hab má:s
and that-one from appears
and consequently it seems

mo heg hékaj 'im hú hab 'i 'e-júccu.
ss that-one by means of away gets done.
that therefore it [sickness] gets done away with.

C wóho hab má:s
And truly appears
And truly it seems

mo 'am a s-hó:ho'id,
ss there enjoys,
that they [women] like it [singing],

hég 'ámjeḍ hab 'e-wúa
that-one from happens
consequently it happens

mat 'ab gáwul o 'i tá:hadt
ss against it differently will stimulate
that they [the women or the way] will stimulate him [patient] differently [stop causing his symptoms]

matp hékid 'am o 'e-'á: g ñé'ij,
ss whenever there will get told the its song,
when its [a kind of dangerous object's] song gets sung,

'í:dam há'akia, gí'ik
these-ones several, four
these four [kind of things]

mañ 'am hab ha-'á:g.
ss I there tell them.
which I have told.

Wústana, blowing and use of fetishes

Our next two texts, 45 and 46, concern the prayerful nature of the nonsinging actions performed in ritual cures: blowing and the use of fetishes. These activities, like songs, are said to appeal to the sensibilities of the causal agent. They are forms of prayer addressed to an intelligent causal agent on the patient's behalf. These texts will explain why ritual curers blow and use fetishes and how these nonsinging activities fit into the total scheme of the curing ritual.

Part A of text 45 identifies the two phases of a maximal level cure. These are the singing component, directed at the landscape of the spirits, and the *wústana* component, directed at the patient's body. Gregorio refers to the phases as distinct units: "And when it [singing] finishes, they [singers] will blow on him [patient]." The verb we translate as "finish" is *kú:gid.* Used as a noun, *kú:g* means "the end of a sequence of action," "the extremity of a tree," "the end of a table," or "the end of a mountain." The *wústana* phase, as described in parts A and B, includes blowing onto the patient and the application of fetishes to his body; for example, whipping him with a horse's tail, mentioned in text 45, or pressing the expelled dirt from gopher holes onto him, mentioned in text 39. (See Appendix for a list of the fetishes and the different methods in which they are applied.)

The result of each action, whether blowing or applying fetishes, may be expressed in two manners.

1. In terms of the patient's own body sensations, for example:

   a. It [the blowing] feels [to the patient] as if it really penetrates in him when he [curer] blows on him. (*Wústana* reference, text 45, pt. A.)

   b. It [strength from fetish?] will enter deeply [into the patient] for that purpose he [curer] presses it, it [curative strength?] does away with it [strength of dangerous object?] if it enters deeply into him. (Pressing a fetish [for ocean way] onto the patient's body reference, text 47.)

2. In terms of a type of thinking, feeling, or spiritual causal agency, for example:

   a. Uh, so that it [strength?] will get done away with, it [causal agent] will never again be desiring something of the patient. (Concrete act of blowing [*'ab wústad*, "to blow against it"] reference, text 45, pt. A.)

   b. Look, he [curer] will whip him with it [creosote bush], but strongly. He [curer] will not go easily on it. Look, and that will scare it [causal agent]. (Cure for whirlwind sickness reference, tape 2.11.)

The second manner of speaking (2) conforms with our interpretation of prayerfulness. The first example (1) expresses a different principle, in which the fetish itself is endowed with curative strength. We have not pursued the problem resulting from this principle with Gregorio: how the task of expelling an intrusive strength from the patient is accomplished by what appears to be the addition of more of the same kind of strength. If the patient is afflicted with ocean strength, how does he benefit from an infusion of strength from an ocean fetish?

We conclude that blowing and the use of fetishes can be prayerful in the manner of singing. It is possible that the prayerful rationale covers all activity performed during maximal cures and the nonprayerful rationale applies to the minimal cures, for in the latter case curers act directly on strength.

TEXT 45 (Tape 9.4)

A

. . .Pégi, kutp hékid ’am o ’e-’á: g ñé’ij,
. . .Well, and whenever there will get told the its song,
. . .Well, and when it’s [object’s] song gets pronounced,

k ’am hékid o ’i kú:gidk, ’ab o wúso.
and there whenever will end, against-it will blow.
and when it [singing] finishes, they [singers]
will blow on him [patient].

T hég a wépo o tá:hadagk
That-one similarly will stimulate
It [the blowing] feels as if

mat ṣ gm hú si wá:p, hégai
ss deeply really enters, that-one
it really penetrates in him [patient]

mat ’ab o wústaḍ, hégai.
ss against-it will blow, that-one.
when he [curer] blows on him.

Ñé:, hab másma ’am hab o ’e-’élidad,
Look, thus there will get intended,
Look, in this manner it [causal agent] will be thinking,

koi, mat ’im hú hab o ’i ’e-jú: ’ab ’ámjeḍ,
uh, ss away will get done about it,
uh, so that it [strength?] will get done away with,

pi 'am hú hab o tá:ccudad há'icu g hémajkam.
not ever will be desiring something the person.
it [causal agent] will never again be desiring something of the person.

B

Ñé:, há'icu hab wuḍ hí jíawul,
Look, something is on the other hand devil,
Look, something [for example] is the devil [ritual cure],

ñ-hab másma 'ep ká:, 'é:p,
I thus also hear, also,
[and] as I have heard,

báhij 'at o bék
its tail will get
he [curer] will get its [horse's or cow's] tail [for a fetish]

matp hékid wuḍ o 'i hégaik,
ss whenever will be that-one,
when it is the time [to do a devil cure],

('o pi hab o 'e-jú:).
(or will not get done).
(or perhaps he won't do it).

K 'am o hímk, 'am o hímk,
And there will go, there will go,
And it [singing] will go on and on,

k 'am hú hébai wuḍ o 'i kú:gajk
and eventually sometime will be its end
and then sometime at the end of it

mat 'am o 'i kú:gt.
ss there will end.
when it [singing] will end.

Ñé:,	'an 'ép o hékaj,	ṣa géwĭta	hégai,	'an wúsotk.
Look,	there also will use,	slightly will whip	that-one,	there blows.

Look, then he [curer] will use it, he will whip him after blowing on him.

K hég	a wépo	o 'e-jú:
And that-one	similarly	will get done

And likewise it [causal agent] does

matṣ gm hú	hab si 'e-jú:,	hégai.
ss away	gets done,	that-one.

that it [causal agent] gets done away with.

Ñé:,	b 'o másma	hab 'e-wúa,	'í:da,
Look,	thus	happens,	this-one,

Look, this is how it happens,

c 'am 'as wóhocud	hégai,	g 'e-cú'ijig
and there is made to believe	that-one,	the its own consequence

and then it [causal agent] believes it [the sickness] is its own doing

mat hékid	'am o 'e-'á:,	abṣ cem háscu
ss whenever	there will get told,	just whatever

when anything [kind of song] gets pronounced

matp háscu	wuḍ o 'i má:s	dúakamk	'ámjeḍam,	hégai,
ss whatever	will appear	animal	from thing,	that-one,

whatever kind of animal it will be from,

hémho a mat 'am a hás	o 'e-tá:t,
necessarily ss there somehow	will get sensed,

it [causal agent] will always feel in some manner,

'am káiok	g 'e-ñé'i.
there hears	the its own song.

upon hearing its song.

Ñé:, há'ap o másma.
Look, that-way thus.
Look, that's how it is.

Text 46 provides further information on the nature of curative blowing and on the relationship between blowing and singing within the total plan of a curing ritual. The ritual under consideration is the scalp bundle curing ritual, in which each member of the group of singers takes a turn blowing smoke onto the patient. The same cigarette is passed from one person to the next. The rounds of curative blowing take place after the completion of each of several phases of singing. Gregorio explains that the number of cigarettes needed for the entire ritual is determined by the number of singers as well as by the number of songs they know. If the group is large and the singers know many songs, then many cigarettes will be consumed in blowings.

From this explanation it seems clear that the ritual curers' blowing has no connection with the charisma of the blower. All singers blow at certain times, as if to punctuate the cycles of songs. We hypothesize – although Gregorio has not affirmed our hypothesis – that the efficacy of curative blowing derives from the nature of the tobacco smoke and not from the breath or heart of the blower.

TEXT 46 (Tape 17.7)

'Í:da mam hab 'á:g, "kú:kpĭ wúsosig,"
This-one ss you tell, "enclosed thing ritual cure,"
This one, which you call, "scalp bundle cure,"

hab másma hab 'e-wúa
thus happens
it happens like this

matp hé'ekia o 'i 'e-ná:to g 'ó:wick,
ss several will get made the cigarette,
that a number of cigarettes get made,

pégi, k 'am o cú:cca, 'am há'icu 'i 'éḍa,
well, and there will stand, there something inside it,
well, and he [curer] will stand them inside of something [e.g., can],

'o 'am abṣ o tóa.
or there just will lay.
or just lay them someplace.

Pégi, k hab 'ẹ-wúa
Well, and happens
Well, and it happens

matp hékid 'am o 'ái g wúsosig
ss whenever there will reach the ritual cure
when it will be time for the curing ritual

matp hé'ekia wuḍ o 'ik,
ss several will be,
if there will be several [curers],

pégi, t 'am héma o méhi, g ha-mó'o 'ám dá:kam.
well, there one of them will light it, the their head there sitting one.
well, then he who sits at the head of them will light one.

'Am gí'iko o si wúso,
There four-times will blow,
He will blow four times,

'am o wústaḍ hég óiḍk, hégai múmkudam,
there will blow that-one along, that-one sick-one,
he will blow along the [body of the] sick person,

ñé:, k 'am o 'i dágǐto,
look, and there will drop it,
look, then he will quit,

t 'an bá'ic 'i dá:kam, héma 'é:p,
there next sitting-one, one of them also,
then the one sitting in line will do it,

b aṣ 'i másma 'am o 'i hí:.
thus there will go.
thus it [the cure] goes.

. . .Kutp hébai o ’i húhug,
. . .And sometimes will stop,
. . .And whenever it [cigarette] is used up,

kói o wé:sijc wústan,
not yet will be everything and blows,
and not everybody has blown yet,

kut ’am héma ’ep o méhi, hégai,
and there one of them also will light it, that-one,
and then he [curer] will light another one,

ñé:, b o ’e-júñhimk.
look, it will be getting done.
look, it will be going on.

Kutp hab o cú’igk
And will be
And it may be

matp hab o cú’igk
ss will be
if it is the case

matp o mú’i s-má:ckad, hégai
ss will many know, that-one
if he [curer] knows many [songs]

matp héḍa’i ’am o ha-ñé’icul. . . ,
ss whoever there will be singing them for it. . . ,
whoever will be singing the [songs] for it. . . ,

pégi, t ’am o a ’i dágĭto. . . .
well, there will drop it. . . .
well, then [after all the songs are finished] they will quit. . . .

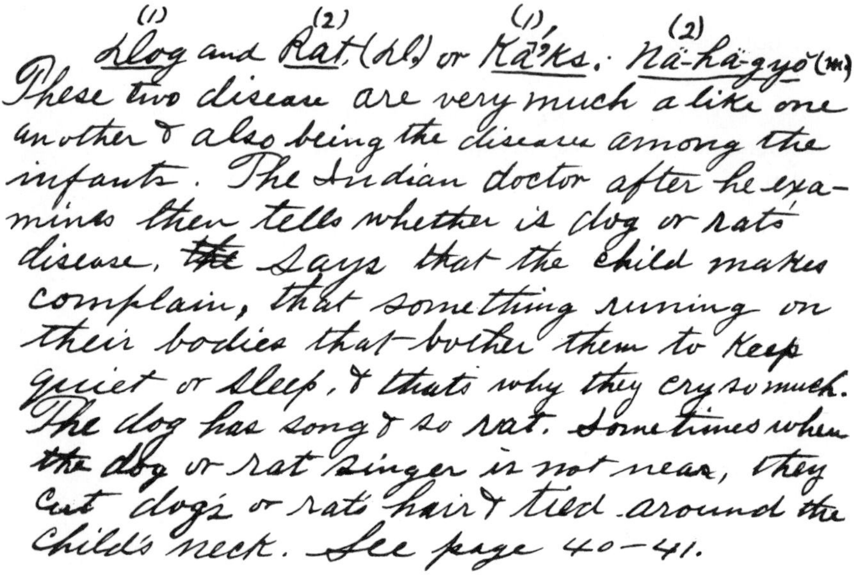

Dog[1] and Rat[2], (Dl.) or Kä'ks[1]: Nä-hä-gyo[2] (m.)
These two disease are very much a like one another & also being the disease among the infants. The Indian doctor after he examins then tells whether is dog or rats disease, ~~the~~ says that the child makes complain, that something running on their bodies that bother them to keep quiet or sleep, & thats why they cry so much. The dog has song & so rat. Sometimes when ~~the~~ dog or rat singer is not near, they cut dogs or rats hair & tied around the child's neck. See page 40–41.

Resorting to the minimal level of cure when a singer is not available. José Lewis Brennan holograph, 1897.

(Courtesy Smithsonian Institution, J.N.B. Hewitt, Collector.)

7. Concluding Remarks on Rationale for Ritual Cure

The patient's quest for a level of curing commensurate with his needs has set the theme for part IV. We demonstrated the necessity for the maximal level of cure and we studied to whom the cures are addressed and how the actions involved in the cure may be construed as prayers.

Our first texts on the levels of curing, texts 38 and 39, demonstrated that the minimal level may be insufficient to permanently rid a patient of a sickness. The most extensive curing ritual, involving the services of *s-wúsos 'ó'odham*, may be required to persuade the causal agent to cease sickening a patient.

Our final text, 47, returns to the minimal cure, this time in order to make quite a simple statement. People may be cured simply by the use of a fetish, and they may resort to this if the proper kind of singer cannot be found. This text, concerning the level of cure which excludes singing, contains a clear account of the nonprayerful use of blowing and fetishes. In effect, the text states a point of view on curing in opposition to the main theme of our discussion. It allows that the elaborately prayerful curing rituals may be forgone in favor of simpler, more direct techniques – techniques analogous to those by which the shaman intervenes directly on strengths. (See pt. III, sec. 6.) Analogous to the shaman's intervention which succeeds only if the causal agent permits it, these pressings and blowings are presumably only sometimes adequate.

TEXT 47 (Tape 12.5)

A

. . .Kut hékid	mat hab o cú'igk
. . .And whenever	ss will be

. . .And if it should be the case

mat pi 'in hú	o míak,	hégai	ñé'edam,
ss never	will be close,	that-one	singer,

that the singer should be inaccessible,

kutp háscu wuḍ o'ik,
and whatever will be,

and [no matter] whatever kind of thing it [sickness] will be,

k 'am a háscu 'á'ap'et, 'ab 'ámjeḍ hégai.
and there whatever is proper, about it that-one.
there will [still] be something proper to do about it.

. . .C 'í:da hab cú'ig, hab másma há'icu
. . .And this-one is, thus something
. . .And this [alternative] is something

mat pi 'an hú wo míak,
ss never will be close,
if he [a singer] is inaccessible,

pégi, kc 'atp g 'íagta 'an o há'icugk,
well, and the fetish there will be present,
well, and there will be a fetish,

pégi, t heg hékaj abṣ o dágĭtpa c o wústan.
well, that-one by means of just will press and blow.
well, and one will just press it on him and blow on him.

B

Ñé:, 'am o há'icu si táṣo hab cú'ig,
Look, there something very clearly is,
Look, there is something very clear [as an example about fetishes],

hab 'ep másma
also is thus
it is thus

mo 'in hú há'icu 'e-béb'e, 'in hú ge sú:dagĭ t 'án.
ss there away something gets gotten, there away the ocean at.
that something [a fetish] gets taken [from] there at the ocean.

Pégi, kc hab 'e-wúa hab másma
Well, and happens thus
Well, and thus it is done

mat heg hékaj abṣ o 'e-dágĭtpa
ss that-one by means of just will get pressed
by means of it [fetish], he [patient's body] gets pressed

mat pi 'am hú o ha-ñé'ikad, hégai.
ss never will be singing, that-one.
if there won't be any singing.

Hí o a wúso,
Of course will blow [cure?],
Of course he will blow [cure him?],

t g gm hú o a wá:
deeply will enter
it [strength from the fetish?] will enter deeply [into the patient]

mo hég 'ámjeḍ 'an dágĭtpag,
ss that-one from there presses,
for that purpose he presses it,

gm hú hab 'i wúa
away does
it [curative strength?] does away with it [strength of sickness?]

mat hég gm hú o wá:.
ss that-one deeply will enter.
if it enters deeply into him.

Pégi, k hég o cé:mo, hégai cú:kug,
Well, and that-one will permeate, that-one meat,
Well, and it [curative strength?] permeates the flesh,

ñé:, k 'am o a 'áp'et, hégai.
look, and there will be-good-for-it, that-one.
look, and it will help him.

C

Cem háscu hab cú'ig
Just whatever is
Just anything [fetish] is like that

mat pi 'in hú o há'icukad g ñé'ikam,
ss never will be present the singer,
if the singer is not accessible,

pégi, t abṣ o wústan,
well, just will blow [cure?],
well, he [curer] will just blow [cure him?],

k heg hékaj o dágĭtpa,
and that-one by means of will press,
and by means of it [fetish] he will press it,

"'íagta," b 'o 'á'aga, hégai. . . .
"fetish," calls it, that-one. . . .
"fetish," it is called. . . .

PART V

PIMAN SHAMANISM AND *KÁ:CIM* SICKNESS

Ever since the missionary began to work here, these medicine men have been an annoyance and a hindrance to his work, but they have inevitably turned out badly.

. . . they . . . have done more to destroy the efforts of Indian agents to improve the condition of the Indian, both in school-work and in moral elevation, than all the other undermining and checking influences combined. . . . the Indians crave excitement and amusement. Since the hunt and chase are things of the past, a substitute of some kind is required.

Among the Pimas or the Mission to the Pima and Maricopa Indians,
Ladies Union Mission School Association, 1893

An Overview

Piman sicknesses

In this study our basic orientation has been the assumption of the existence of a Piman general theory on sickness. Throughout the study we have sought factors common to *ká:cim* sicknesses. When we were concerned with differences, this concern typically involved contrasting *ká:cim* sicknesses with other kinds of afflictions. We have not studied how the *ká:cim* differ from each other.

We stated the *ká:cim* are at the core of Piman thinking on sickness. An examination of the Appendix will show that the core is variegated and not uniform. This variegated core remains to be studied as do the many afflictions we relegated to the periphery because they are not *ká:cim* sicknesses. The latter are no less interesting for the fact that they are not *ká:cim* sicknesses.

Two scenes of action

Before making this study we had assumed shamans were exclusively concerned with spirits. This was the stress of the literature. Eliade, for example, defines no other shamanic geography except that consisting of the three cosmological zones: this world, the spiritual world above, and the spiritual world below. It was understood that shamans are unique in being able to move between this world and one or both of the spiritual worlds (1964).

Gregorio's shamanism appears uniquely sedentary and this-worldly. Rather than journeying between cosmological realms the Piman shaman concentrates on things that are inside the patient. Spirits help him, but only as the ultimate means for solving the problem within the patient.

We suggest considering the patient's body and the spiritual realms as alternate fields of action for future comparisons of shamanic curing. In this manner it may be found that the body has more theoretical import than had been previously thought.*

We are aware of only one example in the literature where the shaman's concern with the patient's body was shown logically and practically to preclude his involvement with the cosmological zones as defined by Eliade.

*Certainly intrusive object theories of sickness are widespread. The problem lies in relating those objects which intrude into the body with entities in the landscape of the spirits.

This example is from the Cuna (Levi-Strauss 1967). The Cuna shaman makes a spiritual journey to be sure, but the place to which he journeys is inside the patient's body rather than out-of-doors into the darkness (Piman landscape of the spirits), the sky, or the underworld.

The Cuna example is interesting because although the shaman's itinerary includes the obstacles and fights typical of spiritual adventures, these things take place inside the patient rather than somewhere beyond. From the Piman perspective we think Cuna shamanism would seem comprehensible because of the interest in the patient's body, but it would perhaps also seem strangely spectacular due to the claim that the shaman's spirit actually enters the body.

Toward a Piman literature for Pimans

We are moving toward a Piman literature on two fronts. The first is in the area of defining ideas crucial to the topical area of sickness. The second is in understanding the Piman language and, more specifically, in understanding how the language may be written.

At present, the progress on both fronts largely has been motivated and evaluated by non-Pimans. Hale taught linguistics to Alvarez because Hale believes the interests of linguistics will best be served by training native speakers to analyze their language. In this study, Bahr asked Gregorio about sickness for analogous reasons.

In each case an outside science – linguistics or the anthropology of religions – has been placed at the disposal of Pimans in the hope they would apply its vocabulary and methods to Piman culture. It may be expected that greater adversity is in store for the science of sickness because the Piman theory of sickness, as we now know it, includes beliefs whose truth will be disputed by Western European doctrine.

We have seen how Gregorio dealt with this problem by explicitly confining the application of Piman theory to the Piman race. Thus he reserves a special place for Piman sicknesses, afflictions that Pimans and only Pimans have over and above all the world's other afflictions. Gregorio's theory implies that *ká:cim* sicknesses are exempt from, or have little to do with, the physical processes accepted by Western European medicine. Therefore, Gregorio is interested in the foreign type of sickness, the wandering sicknesses, precisely because they are so unlike the *ká:cim*. In effect the whole of Western European germ theory provides a background of comic relief against which the undisputed qualities of *ká:cim* sickness can better be illuminated.

We conclude that the Piman theory of sickness is not emerging into existence and seeking a tenable position vis-à-vis the other schools of "outside science." The Piman theory does exist and it has a tenable position. We hope this position will be clarified through further study and that these studies soon will be written by Pimans.

APPENDIX

LIST OF *KÁ:CIM* SICKNESSES

The following alphabetical list summarizes the reported facts concerning the infringements, symptoms, and ritual cures of *ká:cim* sicknesses. Sources are coded as follows:

(G) Gregorio (1972)
(R) Russell (1908)
(U) Underhill (1946)
(B) José Lewis Brennan (1897)

DANGEROUS OBJECT	WRONGFUL ACTION	SYMPTOMS	MINIMAL LEVEL CURE	MAXIMAL LEVEL CURE
Badger	(G) 1. Children bothering its hole, e.g., by sticking their hands in it 2. Killing it 3. Some Pimans (of another dialect group) are said to eat badgers; therefore, they frequently are afflicted with the sickness	(G) Throat swells; in severe cases, demanding maximal cure, entire body swells	(G) Pressing front paw or tail onto patient's neck	
		(R) "Severe throat disease"	(R) Pressing tail on neck	(R) Songs, p. 321
Bear	(G) 1. Stepping on tracks 2. Stepping on feces	(G) Legs swell.		
	(R) One killing a bear without first saying "I'm red," he gets the sickness	(R) 1. Swellings on body 2. Headache 3. Fever	(R) No part of the animal is used in treatment (therefore no minimal level of curing?)	(R) Bear songs, p. 318
Bee	(G) Parent of unborn child eating too much honey	(G) Sores in ears of baby or child	(G) Putting honey in ears	(G) No songs (therefore no maximal level of curing?)
Butterfly	(G) Parent of unborn child killing or injuring it	(G) Only sickens babies and children	(G) Pressing body with butterfly images cut from paper	
		(R) Internal pains	(R) Pressing body with butterfly images made from deer skin.	(R) Songs, p. 205

		(U) Babies have diarrhea and sleeping spells	(U) Pressing body with painted image made from cactus rib	(U) Songs
Buzzard	(G) 1. Anyone killing it 2. Picking up feathers 3. Disturbing corpse of buzzard	(G) Sores all over head		
	(R) Parent of unborn child eating dead animal	(R) 1. Sores, e.g., syphilis 2. Babies have sore eyes	(R) Passing wing feathers over patient	(R) Songs
	(U) Buzzard eating some of a hunter's kill while hunter's wife is pregnant	(U) Children have sores	(U) Using buzzard wing feathers	(U) Songs
Cat		(G) Mucus comes from mouth of baby or child	(G) Wiping mouth of cat, then wipe mouth of patient	(G) No songs (therefore no maximal level of curing)
Cow	(G) 1. Parent of unborn child looking at a dying cow during slaughter of the animal for a fiesta 2. Anyone slaughtering a cow for a fiesta failing to pray properly	(G) 1. Mucus runs from mouth of child 2. Symptoms of adults not described	(G) Sweeping over patients body with cow tail	(G) Songs
	(U) Parent of unborn child tormenting a cow	(U) Fever afflicts infants	(U) Using braided cow tail	(U) Songs

DANGEROUS OBJECT	WRONGFUL ACTION	SYMPTOMS	MINIMAL LEVEL CURE	MAXIMAL LEVEL CURE
Coyote	(G) 1. Anyone eating melon which a coyote has bitten into 2. Anyone killing a coyote		(G) 1. Wrapping coyote feces in bundle, boiling the bundle, then pressing onto patient's body 2. Sweeping over patient's body with coyote tail	(G) Songs
	(R) Parent of unborn child eating melon that coyote has bitten into	(R) Dysentery or blistered tongue afflicts babies	(R) Swinging coyote tail over child	(R) Songs, p. 316
		(U) Itching	(U) Using coyote tail	(U) Songs, p. 289
Deer	(G) 1. Anyone choking while eating deer meat 2. Anyone killing deer in a cruel manner 3. Parent of unborn child killing deer	(G) Afflicts head and neck	(G) Swallowing ashes	(G) 1. *Mé'ijida wúsosig,* "killing it for somebody ritual cure"; A deer is killed and its meat is boiled (without salt) on the patient's behalf; ritual curers eat the meat; the patient and his family do not eat it 2. Use of head and tail as fetishes 3. Songs and dancing

		(R) Diseases of throat and lungs	(R) Pressing tail on patient’s body	(R) Songs, p. 317
	(U) Anyone eating too much deer fat	(U) Coughing (tuberculosis)	(U) 1. Swallowing ashes 2. Pressing tail	(U) Ritual cure described, p. 290
		(B) 1. Sores in throat 2. Swelling of face 3. Worms in ears	(B) Using deer tail	(B) Songs
Devil	(G) Succumbing to devil’s temptation in dreams: devil offers skills at cowboy work to men and skills at making horsehair baskets to women	(G) 1. “Loss of mind,” *gmhú hab wúa g cégĭto’idag* 2. Forgetfulness 3. Seeing things and hearing things that are not there 4. Being bucked by horse 5. Being kicked by horse	(G) Using cow or horse tail	(G) Songs
		(R) Being bucked by horse	(R) Swinging pair of crossed sticks over patient	(R) Songs, p. 329
		(U) Insanity	(U) No fetish	(U) Songs, p. 292
		(B) Pains in the body, especially the heart, caused by intrusive presence of horsehair in heart	(B) 1. Removal of hair by shaman 2. Horse tail fetish	(B) Songs

DANGEROUS OBJECT	WRONGFUL ACTION	SYMPTOMS	MINIMAL LEVEL CURE	MAXIMAL LEVEL CURE
Dog	(G) Parent of unborn child does not pity or defer to pet dog	(G) Hotness in heart afflicts babies and children	(G) 1. Pressing body hair of dog onto patient's body 2. Wiping mouth of dog and then wiping mouth of patient	
		(R) Children become fretful	(R) Tying dog whiskers to a stick and swaying over patient	(R) Songs, p. 315
		(B) Babies or children become fretful and feel as if something is crawling all over their bodies	(B) Tying hair from dog around child's neck	(B) Songs
Eagle	(G) 1. Anyone killing an eagle 2. Picking up feathers	(G) 1. Itchy head 2. Lice		
		(R) Lice	(R) 1. Blowing smoke over head of patient 2. Passing eagle down over patient	(R) Songs, p. 289
	(U) Failure to observe taboos connected with killing an eagle	(U) 1. Nosebleed 2. Lice	(U) Using eagle down fetish	

Enemy: *'ó:b* (things associated with)*	1. Wrongful actions during ritual purification: a. failure of man to remain in seclusion b. Pollution by menstruating woman	1. a. Blood in urine of enemy killer b. Pains in stomach of enemy killer or of member of his family who failed to observe ritual restrictions	Fetishes include: scalp, sticks with red and blue feathers, white clay	1. *'Ó:b cu ŋig wúsosig*, "enemy consequence ritual cure"; Person who knows war orations must recite them over patient; may be done in daytime
	2. Failure to feed or show proper respect for scalp bundle.	2. a. Bundle owner's wife is seduced by spirit of bundle; she loses her mind b. Bundle owner is seduced by female spirit associated with bundle c. Bundle owner is pestered by spirit of bundle; it tickles his feet d. Bundle owner's family is pestered by spirit of bundle; it makes noises and breaks things around the house		2. *Kú:kpĭ wúsosig* (also called *kúmuda*), "scalp bundle ritual cure"; Singing of scalp bundle songs at night

*Each source has mentioned aspects of the sickness(es) associated with enemies. We have summarized them here without attempt to distinguish between the nomenclature used by the various sources.

DANGEROUS OBJECT	WRONGFUL ACTION	SYMPTOMS	MINIMAL LEVEL CURE	MAXIMAL LEVEL CURE
Fly		(G) Babies and children have sores all over head	(G) Curer putting burning coals in mouth and chewing them; then rubbing his hands in front of him, then behind him (like a fly); then spitting onto child's head	(G) No songs (therefore no maximal level cure)
			(U) Rubbing black (not red) embers between hands, then chewing powder, then putting on the sore	(U) Songs, p. 291
Frog [Gregorio denies that frogs are dangerous. He says they are good-natured animals and naturally allied with mankind in loving the rain. One of Gregorio's nicknames is "Frog."]		(U) Sores on body	(U) Wooden image	(U) Songs, p. 290

Gila Monster	(G) Anyone touching, killing, or looking at a gila monster in an unduly curious manner			
	(R) Parent of unborn child killing it	(R) Baby's body becomes red and feverish	(R) Pressing carved image onto patient	(R) Songs, p. 307
	(U) 1. Anyone stepping on it 2. A nursing mother crossing its path	(U) 1. Sore feet 2. Sores all over body	(U) 1. Catching gila monster and tying red rag around its neck, then sending it away 2. Using carved image with red cloth tied around neck	(U) Songs, p. 291
Gopher			(G) Pressing with gopher "diggings"	(G) Songs
		(R) Stomach trouble, particularly children	(R) Pressing with diggings; pressing with deerskin bundle containing eagle down and sticks gnawed by gopher	(R) Songs, p. 319-20
	(U) Women sitting on gopher hill	(U) Menstrual cramps	(U) Using gopher skin on image made from diggings	(U) Song, p. 292

DANGEROUS OBJECT	WRONGFUL ACTION	SYMPTOMS	MINIMAL LEVEL CURE	MAXIMAL LEVEL CURE
Hawk	(G) Anyone eating chicken eggs which hawk has pecked	(G) Nose bleed		
		(R) Hemorrhage	(R) Passing wing feathers over patient	(R) Songs
Horned Toad	(G) Anyone killing or injuring a horned toad	(G) Pains or swelling in feet, legs, hands, back		
	(R) Anyone stepping on one may take immediate remedy: tie red string around its neck and tell the animal, "Eat my blood"	(R) 1. Rheumatism 2. Hunchback	(R) Pressing carved image onto patient	(R) Songs, p. 307
	(U) Anyone stepping on one	(U) Sores on feet	(U) 1. Wooden image 2. Catching live toad, tying red cloth around neck, and releasing it	(U) Songs, p. 293

Húidam: an invisible, two-headed snake that lives underground and can fly for long distances	(G) Anyone cutting it in half while plowing		(G) Curer making stick from tree root, putting stick in his own throat, and then pressing stick onto patient	
		(R) Disease of the throat (Assuming that R's *wheita* is identical with G's *huidam*).	(R) Curer making stick from mesquite root, thrusting it down patient's throat and then pressing it over patient's heart	
Jimsonweed	(G) Anyone touching flowers	(G) 1. Loss of mind 2. Dizziness 3. Sleepiness	(G) Using images of flowers	(G) Songs
Lightning: *wúihom*	(G) Anyone using firewood from a tree which has been struck by lightning	(G) Heat in wrists	(G) Using flint arrow points or bits of lightning-struck tree	(G) Songs
	(B) Anyone using firewood from tree which has been struck by lightning	(B) Open sores, swelling, appearance of having been scorched		(B) Songs

DANGEROUS OBJECT	WRONGFUL ACTION	SYMPTOMS	MINIMAL LEVEL CURE	MAXIMAL LEVEL CURE
Lizard: *cúsukal*	(G) Parent of unborn child or anyone accidentally hitting a lizard with an axe – it lives around woodpile	(G) Whitening of parent's skin or of child's skin		
		(R) Fever in children	(R) 1. Pressing body with image of lizard 2. Killing lizard and rubbing fat on patient's body	(R) Songs, p. 308
Lizard: *jénaṣat* (Also identified by Underhill as "lizard weed," a narcotic plant.)	(G) Anyone stepping on it (It lives among rocks on mountains)			
Mouse	(G) 1. Parent of unborn child eating food which a mouse has gnawed 2. Parent killing or stepping on it	(G) Only afflicts babies and children		

		(R) Children have constipation	(R) Pressing mouse tail on patient's body	(R) Songs, p. 314
		(B) Child feels as if something is running on his body, therefore, cannot sleep	(B) Tying mouse hair around child's neck	
Owl	(G) Succumbing to temptation during dreams in which ghosts appear	(G) Adults or children become sleepy		
		(R) Trances and fits	(R) Swinging owl feathers over patient	(R) Songs, p. 311
		(U) 1. Sleepiness 2. Dizziness 3. "Heart Shaking"	(U) Using owl down	(U) Songs, p. 294
Peyote: *Pihuri*	(U) Anyone getting too close to a little old man (perhaps the personification of peyote)	(U) Trachoma and other eye problems	(U) No fetish	(U) Songs, p. 296
				(R) Songs
Quail	(G) Failure to wash hands after eating quail eggs	(G) Sore eyes		
		(U) Sore eyes	(U) Using topknot for fetish	(U) Songs, p. 294

DANGEROUS OBJECT	WRONGFUL ACTION	SYMPTOMS	MINIMAL LEVEL CURE	MAXIMAL LEVEL CURE
Rabbit	(G) 1. Anyone killing a rabbit and picking it up before it is dead 2. Parent of unborn child killing a rabbit or looking at one while it is dying	(G) 1. Symptoms of adults not described 2. Children: a. Inability to urinate or defecate b. Blisters on skin	(G) Using rabbit tail tied to stick	*Mé'ijida wúsosig* (see deer sickness)
		(R) Open sores	(R) Using tail and whiskers	(R) Songs, p. 314
	(U) Parent of unborn child killing a rabbit	(U) Children have convulsions	(U) Using tail	(U) Song, p. 294
Roadrunner		(U) Pains in side	(U) Using ironwood splinters	
				(R) Songs, p. 312
Saint	(G) Failure to baptize a newly acquired saint's image	(G) Loss of mind		(G) Give a public fiesta with Catholic prayers
Snake (specifically, rattlesnake)	(G) Parent of unborn child or anyone looking at a snake in offensive way, or killing it, or stepping in its tracks			

	(R) Stepping on tracks	(R) Children have kidney or stomach trouble	(R) Pressing body with carved images	(R) Songs, p. 309
	(U) Stepping over tracks		(U) Using carved image (B) Using carved image	(U) Song, p. 294
Squirrel		(R) Nose bleed		
Turtle	(G) 1. Thoughtless killing, etc. 2. Anyone failing to be polite	(G) Pain in chest		
		(R) 1. Sores on body 2. Crippled legs	(R) Using turtle shell rattle	(R) Songs, p. 306
		(U) Sores on feet	(U) Using turtle shell rattle	(U) Songs, p. 295
Water (ocean)	(G) Failing to properly purify salt-getters and their salt	(G) Diarrhea: sensation of water in stomach and vomiting salty water	(G) Pressing fossilized sea foam brought from ocean on patient's body	(G) Recitation of ritual orations, named *hámbḍho*
		(B) Vomiting and coughing salt water		(B) Songs, named *hew-pitco-lita*

DANGEROUS OBJECT	WRONGFUL ACTION	SYMPTOMS	MINIMAL LEVEL CURE	MAXIMAL LEVEL CURE
Whore	(G) Succumbing to temptation in dreams	(G) 1. Loss of mind 2. Inability to see properly 3. Pain in legs	(G) Using male and female dolls	(G) Songs
		(U) Lovesickness	(U) Using female doll made from clay	(U) Songs, p. 300
*Wí:gita**	(G) Failing to maintain ritual constraints concerning food or effigies	(G) Swelling of joints (arthritis)		(G) (R) (U) (B) Performance of miniature ritual on patient's behalf
		(R) 1. Swollen knee 2. Enflamed eyes		
Wind	(G) Anyone running into a whirlwind	(G) Pains in legs or back caused by stones blown in by wind	(G) Whipping patient with greasewood	(G) *'O'ohon k'e-wúso,* "draw and get cured" ritual involving sand paintings
		(R) Pains in legs	(R) Rubbing limbs with ocotillo gum	(R) Songs, p. 324
		(U) Dizziness		(U) Songs

*We have classified Russell's "sun," and Brennan's "stone" and "sun" under *wí:gita*, assuming they refer to artifacts used in the ritual; however, this may not be the case.

Notes

Part II, section 1

1. An estimate of the number of practicing Piman shamans: During Gregorio's lifetime, approximately five hundred Papagos made their home in Gregorio's village of Santa Rosa, Arizona. There were four practicing shamans in that village. This provides a ratio of approximately one shaman per hundred people. In Arizona there are at least fifteen thousand Pimans who make use of Piman shamans. This would provide a total of one hundred and fifty shamans.

Part II, section 2

2. Not all Piman rituals are dangerous. The following ones are:

   1. Prayer stick festival, *wí:gita*, resulting in *wí:gita múmkidag, wí:gita* sickness.
   2. Hunting ritual, *má'amaga*, resulting in *húawi múmkidag*, deer sickness.
   3. Eagle killing purification, *bá'ag 'á'an wúsosig*, resulting in eagle sickness, *bá'ag múmkidag.*
   4. Enemy slayer purification, *síakam wúsosig*, resulting in enemy consequence sickness, *'ó:b cú'ijig múmkidag.*
   5. Salt purification, *'ón wúsosig*, resulting in ocean consequence sickness, *sú:dagǐ cú'ijig múmkidag.*
   6. Saint's image purification, *sá:nto 'ó'ohon wúsosig*, resulting in saint sickness, *sá:nto múmkidag.*

People are afflicted with these sicknesses through looking at, coming too close to, or touching things which are used at the rituals, such as effigies, food, and the inedible parts of butchered animals.

Three of the above ritual sicknesses – deer, eagle, and saint – may be obtained outside of ritual situations. For example, deer sickness may be contracted whenever a deer is killed improperly or from misbehavior at a hunting ritual.

Two other sicknesses from the list, enemy and ocean, can only be contracted from misbehavior during ritual. In principle these rituals include all the occasions during which Pimans come into contact with enemies or the ocean. Thus, these two sicknesses derive from Piman contact with natural objects in the same way as do the first three ritual sicknesses, but they constitute a special case in which the natural objects can only be dealt with in ceremonial or sacralized ways.

Finally, in the case of *wí:gita* we have a sickness for which the dangerous objects are artificial – things produced by people – as opposed to natural. The occasions for becoming afflicted with this sickness are thus confined to the performance of the ritual.

We cannot explain why some dangerous things are encountered only under ritual situations while most others are encountered nonritually, simply during the ordinary course of affairs. Gregorio stated that the former things are dangerous because they were intended to be used by humanity, and the sickness results from improper use; the opposite is true for at least some of the latter. They are dangerous because they should be left alone by humanity. These sicknesses result from deliberate or accidental transgression upon their person or property.

3. Texts on staying and wandering sicknesses.

TEXT 48 (Tape 15.6)

Q

Hás wuḍ 'á:ga, "ká:cim múmkidag"?
Somehow means, "staying sickness"?
What is the meaning of "ká:cim múmkidag"?

A

Ñé:, hab o másma hab 'e-'á'aga há'icu
Look, thus gets told something
Look, something is called like that

m 'ab hé̜'ekia há'icu wuḍ 'i t-múmkidag,
ss several something is our sickness,
of the diversity of our sicknesses,

c pi hébai 'óimmeḍ,
and not someplace wanders,
and it never wanders,

c 'an hab abṣ 'i hég 'éḍa
and there just here that-one in
and it is just right here

mo hébai 'ab míabidc g hémajkam.
ss sometimes against approaches the person.
whenever it is close to the people.

B

Ñé:, mant 'am há'icu hab o 'á: si táṣo,
Look, ss I there something will tell very clearly,
Look, I will explain something clearly,

mo gn hú hía cem wó'o g ṣú:dagĭ,
ss distantly of course just lies the water,
which is that the ocean lies over there,

pégi, ñé:, hég o 'áb 'am si táṣo hab 'e-wúa há'icu
well, look, that-one is against there very clearly happens something
well, look, as for that [the ocean] something is quite apparent

m 'an hab cú'ig, c hég 'ám hab cú'ig,
ss there is, and that-one there is,
that it is there, and there it stays,

c pi hébai 'óimmeḍ.
and not someplace wanders.
and it never wanders.

'An o hab abṣ 'i cú'ig, 'á'ahid 'óidam
There just is, years during
It just stays there through the years

matp hékid 'an 'i wó'iwua, hégai.
ss whenever there lies, that-one.
for as long as it lies, that one [ocean].

C

. . .Pégi, c 'í:ya, hégai há'icu
. . .Well, and here, that-one something
. . .Well, and here there is something

m 'in 'i hé'ekia há'icu wuḍ 'i 'óimmeḍdam,
ss here several something is wandering-thing,
which is all the different animals,

pi hébai 'óiopo,
not someplace wander,
they never wander,

'í:ya 'atp a'i, hég 'éḍa hab má:s
here only, that-one in appears
here is the only place they are

m 'in hab cú'ig, 'í:na.
ss here is, here.
so they exist here.

K wépo, mañ 'ab hab si táṣo hab 'á:g
And similarly, ss I against-it very clearly tell
And similarly, as I clearly explained

matp wuḍ kí:kam múmkidag, hégai,
ss was resident sickness, that-one,
that it is for a resident sickness,

c hab 'e-wúa mo pi hébai 'óimmeḍ,
and happens ss not someplace wanders,
and it never wanders,

c hémho a mat 'ab o 'áb géi g 'ó'odham
and necessarily ss against-it will strike the Piman
and it will always strike a Piman

matp 'am hú	hás	másma	pi 'áp	o 'e-ñú:kud.
ss there ever	somehow	thus	not properly	will get cared for.

if ever he fails to take proper care of himself.

D

Ñé:,	mo 'ép g ṣómaigig	hab cú'ig,
Look,	ss also the snotness	is,

Look, the common cold is such a thing,

táṣo	hab hía	ha-wúa	mo hás	másma	hab 'e-wúa,
clearly	of course	does to them	ss somehow	thus	happens,

clearly it afflicts them, if they do something [to catch a cold],

k 'o héma	hab o ge 'élidad
and one-of-them	will just believe

and if somebody [with a cold] will just think

mat pi 'áp	o 'e-ñú:kud.
ss not properly	will get taken-care-of.

that he won't have to take good care of himself.

. . .T hí	o a 'áp'et	g 'ó'odham,
. . .Of course	will improve	the man,

. . .Of course he will get better,

'am 'ép o 'i hí:,
there again will begin,

then it will start up again,

t 'am 'ép o ṣómai	há'as hú 'áli.
there again will get snotty	a little bit later on.

then he will have a cold again after awhile.

E

. . .Ñé:,	mo 'am há'icu	'ép táṣo	maṣ há'icu	wuḍ bá'ag,
. . .Look,	ss there something	also is clear	ss something	is eagle,

. . .Look, another thing is [a] clear [analogy], which is the eagle,

c 'ía 'e-ná:to,	'í:ya,
and here got made,	here,

and it was created here,

héu'u	matp hía	hímk	hébai	kí:,
yes	ss of course	went and	someplace	lives,

yes of course it [eagles] went away and lives elsewhere,

k abṣ hab-a 'am a hás 'á:gk
but there somehow means
but there is an explanation

. . .mo 'in a 'i wúṣk'e mo wuḍ a'i 'í:ya, 'í:da.
. . .ss here emerges ss is only here, this-one.
. . .[namely] that it [eagles and their way] have their origin here and only here.

Héu'u matp hí g 'i gáwul másma
Yes, ss on the other hand differently thus
Yes, maybe it is different

. . .mo hab másma 'am 'ép hí:,
. . .ss thus there also goes,
. . .since it has gone [to live among other peoples],

k abṣ hab-a g kí:kam 'i hab má:s.
but the resident appears.
but the resident [eagle, the kind that remains with the Pimans] is like this.

F

C hég hab wuḍ ká:cim múmkidag, hégai mo pi hébai 'óimmed.
And that-one is staying sickness, that-one ss not someplace wanders.
And that's the ká:cim sickness, the one that never wanders.

TEXT 49 (Tape 15.13)

Pégi, k wóho mo hab 'e-wúa
Well, and truly ss happens
Well, and it [shaman's treatment] happens

mo 'am hás 'am 'i 'e-júccu, 'e-wí:ñhun,
ss there somehow there does, gets sucked,
that something is done to it [wandering sickness] it gets sucked,

. . .pégi, 'atp héms hab háhawa abṣ o 'e-jú:
. . .well, perhaps then will get done
. . .well, perhaps it will happen

mat 'im hú hab abṣ o 'i jú:.
ss there away just will do.
that he [shaman] will do away with it [strength].

K abṣ hab-a 'éḍa wuḍ 'óimmeḍdam,
But yet is wanderer,
But yet it is a wandering sickness,

k 'im hú bá'ic c hékĭ hú 'ab'e-ná:to,
and away beyond and long ago against-it got made,
and it was made far away and long ago,

b o 'e-júñimk, gm hú hab aṣ o 'e-mé:kod,
will be doing, away will get distant,
it will continue existing [as an epidemic sickness] for a long time,

pégi, k 'ab háhawa o ha-'áb, 'im hú bá'ic
well, and against it then will be against them, away farther
well, it will continue on to other people

mat hab o 'e-'élidad.
ss will get wished.
if it wants to.

TEXT 50

(Tape 12.13)

. . .Há'icu 'aṣ hab wuḍ híhiwdag,
. . .Something is sores,
. . .Something is small pox,

. . .pégi, t g ga hú o 'í himad.
. . .well, that-one distantly will be coming.
. . .well, it [epidemic] will be coming from far off.

'Atp 'i hú hébai héma hab o 'i 'e-jú:
Here sometimes one of them will get done
Sometimes somebody here will do something [inoculation]

mat – hégai, 'al bí:talig 'ab o 'al béi,
ss – that-one, a little of the filth against-it will a little bit get,
he will take a little of the pus,

. . .'i hébai o 'al mágkaḍ, 'í:ya.
. . .someplace will make a little hole, here.
. . .he will make a little hole here [in patient's arm].

[At this point Gregorio shifts to English.]
Right here [on the arm], I'll put that [pus].
or, if it's [the pus] dry, well, put in there [on arm],
or wet, and put it there [on arm], and rub it on.

They call it "cékidaḍad" [inoculation].
Let's see,
now wait 'til I finish.

Hab wuḍ 'á:ga
It means
It means

matp 'am hú o cem 'á'ahek,
ss there ever will try to reach it,
if it [small pox] tries to reach him [inoculated person],

pi hab másma o 'á'ahe,
not thus will reach it,
it won't get to him [seriously],

heg hékaj mo cékidaḍad.
that-one by means of ss is inoculated.
because he is inoculated.

Hí a ṣa 'al hás 'atp o 'e-jú:,
Of course slightly somehow may get done,
Of course it [sickness] may do just a little bit,

abṣ o 'áp'et, hégai,
just will get better, that-one,
but he will get well,

'o héms abṣ 'ép pi o 'ái.
or perhaps just also won't reach it.
or perhaps it won't even reach him.

The following citation from Russell shows that the Pimans have practiced inoculation for at least the last hundred years (1908:267-68). It describes the *'óimmeḍdam* sicknesses as free and relatively indiscriminate agents.

> Children are intentionally exposed to smallpox and measles, that they may have the diseases in lighter form. Smallpox was regarded as an evil spirit of which they did not dare show fear. They said 'I like smallpox', thinking that he would be thus placated. At one time they attempted inoculation from persons that had light attacks, but the experiment resulted in many deaths. From 1870 until the Government sent a physician to the agency, the missionary, Rev. C. H. Cook, supplied the Pimas with vaccine. They retained some of their old dread of the demon and continued to place the bandages with which the arm had been dressed upon a certain mesquite tree, not daring to burn them for fear of offending.

4. *Kí:dag* is an abstraction from the word *kí:*. As a verb, *kí:* means "to live" or "to reside," – as opposed to *'óimmeḍ*, "to be domiciled" or "to be staying at a place temporarily." As a noun *kí:* means "house." The English words "residence" and "society" are needed to translate the different senses of *kí:dag*. The word *kí:kam*, "resident," may designate residency in the following senses: member of a

household, resident in a village, or member of Piman society as a special species of social creatures commanded to uphold the Piman way. We understand that *kí:kam* sicknesses are those which are incumbent upon people as members of Piman society.

5. The Herzog text included in this study has been edited by Alvarez and Bahr. The coauthors have changed a portion of the transcription and the translations.

Part II, section 3

6. Gregorio has used the term *pi cú'ikodag* with reference to two different contexts. The first concerns men and women as parents and the second concerns men as the obtainers of certain raw materials which are necessary to sustain Piman society. The situations in which a person is *pi cú'ikodag* are:

   1. For men and women: during the wife's pregnancy until their child is born and given the purifying ritual.
   2. For women: having menstruated for the first time.
   3. For men: having killed an enemy (as opposed to a fellow Piman), having captured and taken feathers from an eagle or having brought salt from the ocean. These three activities only apply to men and only on the condition that they are not *pi cú'ikodag* on the grounds described in 1. Furthermore, Gregorio has spoken of them as activities which men should do, for the first time at least, before they get married. For example, married men are prohibited from becoming "enemy killers" in the mock battles which presently substitute for actual warfare. Broadly speaking, then, these three activities serve to initiate boys into their roles as men who will father children and who will take from nature the things necessary to sustain Piman society. The regime of *pi cú'ikodag* precludes a man from doing both things simultaneously.
   4. For men: having supervised or participated in a ritual called *wí:gita.* We distinguish this ritual from the rites of passage into manhood grouped under 3 on the shallow grounds that: (a) it does not involve an arduous journey by young men in pursuit of commodities belonging to an alien locale – the land of the enemies, the ocean, or the sky – and (b) it is a harvest ritual. The ritual concerns the maintenance of human lives, however, and adolescent girls and boys have roles in the ritual. The myths commemorated by it refer to the sacrifice of children in a spring (Underhill's "northern version") and children being swallowed by an aquatic monster (the "southern version").

7. The best documentation of the techniques and mood of sorcery consists of Russell's Piman-English texts of war orations. These texts describe sorcery in the sense of incapacitating enemies, giving numerous examples of the devastations caused by shaman's spirit helpers. Each of the other four varieties is discussed by Underhill (1946).

8. We suggest that the possible subjects of sentences with the verb *híhwoi* – that is, the things spoken of as causal agents – are always people. Thus, they contrast with the causal agents spoken of in sentences with *múmkicud*, which are always the way or strength of nonhuman objects.

   A topic which remains to be studied is whether some of the things defined as dangerous objects with reference to *ká:cim* sicknesses may also serve as the means for accomplishing sorcery. This is probably true of owls or ghosts, which in some unexplained sense are the same. Afflictions diagnosed as owl sickness commonly are blamed on the patient for grieving too much or on the ghosts for tempting or haunting the patient. However, ghosts may also serve as sorcerers' agents. In this case we suggest the sickness would be blamed on the sorcerer, but the patient would still require a cure for owl sickness. Such an affliction could perhaps be described: "owl way sickens the person because somebody has sorcerized him by means of the owl."

Part III, section 2

9. This classification, which will be borne out in Gregorio's texts, leaves the divination with ashes unaccounted for. This was an act directed at water in a bowl, not at strength in the body nor at spirits in the darkness outside. One can say that objects of this divination are in between the two fields of action, outside the patient's body, but still inside the house. We will not, however, argue for this interpretation which could only be supported by information, presently lacking, on the forces that make ash divination succeed. See section 8 for our interpretation of these forces within Gregorio's theory.

Part III, section 5

10. This usage seems to contradict the *'óimmeḍdam/ká:cim* distinction in that it refers to a staying sickness as a "wanderer." Examples of the same usage are found in two other texts (text 2 and tape 19.16).

> It [*ká:cim* sickness] never wanders, it only goes around [*'óimmeḍ*] here, because it was established here (text 2).
> And it [*ká:cim* sickness] will be the kind of thing that goes around [*'óimmeḍ*] here (tape 19.16).

This usage is justified by the following explanation: The term *ká:cim múmkidag* is used only when one wishes to distinguish Piman sicknesses from those alien ones whose origins are outside Piman society; when this distinction is not at issue, as in the above examples, then the movements of bona fide Piman sicknesses may be refered to as "wanderings."

Part III, section 7

11. Texts on the recruitment of shamans.

TEXT 51 (Tape 10.16)

Q

K háscu wuḍ hégam há'icu dúakam, 'o abṣ cem háscu mo 'am 'e-wépogid,
And whatever is those-ones something living thing, or just whatever ss there gets shown up,
What are the animals or whatever they are which appear [in visions],

k 'am há'icu máṣcam g hémajkam?
and there something teaches the person?
and teach something to a person?

A

Héu'u, ná'as hab má:s a wóho,
Yes, seemingly appears truly,
Yes, it seems to be true,

mú'i há'icu 'atp hab cú'ig,
many something existed,
many things are like that,

a wóho 'ab 'ámjeḍ
truly about it
it's true about it

matp háscu wuḍ o'ik g há'icu dúakam.
ss whatever will be the something living thing.
whatever kind of animal it may be.

'Am o tá:gio 'i wú:ṣ, hégai
There will in a confrontation emerge, that-one
It [animal] will confront one [person]

matp héḍai hab o 'i 'élidad
ss whoever will be wishing
whoever [animal] will be desiring

mat hég o máṣcamc,
ss that-one will cause it to teach,
that it [animal] will be caused to teach him [a person],

k hás másma hab o jú:.
and somehow thus will do.
and somehow he will do it.

K abṣ s-péhegĭ o béi
And just easily will get
And he [person] will easily acquire it

matp háscu wuḍ o'ik
ss whatever will be
whatever [teaching] it will be

matp hás 'i má:s o hímdagk, hégai há'icu dúakam
ss somehow appears will be a way, that-one something living thing
whatever the way of the animal will be like

matp háscu wuḍ o 'ik.
ss whatever will be.
whatever [animal] it will be.

Pégi, k hémho a mat 'am hég 'óidk hab o 'e-jú:
Well, and necessarily ss there that-one during will get done
Well, and during that [teaching] it will have to be done

matp hás 'i má:s hímdag.
ss somehow appears way.
if it is some kind of [animal's] way.

B

Hébai hab 'ép 'e-wúa hab másma,
Sometimes also happens thus,
Sometimes it happens thus,

ñé:, matp héms hab o má:sk
look, ss perhaps will appear
look, if perhaps it [teaching] is thus

mat háscu 'i m 'in wuḍ jéwedo méḍdam 'i há'icu,
ss whatever ss here is earth-on running thing something,
if whatever [animal], such as [those which are] runners on the earth,

k hég 'am hú hébai o 'i nám,
and that-one there ever sometimes will meet,
and it [animal] sometimes will meet one,

k 'am há'icu o i 'á:
and there something will tell
and it will tell him something

m o 'i béi 'am hébai húgkam,
ss will get there sometimes finally,
and it will take him just so far,

k 'am hébai o cé:gĭ
and there sometimes will show
and show him

matp hás 'i másma há'icu 'am hab má:s.
ss somehow thus something there appears.
how something is.

Pégi, k 'atp héms hab o cú'igk
Well, and perhaps will be
Well, and perhaps it will be the case

mat g ñéñ'ei 'am háhawa abṣ o má:cul.
ss the songs there then just will teach.
that it will teach songs to him.

Kut hég wuḍ 'o 'ámjeḍkam, hégai,
And that-one will be from-thing, that-one,
And that [animal] will be the source of it,

hég wuḍ o ñé'idaligk, hégai,
that-one will be song-attribute, that-one,
it will be the musical characteristics of it,

wuḍ o wúsosig 'á:gak,
will be curing ritual meaning,
it will be intended for ritual curing,

'o wuḍ o dúajida 'á:gak
or will be dúajida meaning,
or it will be intended for the dúajida

matp hás o 'i má:sk.
ss somehow will appear.
however it may be.

c

Ñé:, cem háscu hab má:s,
Look, just whatever appears,
Look, just anything [animal species] is like that,

abṣ cem háscu k 'áb g há'icu dúakam
just whatever and is against the something living thing
it can be any kind of animal

matp háscu wuḍ o 'ik,
ss whatever will be,
whatever kind it may be,

c o nám g 'ó'odham.
and will meet the man.
and will meet the person.

Pégi, k hémho a mat hég 'óidk 'am o 'i bébehi
Well, and necessarily ss that-one during there will get
Well, and during that [teaching] he [person] has to get it [knowledge]

matp hás 'i másma o s'e-'ámicudad,
ss somehow thus will get understood,
however he [person] will understand it,

pégi, t hég o má:, hégai.
well, that-one will give, that-one.
well, and it [animal] will give it to him.

Ñé:, há'ap · o másma hab cú'ig.
Look, that-way thus is.
Look, that's how it is.

TEXT 52 (Tape 10.17)

Q

T háscu 'á:gk o dágǐto, hégai há'icu mat 'am má:cul g hémajkam?
Whatever means and will drop it, that-one something ss there taught the person?
What is the reason why a [animal or spirit] teacher will quit a person?

A

Héu'u, b 'o hía másma,
Yes, of course thus,
Yes, of course it's like that,

'atp a wóho hab 'ép má:s, hégai
truly also appeared, that-one
it may truly be like that

matp hébai hab 'e-wúa.
ss sometimes happened.
when it happens.

. . .K abṣ hab-a 'ab héjel ha-'áb, hég 'ámjeḍ, hégai
. . .But itself is up to them, that-one from, that-one
. . .But it [decision to cut off instruction] is up to them [teachers]

mat pi hab o 'e-'élidad,
ss will not be wishing,
if they don't intend to [continue teaching],

pégi, k pi 'am hú hab o 'e-jú: 'am hég 'óidk
well, and never will get done there that-one during
well, then they won't have to continue with it

matp háscu 'am o' i,
ss whatever there will be,
whatever it will be,

'am wuḍ o cem hégaik g máṣcamaḍagk,
there will be just that-one the teaching,
it will be the teachings,

'am 'amjeḍ, hégai
there from, that-one
from that [animal]

matp héḍai hab o 'i 'élidad,
ss whoever will be wishing it,
whoever wishes,

c 'am o 'i wáñim hég 'óidk.
and there will lead that-one during.
and will lead him [student] through it.

B

'O 'é:p, mat héjel hab o 'e-jú:
Or also, ss itself will get done
Or else he [the student] may do it himself [cause the instruction to stop]

mat 'am abṣ a pi 'am hú o 'áp 'e-ñú:kud
ss there just never will properly get taken care of
if he won't take proper care of himself

mañ 'am hú hékĭ hú hab há'icu ṣa 'á:g
ss I there already something slightly told
as I have already explained

maṣ há'icu wuḍ húhulga,
ss something is menstruation,
that there is a thing, menstruation,

s-ta-'é:bidama,
fear-inducing,
dangerous,

pégi, pi 'o táccu, hégam hab cú:cu'igam hémajkam
well, doesn't want it, those-ones existing kinds of persons
well, that is not liked by those kinds of persons

mas hég 'óidk 'am o'i wáñim, hégai,
ss that-one during there will lead, that-one,
who will be leading him through that [instructions],

hémho a mat 'am o a'i dágĭto.
necessarily ss there will only drop it.
they will have to drop him.

Ñé:, ñ-hég hab hí pi mámci
Look, I that-one on the other hand don't know
Look, on the other hand, I don't know

mat hébai hab o 'e-jú:
ss sometimes will happen
whether it could happen

mat o ha-múmkic.
ss will sicken them.
that it [animal teacher] will sicken him [It is known that the teacher may drop the student, but it is not known whether it will sicken him.]

Pégi, tp abṣ hab-a o a 'áp'et,
Well, but it will be proper,
Well, but it will be all right,

k hab hí o ṣa má:skad há'ap
and on the other hand will slightly be appearing that-way
and on the other hand it is pretty certainly like that

matp hég hab o ṣa 'ábk, hégai,
ss that-one will slightly be up to it, that-one,
if [sickness] is against him [student],

pégi, k abṣ s-péhegim hab hí o 'e-jú:
well, and just easily on the other hand will get done
well, it's fairly easy to do it

mat hég gam hú o 'i 'e-wú:ṣad, hégai.
ss that-one away will get removed, that-one.
to get it [sickness] removed.

Ñé:, há'ap o a'i másma hab cú'ig, 'í:da.
Look, that-way will only thus be, this-one.
Look, that's how it has to be.

TEXT 53 (Tape 13.6)

Q

'An o káidag mat o kúḍu g 'ó'odham 'í:bdag, hégai há'icu má:culig,
There is said ss will bother the man heart, that-one something caused to know,
It is said that the thing [spirit or animal] which teaches a person may bother his heart,

'ói a abṣ héjel pi o 'á'apet 'ab 'ámjeḍ,
then just itself will be damaged about it,
he [the person] just damages himself,

k héḍai wuḍ cú'ijig, hégai?
and who is instigator, that-one?
and who is responsible for it?

Hégai 'ó'odham mo s-hó:ho'id,
That-one man ss enjoys it,
The man who enjoys it [instruction],

c 'éḍa pi o 'e-náko, hégai?
and yet does not endure it, that-one?
although he cannot endure it?

'O héms hég wuḍ cú'ijig g há'icu dúakam,
Or perhaps that-one is instigator the something living-thing,
Or perhaps it is the animal's responsibility,

no pi hég 'e-kuḍút 'ab 'ámjeḍ?
because that-one got bothered about it?
because it got bothered about it?

A

Héu'u, mo a wóho hab má:s, hégai
Yes, ss truly appears, that-one
Yes, it really is like that

. . .matp 'ab o há'icu 'ab 'úlink
. . .ss against-it will something hold out
. . .if he is inclined towards something

mat háscu o 'i mái.
ss whatever it learn. .
whatever he will learn.

B

. . .Pégi, kc hab cem cú'ig
. . .Well, and just is
. . .Well, and it ought to be the case

matp 'am hú hébai 'i hímdam hab o a cem má:sid
ss ever sometime later will just appear
that later on it will become apparent

mat 'am o húgkad, 'ámai,
ss there will terminate, there,
that it [instruction] should stop at a certain point,

pégi, t 'am o 'i cíkp, hégai.
well, there will start to work, that-one.
well, then he should start working on it [shamanism].

K 'ói a hébai hab 'e-wúa 'atp héma,
And then sometimes happens one of them,
And then sometimes it happens to one of them [students],

hég 'ámjeḍ 'am hab pi 'á'ap'et
that-one from there is damaged
because of that [instruction] he gets damaged

matp hab o ge 'élidad
ss will be wishing
if he happens to wish

mat há'icu si táṣo 'am hab o 'e-jú:, hégai.
ss something very clearly there will get done, that-one.
for some very definite thing to be done by that [teacher].

c

Pégi, kutp 'am hab háhawa o 'e-jú:,
Well, and there then will get done,
Well, and then it [damage] will happen [to the student],

'éḍa hab wuḍ cem 'á:ga,
yet just means,
yet, it should be understood,

hab wuḍ a cem má:s, há'icu,
just appears, something,
the thing [spirit teacher] just appears to be something,

pi 'at hékid há'icu
never something
but it isn't something

mac 'in hab cú'ig, c 'in 'ó'odhamak.
ss we here are, and here being mankind.
like we are around here, [namely] people.

Hébai héma 'i t-nánamek,
Sometimes one of them us meets,
Sometimes we [real people] meet one another,

c háscu 'i t-wé:m ñíok,
and whatever us with talks,
and we talk with each other,

pégi, pi 'o hab má:s, 'í:da hab cú'igam há'icu.
well, not appears, this-one kind of something.
well, this thing [spirit teacher] is not like that.

Cúhugamk 'éḍa 'o 'e-ná:to, hégai,
Darkness in will get made, that-one,
It is made in the darkness,

c abṣ hab-a 'éḍa wuḍ a wóhokam.
but yet is true thing.
but yet it is real.

D

Wóho, 'at hab o 'e-jú:
Truly, will get done
It really happens

mat hás 'i másma há'icu o 'e-ñéidad,
ss somehow thus something will get observed,
that somehow something [spirit] gets observed,

pégi, c 'atp 'am hab o a cem cú'igk hab másma.
well, and there will be thus.
well, and it should be like that [the student should remember that only people and not spirits are proper companions].

'Ói a hab o 'e-jú:
Then will get done
Then [otherwise] it will happen

matp hékĭ hú o 'i 'e-bá'iwc
ss already will get surpassed
that he [student] will already have passed it

matp hébai húgkam o cem híwgidask
ss sometime terminally will have been permitted
if there is a limit to what has been permitted

mat 'am húgkam há'icu o s-má:cid.
ss there terminally something will be known.
if there is a limit to what he [student] will know.

Pi abṣ o si 'e-bá'iwc,
Not just will surpass,
He shouldn't exceed it,

pi 'at hab o a 'ap'et, hégai.
not will be right, that-one.
it won't be right.

Pégi, k 'ói a wuḍ hégai
Well, and then is that-one
Well, and that's what it is

mo heg hékaj 'am pi 'áp'et g hémajkam,
ss that-one by means of there damages the person,
which is the reason why the person is damaged,

ge múmkicud hég 'ámjeḍ, hégai há'icu má:cigaj
just sickens it that-one from, that-one something its knowledge
it just sickens him because that thing, his knowledge

mat pi 'ói 'am hú 'i cíkpan.
ss not immediately ever begins to work.
if he does not begin to work [at shamanism] soon enough.

E

Pégi, k pi héḍai wuḍ 'ámjeḍkam,
Well, and not somebody is from thing,
Well, and nobody [except the student] is the source of it [the damage],

pi héḍai wuḍ cú'ijig,
not somebody is instigator,
it's not anybody's fault,

mo pi wóhocud, 'aha ṣá: 'o hú 'i másma,
ss doesn't believe, what manner of thing ever is thus,
that he doesn't acknowledge how it is,

c 'éḍa 'am hab a cem 'e-júñhim 'ab hég 'óidc
and yet there tried to be doing against-it that-one along
and yet he is trying to do it [to learn things] of that kind

matp háscu 'ab 'e-cé:gidahim 'am hímdaḍ 'éda.
ss whatever against-it was getting shown up there its way in.
whatever [spirit] was showing up in his [student's] experience.

Pégi, k 'am a cem s-hó:ho'id,
Well, and there just enjoyed it,
Well, and he [student] likes it,

c 'am hab 'e-júñhim,
and there getting done,
and he is doing it,

'ói a gm hú'i mat 'am pi 'am hú hab o 'e-jú:
then later ss there never will get done
then later on he fails to do it [start working]

k 'am héjel o 'ái, hégai pi 'e'áp'edag. . . .
and there itself will reach, that-one itṣ own impropriety. . . .
and he himself reaches his impropriety. . . .

12. We have no evidence that the patient's heart, *'í:bdag*, has such soullike attributes as a disposition to become lost from the body or the ability to notice activities in the world. For the present we conclude *'í:bdag* refers to no more than an organ in the patient's body which must be protected from intrusive strengths.

Part III, section 8

13. There is no evidence that the word *'í:bdag* refers to a displacable soul as well as, or instead of, the flesh and blood heart inside the shaman's body. Thus, as far as we know all of the actions within the landscape of the spirits are performed by creatures who reside there and nowhere else. There are no living people, or spiritualized parts of people, in the landscape of the spirits.

Part IV, section 1

14. It is possible that the word *wúsosig*, which we have not been able to differentiate from *wúsota*, refers exclusively to the maximal level of ritual curing. Whenever Bahr asked Gregorio to describe a certain kind of *wúsosig*, he responded with the fullest possible account of a cure for that kind of sickness, i.e., an account involving singing, *wústana*, fetishes, and whatever other ceremonial actions are prescribed for the cure.

Part IV, section 3

15. This specification of objects holds only within the discourse on sickness. Other possible objects of *wústana* include:

    1. Natural objects undergoing ritual purification, for example, salt, scalps, or images of saints
    2. People who have obtained the above natural objects
    3. Flames, dust, and other secular things

Part IV, section 5

16. The most common method for the procurement of fetishes is probably as by-products of maximal level cures. Thus the patient with gopher sickness will get cured by a combination of singing, *wústana*, and fetishes made expressly for the occasion of his cure. He keeps the fetish for future use. Other methods of fetish procurement are borrowing them or making them for oneself without undergoing the maximal level of cure.

17. In informal conversations, Lopez granted the possibility of inquiring into the *ñé'idalig*, "attributes of the singing," of each kind of dangerous object. He suggested that the songs for some species dwell on the meanness of the species; other species "like to hear" songs about their "funny actions."

Part IV, section 6.

18. In addition to his discussion of the spiritual women as phenomena of the darkness, Gregorio has spoken about how infants are sometimes frightened by the shadow of the darkness, which covers them during the daytime. He says the darkness is like a cloud of smoke. For a discussion of spirit teachers as phenomena of the darkness see text 53, pt. C.

19. It is possible that these women are identical with or related to whores: *cé:cpa'owĭ*, "whores," or *ce:cpa'owi 'ú'uwi* "whores women;" also called *púputa*, from the Spanish *puta*, "whore." "Women of the darkness" is our designation, not Gregorio's. He merely refers to them as "women." We suspect that these women are in fact the ones called *cé:cpa'owĭ* and that Gregorio simply chose not to identify them as such. When asked to verify this reasoning he did not offer a positive response, but perhaps Bahr's question was ill-formed.

Whores are dangerous objects in their own right. There is a *ká:cim* sickness named for whores. Thus, it is strange and presently unexplained why Gregorio did not list "whore ritual cure" among the group of cures whose songs elicit the uncanny chiming in. Our analytical separation of the spirit of the way from spiritual women would be jeopardized if the whores do not have a distinctly conceptualized way which responds to the curer's action in addition of the individualized, uncannily real whores themselves. We have not resolved this point.

Finally, we note that references to whores occur in examples of the following kinds of curing songs published by Russell: gila monster, black lizard, badger, scalp bundle, and owl. Furthermore, the text of at least one of Russell's devil songs probably refers to whores, although they are not named. There are no examples of ocean songs in Russell's collection. Thus, the whores are referred to not only in three of the four kinds of cures singled out by Gregorio, but also in songs addressed to certain of the animal group of dangerous objects.

We may speculate that women of the darkness are identical with whores. These women are heard singing in conjunction with each of the several kinds of curing songs in which whores are mentioned.

It still remains to be established, however, if the spirit who accomplishes the cure is the way or the whores. For example, whores may be mentioned in devil songs, not because they are responsible for the patient's affliction with devil sickness, but simply because whores are notable parts of the environment of devils as well as humans. The spiritualized representative of devil way may enjoy hearing songs about how devils get involved with whores. He may be proud of this quirk of his way and withdraw his strength from the patient in response to this pleasure.

On the other hand, we know from text 44 that the women of the darkness (or whores) also like to hear curing songs of the four ways cited by Gregorio and that they may cause the patient to be cured on their own accord. Thus they seem to have the same curative efficacy as the spiritualized ways.

20. The word we translate as "to purify ritually" is *kégcud*. Its literal meaning is "to cause it to be good," "to cause it to be clean." In Gregorio's texts about this ritual, the objects of the verb may be either the men who have returned from getting the salt or the salt itself. In text 43 Gregorio speaks only of the salt as an object of purification.

The word *wúsot*, also used in this context, may be interchangeable with *kégcud*. Thus, the objects of *wúsot* as used in this sense may be either the men or the salt they have obtained. Referring to the men, this seemingly distinct sense of *wúsot* has the idiomatic meaning, "to purify a person who is 'not-free'." For example:

Mat o wúso, mat o kégc g pi cú'ikokam.
Ss it will purify it, ss it will purify it the not-free-one.
If he [ritual curer/purifier] will purify him [man returned from salt-getting], if he will purify the one who is in an unfree state.

See note 6 for a discussion of the usage of the related term, *pi cú'ikodag*. It is probable that the above sense of *wúsot* can be differentiated from the sense pursued in this study by showing the differences between the aforementioned sentence and the following sentence.

Mat o wúso, mat o 'ápc g múmkudam.
Ss it will cure it, ss it will cause-it-to-be-proper the sick-one.
If he [ritual curer] will cure him [patient], if he will make the sick person be proper [or healthy].

The problems are how "to purify" differs from "to make proper" and how "person in a sacred state" differs from "person who is sick."

Bibliography

PUBLISHED MATERIAL

Alvarez, A., and K. Hale

1970 "Toward a manual of Papago grammar: some phonological terms." *International Journal of American Linguistics* 36, no. 2, pp. 83-97.

Cook, C.

1893 *Among the Pimas or the Mission to the Pima and Maricopa Indians.* Albany: Ladies Union Mission School Association.

Densmore, F.

1929 *Papago music.* Washington, D.C.: Bureau of American Ethnology, Bulletin 90.

Eliade, M.

1964 *Shamanism.* New York: Bollingen.

Levi-Strauss, C.

1967 "The effectiveness of symbols." In *Structural Anthropology.* Garden City: Doubleday Anchor.

Mathiot, M.

1968 "An approach to the cognitive study of language." *International Journal of American Linguistics* 34, no. 1, pt. 2, Publication 45.

Pilcher, W.

1967 "Some comments on the folk taxonomy of the Papago." *American Anthropologist* 69, no. 2, pp. 204-208.

Russell, F.

1908 *The Pima Indians.* Washington, D.C.: Bureau of American Ethnology, Annual Report 26. Reedition 1974. Tucson: University of Arizona Press.

Saxton, D. and L.

1969 *Papago & Pima to English, English to Papago & Pima Dictionary.* Tucson: University of Arizona Press.

Underhill, R.

1939 *The social organization of the Papago Indians.* New York: Columbia University. Contributions to Anthropology, vol. 30.

1946 *Papago Indian Religion.* New York: Columbia University Press.

UNPUBLISHED MATERIAL

Alvarez, A.

1969 "*'Ó' odham ñé'okĭ ha-káidag* [The Sounds of Papago]." English version by Kenneth Hale. Boston: Massachusetts Institute of Technology, Department of Linguistics.

Brennan, J. L.

1897 Papago material of José Lewis Brennan, Piman Stock, Collector J.N.B. Hewitt. Washington, D.C.: Smithsonian Institution, Archives of the Bureau of American Ethnology, no. 1744, vol. 2.

Hale, K.

n.d. Papago texts.

Herzog, G.

n.d. Piman texts. Philadelphia: American Philosophical Society Library. Franz Boas Collection of Materials for American Linguistics, ms. 269.

Acknowledgments

The research leading to this study began in the summer of 1960 and continued sporadically until 1969 under the sponsorship of the following institutions:

University of Illinois. Summer 1962 (Bahr).

University of North Carolina. June 1963 - August 1964 (Bahr).

National Institute of Mental Health, fellowship no. 5 F1-MH-30, 294-02 (BEHA) (sponsored by D. Oliver, Harvard University). January - June 1967 (Bahr).

Massachusetts Institute of Technology. October - December 1969 (Alvarez).

Arizona State University. October - December 1969 (Alvarez and Bahr).

We wish to acknowledge the contribution of Kenneth Hale, of MIT, in the preparation of the texts. He proffered advice on translation and transcription when Lopez and Bahr were at the stage of first writing the texts and rendering them into English.

We wish to thank the following anthropologists for their assistance at various times during our acquaintance with Pimans: B. Alpher, B. Fontana, W. Kelly, J. Martin, D. Metzger, R. Nonas, D. Oliver, R. Patrick, R. Ruppé, R. Underhill, and E. Vogt.

We wish also to thank Lambert Fremdling, OFM, for his friendship and assistance.

Additionally, we wish to express appreciation to the University of Arizona Press for effecting publication with particular thanks to editor Susan Adler.

Finally, we express our gratitude to the Piman Indians.

D. M. B.

Index

Accidents: as foreboding, 53
Adulthood: sicknesses of, 114, 283-98; and not-free-ness, 206. *See* basket making; cowboy; enemy killer; menstruation; parent; pregnancy
Afflictions, 19-20, 22 (table 1), 279. *See* nonsickness; sickness
Angelo, Sam, 201
Anglo-American: contact with Pimans, 14; versus Piman concept of sickness, 48. *See* non-Indians
Animals: bites of, 69-73, 79; as dangerous objects, 21, 25, 29-32; in deformities, 90-98; in forebodings, 53; recruit shaman, 307-10; as residents, 301; in songs, 242-43, 318; species versus individuals, 31-32, 90. *See* causal agent, way
Apaches, 251. *See* enemy
Arthritis: in *wí:gita* sickness, 297
Ashes: in deer cure, 289; in divining, 118-19, 307
Awareness (*tá:t*): in animals, 69, 70-73, 148-49; in causal agents, 243-44, 244-46; of nonsickness, 108; of sickness, 116, 149-55; of past actions, 76, 77, 113, 138-41, 143, 144-48, 171; of permeation, 131-32, 134-35. *See* patient

Babies: baptism, 49, 53-54; 55-61; frightened by darkness, 319; harmed by parents, 76-77, 91; retardations of, 98-105; sicknesses of, 29-30, 283-98
Back: pain, 164, 292, 298; swelling, 292
Badger: sickness, 26 (table 2), 30, 285; and whore songs, 319
Baptize: babies, 49, 53; failure to, 49, 54-61, 295; saints, 49
Basket making: devil sickness, 287
Bathing prohibition, 53
Bear sickness, 26 (table 2), 33, 91, 284
Bee sickness, 27 (table 2), 285
Bites: contrasted with sickness, 19, 22, 69, 79-84. *See* nonsickness
Blacks, 90-91
Black widow, 80-84
Bleeding: in eagle sickness, 288; in enemy sickness, 289; in hawk sickness, 292; in squirrel sickness, 297. *See* menstruation
Blisters. *See* sores
Blowing (*wústana*): in baptism, 97; in diagnosis, 119, 170, 188, 189-91, 195-98, 204-6, 219-28 (tables 3 and 5); noncurative uses of, 204, 318; Piman words for, 188-91, 224-26, 228 (table 5); in ritual cure, 97, 123, 191-92, 219-28 (tables 4 and 5), 264-69. *See* breath, divination, *dúajida*, ritual cure, ritual curer, shaman
Body: blowing on, 119, 189; contrasted with landscape of spirits, 170-71, 230-31 (table 6), 233; divination into, 195; in *kúlañmada* and *dúajida*, 119, 138, 169-70, 220 (table 3); pain in side, 295; permeated strength in, 132, 134-35; red and feverish, 291; in ritual cure, 219, 221 (table 4), 279-80; sores, 285, 290, 291; stratified strengths in, 114, 131, 134, 136; swelling of, 284
Boils. *See* sores
Breath: augmentation of, 189-91, 198-206, 224-27, 228 (table 5); and ritual curer, 226; and shaman's heart, 189-90. *See* blowing, heart, tobacco, tools
Brennan, José Lewis: biographical data, v; holographs, 66, 114, 120, 243, 272; list of sicknesses, 283-298
Butterfly sickness, 26 (table 2), 30, 284
Buzzard sickness, 23, 26 (table 2), 33, 285

Car accidents, 53
Caterpillar, 27 (table 2)
Cat sickness, 27 (table 2), 285